Saint Mother Theodore Guérin

Woman of Providence

Sister Diane Ris, SP and Sister Joseph Eleanor Ryan, SP

authorHOUSE®

AuthorHouse™
1663 Liberty Drive
Bloomington, IN 47403
www.authorhouse.com
Phone: 1-800-839-8640

First published by AuthorHouse 8/31/2011

ISBN: 978-1-4567-3604-0 (e)
ISBN: 978-1-4567-3605-7 (sc)

Printed in the United States of America

This book is printed on acid-free paper.

Cover design by Pam Lynch
Sculpture by Teresa Clark
Photos courtesy of the Sisters of Providence Archives

Acknowledgements

There are particular persons to whom I owe much gratitude.

- Kathy Lubeznik who graciously offered to type the entire manuscript
- Cordelia Moran, SP, Joan Slobig, SP, Mary Montgomery, SP and Ann Xavier Hau, SP whose editorial expertise has been a true gift to me
- Marianne Mader, SP whose thematic collection of Saint Mother Theodore quotes has enriched this biography
- Dave Cox who shared his memories of the Beatification and Canonization
- Hannah Corbin, SP who set up the Table of Contents pages of this book
- Pam Lynch who designed the beautiful cover showing Mother Theodore's spirit still present within our Woods
- Juanita Crouch and Roberta King whose assistance with printing was invaluable
- Teresa Clark who's magnificent image of Saint Mother Theodore graces the cover of this beloved saint's life story
- Jennifer Drake and Paul Beel who's highly proficient computer skills saved me many hours of grief
- The prayers and encouragement of my Sisters of Providence, friends and family who were there for me when I needed them. Thank you one and all!

Contents

Chapter 1

It was the second day of October 1798. Dawn was just breaking over the northern coast of Brittany, waking the seaside canton of Etables, lighting the cliffs and the caves, the stretches of sandy white shore, and the thatched roofs of the cottages in the little village of Sous-le-Bourg.

In one of these cottages, Number three on the rue d'Etables, Isabelle Guérin embraced her newborn daughter, her second child. "We will call her Anne-Thérèse," she whispered to Marguérite Bosché, the kindly, competent neighbor bending over her bed. She added, with a little sigh, "If only her father were here to see her!"

Laurent Guérin had been on leave, a year and a half ago, to welcome his first-born, Jean-Laurent. How long it seemed since he had set off on his present tour of duty! He had left on the morning of March 19, bound for Brest, where he was to embark on the <u>Redoubtable.</u> [1] Now it was the beginning of October; more than six long months had passed, and there was no way of foreseeing how many more months would go by before he had the joy of taking his little daughter into his arms.

Early the next morning Marguérite carried the child to the town hall, to be registered as one of the new little citizens born in the "Year Seven of the French Republic." [2] Julien Guérin, Laurent's 18 year-old nephew,

1

represented the absent father. There could be no ceremony around the baptismal font in the old church dedicated to Our Lady of Etables, in the parish of St. Jean-Baptiste. Like so many other churches, it had been plundered during the Revolution, and it still remained closed. During the turbulent Directory days, priests rendered their services in secret, when in constant danger of their lives. Staunch Breton families, courageous and indomitable, preserved at home the treasure of their centuries-old faith. Anne-Thérèse, daughter of parents noted for their piety even among the good parishioners of Etables, would have been baptized at home before being officially enrolled as a child of the new Republic.

It is possible that the sacrament was administered by the Abbé Laurent Tréguy, [3] who labored in his native canton all during the years of turmoil. In one disguise or another, he moved about, finding means of visiting the sick, offering mass from time to time, baptizing and hearing confessions. There were always trustworthy persons in every part of the parish to act as a safe and dependable liaison between the devoted priest and those in need of his services. When time and circumstances permitted, some record of a baptism was left with the family, but such records, if they were made, were often lost. No record has been found for Anne-Thérèse, but the reputation for deep faith and the exemplary lives of the Guérin family leave no room for doubt. [4]

That same day Isabelle, who was deeply devoted to the Blessed Mother of God, joyfully consecrated her new little daughter to Mary. The tiny garments she fashioned for the infant, and the dainty frocks in which for the next ten years she would clothe her dark-eyed, lively little sprite, would always be white or blue. Anne-Thérèse would be taught that she was "the Blessed Virgin's little girl," a title in which she found delight. [5]

It was also a title, which, as her mother intended, and as Anne-Thérèse was soon to discover for herself, entailed responsibilities. When, for instance, she might otherwise have made her own small but determined will prevail, the simple reminder that "the Blessed Virgin would not be pleased with her little girl" always served to curb her childish willfulness.

With the birth of Anne-Thérèse, Isabelle Guérin had two small children in her care. In the intervals of her domestic and maternal duties she occupied herself at her spinning wheel in order to help provide for the needs of the little family during the father's long absences. There was little time for yielding to the inevitable loneliness caused by his absence. Isabelle could try to fill in the hours of awaiting his return with dreams of his pleasure in their children, of his surprise and delight at their growth and their small accomplishments. There were relatives nearby, too, with whom she might share experiences. There was her sister Julie, 12 years her senior, who had taken their mother's place and whose husband, Pierre Heurtel, had been Isabelle's childhood guardian. Julie's youngest child, Marie-Anne, like Isabelle's own Jean-Laurent, was just a year and a half older than Anne-Thérèse, Julie's little Agatha Marie, six years old, and her two little boys, Julien, eight, and Pierre, 11, would have played with their tiny cousins in the Guérin courtyard or in their field beside the sea.

Anne-Thérèse was almost a year old when on a happy day in September 1799 Laurent Guérin came home on a short leave. For three weeks the little family was together, weeks entirely too brief for the sharing of so many experiences. The father marveled at the growth of sturdy little Jean Laurent, now two and a half, and to make the acquaintance of his little Anne-Thérèse, already beginning to walk and talk. Then, on Sept. 26 he had to set off once more to board ship at Brest, and Isabelle was left to another period of anxious waiting.

Hard as this parting was, neither Laurent nor Isabelle could have anticipated the tragedy that was to intensify the bitterness of their separation. Laurent had been away for a year, and once again it was Oct. 2, Anne-Thérèse's birthday. Isabelle had sent her two little ones to bed and had retired herself, only to be awakened to the realization that her little home had become prey to one of the fires that were a constant threat to the thatched cottages of the canton. Destruction was usually swift and complete, since the only means of extinguishing a blaze once it was discovered was the primitive one of the fire-chain. The Guérin cottage was destroyed. Little Jean-Laurent lost his life, and Anne-Thérèse, was rescued somehow. All her life she retained the memory etched on her childhood consciousness concerning that night. Long years later, when fire again took toll of her surroundings, she would write, "It was forty-two years ago at that same hour that a fire consumed my father's house and took from me my older brother. I was saved in an extraordinary manner." [6]

The child so providentially spared became doubly her mother's concern and consolation. Anne-Therese was a lively, precocious child, quick to respond to her mother's affection, and no doubt unconsciously sharing her unexpressed emotions. Isabelle Guérin was a quiet, sensitive young woman, long accustomed to separation and loss, and deeply pious. She herself had been well instructed, and she enjoyed teaching her little daughter, who between her father's brief furloughs was her only companion during the next three years.

On Feb. 9 1803, [7] another daughter, Marie-Jeanne, came to share the mother's love and attention. Anne-Thérèse was then five years old. The little that can be known of her childhood and girlhood will be learned chiefly through the recollections that Marie-Jeanne was to confide to her own daughters over the years.

Madame Guérin was Anne-Thérèse's first instructor, introducing her to her catechism, teaching her reading, writing and the history of her country. Her mother laid the foundation for that life-long love for Holy Scripture and the lives of the Saints that was to characterize the future educator and foundress. It was a pleasant way to have lessons, learning at one's own pace, free to question and always confident of her teacher's interest and understanding. There was also the distraction, now and then of Marie-Jeanne's presence, and the delicious grown-up feeling that came with passing on some of her own learning to her little sister.

Madame Guérin herself had, in all likelihood, been a pupil of the Daughters of the Holy Spirit, [8] who taught in Etables from 1761 until 1793, when they were driven out by the Revolution. When the Concordat of 1801 made possible the reopening of religious schools, the sisters once again took up their work, returning to Etables, according to their community records, no later than 1803. The sisters taught the little girls to read, to write, to do simple arithmetic and encouraged proficiency according to each child's abilities. Above all, they strove to instill habits of faith and piety and to instruct these future homemakers in the tasks of the household and in the simple handcrafts, which would help them contribute to their own support.

Madame Guérin's own deep faith, her interest in her daughter's Christian formation, and the proximity of the school to the Guérin home all would indicate that little Anne-Thérèse had at least for a time the benefit of the careful, loving training offered by the Daughters of the Holy Spirit. Anne-Thérèse's attendance at their school, logical though it seems, must remain at most a conjecture. The course of study was, as we have seen, very elementary. Perhaps that is why, when a young woman opened a little school in the village, Madame Guérin enrolled Anne-Thérèse, then nine years old.

The little girl found it hard to adjust. Her active little mind had already mastered the lessons offered. Faced with no adequate outlet for her energies, she suddenly discovered, and put to immediate use, a decided gift for leadership as well as a considerable talent for harmless mischief. She enjoyed her ascendancy over her companions and the eagerness with which they followed her lead, but the lessons she found boring. There was more to interest an energetic little person, more to feed a lively intelligence and imagination, to be found outside the classroom. She loved rambles through the meadows, on the beach, atop the high rocks, and in the beautiful caves along the shore, where one could look out over the great expanse of the sea. Anne-Thérèse cherished these rambles, often stolen, and the long thoughts that came to her as she contemplated the waves that had claimed so many of her ancestors, and still carried her father off in his service of his country. She loved to look out in wonder at the vast ocean that her mother had told her was the symbol of eternity.

She had to learn, however, that following in one's fancy could not always take the place of doing one's duty. Absenting oneself from school where one belonged was one of the ways of displeasing God and his Blessed Mother. Once impressed with this knowledge, she was careful not to repeat her misdeeds. "I always had a horror of sin," she confessed later. "As soon as I understood that it was wrong to play hookey, I was careful not to begin again the things for which I had been punished so often." [9]

Happily for Anne-Thérèse this particular experiment in education did not last long. Before a year had ended, the well-meaning schoolmistress abandoned her project. Anne-Thérèse could take up again at home the lessons she really loved. Providentially, a young relative, one of the seminarians forced by circumstances to interrupt his studies, found hospitality in the Guérin home. His stay was to be of mutual advantage. He himself enjoyed for a time, life in a pious Christian family, close to relatives and friends. Madame Guérin and her little daughters benefited by his help in the house and in the field which they tried to cultivate. In addition, the young man appointed himself Anne-Thérèse's tutor. This occupation, too, would be of double advantage, for while he was instructing his little cousin he could review and refine his own knowledge. Anne-Thérèse proved an ideal pupil. Before long he considered his "little theologian" sufficiently prepared for her First Communion. [10]

Again, there remains no record or description of Anne-Thérèse's First Communion day. She herself, unlike other girls of her age who prepared for the great occasion has left no notes of her impressions. If her mother, like other mothers of her era, committed to writing her own reflections on this joyful family festival, no trace of her notes or correspondence remains. All we know of this great day in Anne-Thérèse's life is that she was permitted to receive her First Communion at the age of ten, at that time a privilege which gives evidence of her dispositions and preparation. On that solemn day she promised to belong henceforth to God alone. This promise had the approval of her confessor, very likely the Abbé Marc-Etienne Duval-Villebogard, [11] appointed to Etables in 1804. The confessor encouraged the aspirations of the little first communicant, assuring her that God would help her one day to realize her great desire if she did not take back the heart she offered him that day. For Anne-Thérèse, the offering was not merely the overflow of passing childish enthusiasm. She treasured her hope and her confessor's assurance. From time to time she would declare, "I have a secret which no one can guess!" [12]

She kept her secret well. Outwardly she remained the same lively, impetuous, amiable young girl busy with her lessons and her small household tasks. She was always happy to escape to one of the little caves along the shore. There, in delightful solitude close to the mysterious sea, she learned something of meditation and of prayer. Prayer, indeed, was a regular part of life for the Guérin family. Morning and evening they prayed together. In the parish church, once it could be reopened and the ravages of the Revolution repaired, the Abbé Duval-Villebogard gathered his parishioners for Forty Hours Devotions, and established the Confraternity of the Rosary and Perpetual Adoration of the Blessed Sacrament.

From her mother, Anne-Thérèse learned devotion to the Blessed Virgin and to the Guardian Angels. She had her own little altar in her bedroom, where around her small statue of Mary she arranged the wild flowers, shells, pretty pebbles or bits of seaweed that she had gathered in her rambles. It was where she knelt in prayer the last thing every night. She would not forget the day when, as a substitute for the blossoms, she had adorned her altar with brilliant butterflies, strung by their jeweled wings. Her mother's cry of dismay, "Anne-Thérèse, how could you be so cruel?" brought realization of her thoughtlessness and quick, contrite tears.

Thus the years were slipping by, the little girls were growing, and in 1809 the birth of a little brother, Laurent-Marie, [13] brought new interest and excitement into their lives. Madame Guérin found herself leaning more and more on her elder daughter, who seemed with the passing years to become more affectionate, more dependable and more resourceful. Serious and thoughtful beyond her years, Anne-Therese also knew how to liven the little cottage with her high spirits and her laughter.

During the years the French national scene continued to change. With the dawn of the Empire, the Emperor made his influence felt throughout Europe. Something of the excitement of the times invaded the Guérin home during Laurent's furloughs. The little girls could not hear enough of his adventures: captured by the British, liberation, embarkation and debarkation at Brest or St. Malo. He had long weeks at sea amid storms and conflict. He told them the fascinating names of the ships: Dorade, Créole, Constante Amitié, and Regulus. The father's visits were bright and festive occasions, shadowed only by the thought of imminent parting and the uncertainty of his return.

He had been away for two years when, in 1813, tragedy struck the fatherless home. Once more Isabelle witnessed the accidental death of a little son, in circumstances heartbreakingly similar to those which surrounded the death of her first-born. During the night of November 19, little four-year-old Laurent-Marie perished when his bed covers caught fire. He was buried the following day. [14] All the sympathy and gentle understanding, which underlay Anne-Thérèse's vivacious, buoyant disposition, now came to the support of her bereaved mother. Her solicitude was made all the more necessary by the fact that there seemed no prospect of the father's early return.

At that time Laurent Guérin was aboard the vessel <u>Austerlitz</u>, involved in the Napoleonic blockade of the continent against England. On April 6, 1814, the defeated Emperor abdicated at Fontainbleau; the French forces were demobilized, and Laurent, having disembarked from the <u>Austerlitz</u> at Toulon in mid-June, began his homeward journey. He was never to reach his family. On June 17 he was attacked and assassinated by highwaymen, at Evenos, in the Province of Toulon. [15]

The news of his tragic death left Isabelle broken in body and spirit. Anne-Thérèse, not yet sixteen, was now not only companion and consolation, but also nurse and support of her widowed mother. With characteristic energy and devotion, she assumed at once the care of the home and the instruction of her sister, while she continued her affectionate, understanding ministry to her mother. During the five years which followed, all thoughts of her own life plans had to be laid aside while she dedicated herself totally to the needs of her mother and her sister.

Family circumstances were strained. Madame Guérin had been accustomed to supplement her husband's stipend at her spinning wheel; now that his support had been entirely taken away, the family faced real need. As soon, therefore, as Marie-Jeanne was old enough to help with the household duties and the care of her mother, Anne-Thérèse set about finding work that would secure them a some small income. Energetic, and trained in the use of the needle, she would have had little difficulty in finding employment in a town which occupied itself during a good part of the year in the equipment of sailboats and schooners for the great fishing season. Fabricators of sails and ropes plied their trade at Etables. There were weavers and tailors also, who would be in need of the services of seamstresses. Anne-Thérèse, her niece was later to record, worked for a time as a seamstress. That is all that we can know definitely of her occupation outside her home.

Throughout these years, of which so many details are still obscure, the young girl still cherished the dream of her First Communion day. For ten long years she had treasured her secret. But now Marie-Jeanne was almost 16, the age at which she herself had assumed responsibility for the home and their ailing mother. Madame Guérin was recovering her health and her spirits. It would be good for Marie-Jeanne to taste responsibility, and she was fully capable of handling it. It was time for Anne-Thérèse to speak of her own vocation. In her love for her mother and her desire to spare her any pain, she pondered and prayed over the kindest way to approach the subject.

Then, one day, there occurred an event, which served to precipitate the important discussion. Anne-Thérèse later confided that her long-guarded secret was wrested from her quite by surprise. She was with a group of her young friends, who like girls everywhere were discussing the perennial topic: the ideal life companion, his rank, his occupation, and his sterling qualities. Anne-Thérèse, usually the most animated and entertaining of them all, remained silent, suddenly overcome by the deep yearning she had so long carried hidden in her heart. Amazed at her lack of response, and unaware of any trespassing, one of her companions demanded, "What about you, Anne-Thérèse?"

So deeply had Anne-Thérèse withdrawn into the depths of her heart that it was from those depths she now spoke. [17] "My spouse will be a king!" she declared, to the surprise of everyone, herself not the least. There followed, of course, great consternation and excited surmise. Anne-Thérèse, knowing that it would not be long before her strange declaration reached her mother's ears, welcomed the opportunity to speak at last of her real aspirations.

It is hardly likely that Madame Guérin was taken by surprise. In the years they had shared so intimately the mother could not have remained entirely unaware of her daughter's inclinations. Yet in spite of her piety and her love for Anne-Thérèse, she could not bring herself to yield to a higher claim on the girl's devotion. To Anne-Thérèse's repeated pleadings over the next few years she consistently used the formidable weapons of her delicate health, her widowhood, her complete dependence on her elder daughter. Her losses had already been too heavy. Marie-Jeanne was still so young; she, too, needed her older sister.

It may well be supposed, considering Anne-Thérèse's tendency to seek counsel, that in yielding to her mother's entreaties she was following not only the dictates of her own affectionate heart, but more specifically the advice of her confessor. The Abbé Duval-Villebogard was still near enough to be consulted, having retired to Saint-Brieuc in 1818. Confident, however, that God would somehow find a way for her to realize her aspirations, she began little by little to make the necessary preparation. When her mother gave her consent, Anne-Thérèse would be ready. Meanwhile she would continue to hope and to pray.

Five years passed before her prayers were answered. Then the answer came, unexpectedly, apparently unaccountably. One evening, night prayers were over, Madame Guérin turned to her daughter just as she was about to retire. "Anne-Thérèse," she said gently, calmly, "you may go! You have your mother's permission and her blessing. I can no longer refuse the good God the sacrifice he is asking of me!" [18]

Given the tragic figure of Isabelle Lefevre Guérin, the separation involved would indeed be a sacrifice difficult to overestimate. Throughout her life she had been deprived, one by one, of those she loved: father, brothers, mother, sons and then finally and most cruelly, her husband. It was not surprising that she had grown to depend, perhaps too much, on Anne-Thérèse's affection and her patient, generous devotion. In parting with this daughter, she would be losing the one who had done her best to substitute for all the others, both in her mother's service and in her affections.

Once the sacrifice had been made, Madame Guérin, from whom her daughter had inherited some of her courageous spirit, never took back her offering. A few years later, Marie-Jeanne's husband, meeting his wife's sister for the first time, offered to see what he could do to have so charming a person restored to her family. Madame Guérin cut short his proposals, reminding him gently, "Never take back from the altar the victim that has been offered." [19]

In her dreams of religious life, Anne-Thérèse had always placed herself in Carmel, among the daughters of her patron, St. Teresa, in a life of solitude and prayer. What led to her ultimate choice of congregation must be left to conjecture. All her life she possessed the gift of going out to others and drawing others to herself; it was impossible for her to remain indifferent in the presence of poverty, ignorance or pain. As time passed, she became more and more aware of the magnitude and the extent of the challenge of the times, and of her own need to respond.

She did not abandon her desire for a life of solitude, penance, and prayer; her whole longing was still for intimate union with God. But the God she loved had walked among his people, healing, instructing, consoling. She began to understand and to appreciate the dedication of the young women of her age who were devoting themselves unsparingly in imitation of Christ.

She would have met some of them in the course of her ministrations to the poor and the unfortunate, and would inevitably have spoken of her own aspirations. There were Daughters of the Holy Spirit in her native village, in the cathedral city of Saint-Brieuc. In other towns of Brittany, there were Sisters of Charity in nearby St. Jacut-sur-mer. In St. Servan a group of Daughters of the Heart of Mary engaged in the work of education under the direction of the holy Abbé Jean-Marie Lamennais.

In 1818 a Breton noblewoman, Zoé Rolland du Roscoät, who had long devoted her time and her resources to the service of the poor, had traveled from her family chateau at Pléhédel to the episcopal city of Saint-Brieuc, to attend a mission preached by a Jesuit Father de la Chapelle from Laval. Zoé had opened her heart to the missionary, who advised her to join a group of pious young women laboring toward the same ministry under the direction of the zealous Cure of Ruillé-sur-Loir, in the diocese of Le Mans. Father Dujarié's little group, the Jesuit assured her, was without doubt the poorest and the humblest in France. [20] The vocation of this highly-respected young woman from one of the oldest and noblest families of Brittany, kindled in the Province awareness of this timely and hitherto unknown society, not yet a religious community.

In 1819 two sisters from Ruillé-sur-Loir opened their first establishment in the Province of Côtes-du-Nord, at Paimpol, [21] on the coast due north of Etables. We cannot know whether, like Zoé du Roscoät, Anne-Thérèse Guérin ever attended a mission at Saint Brieuc. Her confessor had retired there, and it is reasonable to suppose that she sought him out from time to time. There can be no doubt, however, that she did meet one of the two sisters first assigned to the little house at Paimpol, Sister Marcelle Madeleine. We have her own word for it, and more than a suggestion of the importance to her of that friendship formed on the seacoast of Brittany, in a note which she sent back from across the sea some thirty years later.

"My good Sister Marcelle," she wrote, "this letter is for you as well as for Sister St. Eloi. May it convince you that I have never forgotten what I owe you, and that I have never ceased to regard you as my first Mother. Was it not indeed with you that I began my journeyings? Do you remember the trip we made together atop a cartload of flax, in the scorching heat of a July sun? How long ago that seems!" [22]

Unfortunately she did not mention the purpose of the trip, or the destination of the two young women. The picture evoked tells us a great deal about the young girl who was Anne-Thérèse Guérin. It indicates, too, the simple means that Providence so often uses to accomplish its ends.

During her years of waiting, Anne-Thérèse, after prayer and reflection, had developed for herself a plan of life which she hoped would reconcile the seemingly opposing needs of her soul: her attraction for a life of prayer and contemplation, and the imperious call to works of mercy. What God was asking from her at that moment, she reasoned, was to give herself to his people in their desperate need. For ten years, she decided, she would labor as a Sister of Charity, in whatever work might be assigned her. Then she would withdraw into the cloister to devote herself to a life of solitude, prayer, and penance. [23] In her youth and inexperience she did not realize that she was trying thus to solve the perennial problem of the loving soul drawn at once towards contemplation and apostolic action, life in God and for God. Like so many other earnest disciples of the Lord come to dwell among his people, she would learn with time and fidelity to resolve the apparent contradiction. Meanwhile, she prepared to take the first step towards the fulfillment of her life plan.

On Aug.18, 1823, she entered the Congregation of the Sisters of Providence of Ruillé-sur-Loir. [24] She was almost 25 years old, pious, generous, capable, intelligent and well informed. Above all, she was already acquainted with privation, sacrifice, and hard work. She brought with her the simple wardrobe she had been assembling, little by little, as she awaited the permission she had always been confident her mother would give, and a dowry of one hundred francs, all that the financial situation of her family could provide.

Chapter 2

The community, which on that August day in 1823 welcomed Anne-Thérèse Guérin into its novitiate, had its beginnings less than 20 years earlier in the zealous efforts of a country pastor to provide for the pressing needs of his scattered flock. [1] It was one of numerous similar institutes established in France in the early 19 century, the visible response of a merciful Providence to the appeal of a suffering people. In post Revolutionary France the needs of the people were boundless, and their only resource was Providence, which could find its human instruments in many instances among the poor themselves, among the simple, the unlettered, those possessed of no means of their own. Wherever two or three of these workers gathered, it seemed only natural to speak of the center of their ministrations as a "Providence." [2] As St. John Eudes had set up "refuges" for those in need of protection or reclamation, zealous souls now set up here and there for a "Providence" for the dispensing of spiritual and bodily nourishment to the poor and the sick. Thus the Abbé Jean de Lamennais had established the Providence of Ploermel and Mother Jamin the Providence of La Flèche, to name but two.

When in 1806, the Abbé Jacques-Francois Dujarié, parish priest of Ruillé -sur-Loir, succeeded in establishing such a center for the care of his poorest parishioners, he called it the "Little Providence." Everything about it was little, humble, unassuming. Father Dujarié's congregation included not only the inhabitants of the town, but also many families scattered in small hamlets, separated from the town by barren fields and miserable roads. His chief concern was for these people, poor, indifferent, even hostile to religion, their children growing up without instruction of any kind, their sick lacking competent care. In the town itself two Sisters of Charity of Evron administered a little "Bureau of Charity" where they cared for the sick and instructed the children; [4] but these Sisters were unable to reach the needy on the outskirts of Ruillé.

While he set about repairing the parish church, largely at his own expense, seeking to render it fit for mass, Father Dujarié was casting about also for some means of bringing the word of God and the assistance of Christian charity to these neglected souls. He concentrated upon the "Heights of Ruillé," a hamlet comprising about 15 families, two and a half miles north of Ruillé, where the pasturage was poor, the fields unproductive.

Even before his appointment to the parish, he had interested himself in the children of this region, abandoned to ignorance, growing up without hope. [5]

Now that he was responsible for the welfare of the entire parish and could no longer devote as much time as formerly to his catechetical efforts, he looked about for assistance. Like other parish priests of every era, he realized that the help he needed could be found only in the cooperation of devoted women among his parishioners. Seconded by two humble women whose very names have not been recorded, he began work the extent of which he himself could not foresee. [6]

Their first headquarters was a rented house, which was soon found to be too small. "Considering the large number of children gathered for instruction in that house," Father Dujarié later recalled, "and foreseeing the advantage it would be to the parish to have an establishment in this region, I determined to have a house built there." [7] He already possessed a property on which to build, an isolated tract on the Heights of Ruillé, the gift of the Count Jules de Beaumont, proprietor in the area and a generous benefactor of the parish.

Given the circumstances of Father Dujarié's parishioners, contributions toward the expense of the actual building were necessarily meager. But the fields were strewn with stones, and the pastor, "putting in his pocket an apple and a piece of bread for his lunch," set out from time to time with some of the children to gather these natural building blocks. Friends did not want to haul the little piles left here and there to the site of the future "Little Providence." [8]

And so the house was built. It was small but substantial, roofed with tiles, and consisting of a ground floor divided by a narrow entrance hall into two rooms, a kitchen and a schoolroom. Above there was a low attic, so low indeed that one could scarcely stand upright. This attic, exposed to the torrid heat of summer and the frigid blasts of winter, served as dormitory. Outside the sturdy little stone house there was neither orchard nor garden, and the nearest well was about two miles away. The lives of these first servants of the poor rivaled in poverty and inconvenience that of the people they served. [9]

Throughout the week, the catechists spent the days visiting the sick on the scattered farms, giving what nursing assistance they could manage, rendering the most menial services to the aged and the handicapped, gathering together the children, with whom they strove to share their own limited store of knowledge. They could indeed, by example as well as by word, impart the basic lessons of Christian doctrine and piety. For the rest, their instruction was most elementary: a little reading, a little writing, and the simplest arithmetic. In this respect their little pupils fared no worse — indeed even better - than their counterparts throughout the land where it was admitted "the new generation which has just reached its twentieth year is irrevocably sacrificed to ignorance. Primary schools do not exist; most of the nation is without instruction." [10] Primary education had been, in fact, "one of the first victims of the overthrow of society in 1789." [11]

The busy pastor somehow found time to oversee the labors of his associates, advising and instructing them on his visits to the Little Providence or in the presbytery on Sundays, when the young women, arising at 4 o'clock, took the long arduous road to the parish church. There they could assist at Mass, receive the sacraments, consult with their spiritual father, and then perhaps recreate themselves a little in the garden while waiting to participate in the afternoon offices. After Vespers they set out again for Little Providence, carrying with them as their week's provisions what supplies they might secure from Madelon, the testy servant at the presbytery, or from kindly and devoted Madame Aubry, the good neighbor in whose house Father Dujarié had found refuge during the darkest days of the Terror. The provisions would consist of bread, cheese, some vegetables and fruit according to the season, sometimes a little meat or butter. With these the young women had to make do until the following Sunday brought them once more into the town. [12]

It was not until 1811 or 1812 that Father Dujarié succeeded in adding to the stone house a tiny chapel. Here he reserved the Blessed Sacrament and here, two or three times a week he celebrated Mass. The chapel measured 20 feet by11. Its interior walls were whitewashed. Above the altar a picture of the Nativity of touching simplicity focused attention on the patrons of the enterprise: the infant in the manger, Mary and Joseph beside him sharing the humility and the poverty which were his choice and which were to be the portion, also, of those who came to share the life of "Little Providence." [13]

During these early years this life was assuming gradually, almost spontaneously, the aspect of a religious community. Providence was leading the zealous Cure farther than he had envisioned when first he gathered about him his little group of "pious women associated without any definite commitment, to work under his direction." [14] It was not long before those to whom the inhabitants of the Little Providence ministered were calling their benefactresses "Sisters." New recruits arrived to join the first generous laborers; Father Dujarié was finding ever-new needs in other corners of his widespread parish, and neighboring pastors were looking to him for assistance. Father Dujarié saw his work taking a form and demanding an organization that he had not foreseen. He soon realized that these country girls, although filled with good will, had need of a certain formal training, both spiritual and professional, for the life that the Spirit was opening to them. Where could he find for them a house of formation and a good director?

He had not far to look; in the little town of Baugé, in the diocese of Angers, there existed, even during the Revolution, a hospital for incurables under the direction of a woman of outstanding virtue and ability, Mademoiselle Anne Hardouin de la Girouardière, foundress, with the Abbé René Bérault, of the Daughters of the Sacred Heart of Mary, a community completely devoted to works of self-sacrificing charity. [15] Mademoiselle de la Girouardière and the Abbé Bérault enjoyed a wide and well-deserved reputation. Father Dujarié, however, would have had personal experience of their virtues and their talents. It was on the estate of Mademoiselle de la Girouardière's father that the proscribed clergy, the young Dujarié among them, had found refuge during the first Terror, as had his seminary master, the Abbé Meilloc.

René Bérault had been, like Jacques-Francois Dujarié, a seminarian at Anger. Both had early in life been inspired by their teachers with that devotion to the Sacred Heart and to the Heart of Mary which were characteristics of the followers of St. John Eudes. Father Dujarié begged the saintly Superior of Baugé to undertake the formation of some of his catechists. [16]

Mademoiselle de la Girouardière graciously received the seven postulants whom Father Dujarié sent her and taught them both the principles of religious life and the art of caring for the sick. After a stay of several months in this atmosphere of regularity and zeal, under the motherly direction of Mademoiselle de la Girouardière, the seven returned to Ruillé, wearing a religious habit, and eager to put into practice the lessons they had received. Henceforth, like the Sisters of Baugé, they recited the Office of the Sacred Heart of Mary, which Father Dujarié had printed for his little community.[17] He borrowed also the primitive Rule of the Sisters of Baugé to assist him in drawing up Rules for his own Sisters of Ruillé. [18]

The first Rules were to remain for some time only provisional, the founder retaining the single hand-written copy and reserving to himself the privilege of modifying them as occasion might demand. The sisters meantime continued as simply a pious and charitable association, without vows and without definite rules. The formation of a true and stable religious congregation would require rules and constitution outlining a definite program of life under the direction of a competent superior. But day-to-day concerns absorbed all of the pastor's time; besides, he had not yet found among his auxiliaries one who could suitably fill the place of superior, directing in his place the internal affairs of the Community, which in 1818 numbered 18 sisters working not only in the Little Providence but also in seven neighboring parishes. [19]

In July of that year, however, there came to Ruillé a postulant who seemed to have been specially prepared by divine Providence to bring to the fledgling community the form and direction it needed. This was Mademoiselle Julie-Josephine Zoé du Roscoät, [20] daughter of Count Louis Rolland du Roscoät, of Pléhédel, and Francoise Exaudy de Kerbiquet, of

Nantes. Zoé, 37 years of age, brought with her her heritage as daughter of a truly noble family, utterly devoted to its Catholic faith, a family which had enjoyed the privileges of wealth and position and endured the indignities and the hardships of victims of the Revolution. She brought her experience as catechist at home, as teacher in the school her mother had been compelled to open for their support during the Revolution, and finally as angel of mercy among the poor and the ignorant of her native Brittany.

When, after the Revolution, the family fortunes were partially restored, the school in Rennes closed, and the family returned to the chateau at Pléhédel. Zoé was free to devote herself to the work dearest to her heart, the service of the sick and the instruction of little children. She was one of the generous young French women of her period who, for love of God, gave of their own means, but more importantly of their time and their tenderness to the service of the destitute and the helpless.

For Zoé, however, this was not enough. She longed to give herself completely to a life of charity, away from her comfortable home and affectionate family circle, and she took occasion during a retreat at Saint-Brieuc in 1816 to ask for direction. The retreat master, a Jesuit of Laval, Father de la Chapelle, offered her the advice she was seeking. A friend of Father Dujarié and acquainted with the work at Little Providence, he hastened to assure Mademoiselle du Roscoät that it was there she would find what she was seeking, for it was indeed the poorest and the humblest community in France.

It was not until two years later, after the death of her father, that Zoé succeeded in winning her mother's reluctant consent. In July of 1818 she arrived in Ruillé delighted with what she found there, she thus described the little establishment:

> I have the honor of finding here a guide who is all I could
> desire and a true father; he has all the kindness and all the virtues

of an enlightened priest. The rule he has given to our Sisters is very wise, and breathes charity and his zeal for their perfection. I have found them much better informed than I had anticipated in all that regards their state of life.

At the Providence we have a little pharmacy and we instruct children. I am trying to learn something so as to be useful in the future. The Abbé Dujarié, our Father, has given us an excellent manner of instructing the little children. His zeal for the glory of God is great, and his dedication will lead him to undertake all that he can to procure it in our land. I must tell you that we have the happiness of preserving the Most Blessed Sacrament in our little chapel. [21]

Father Dujarié recognized in his new postulant the aide chosen by God to give at last the needed form and direction to his work. Despite her own humble assessment, Mademoiselle du Roscoät was in every way a gift of Providence. Older than her companions, highly educated, experienced, spiritually mature, she had need of all the generosity and abnegation she had acquired in her years of selfless service. She adjusted admirably to the primitive circumstances in which she found herself: the rough terrain, the crowded quarters, the plain and scanty nourishment, the mannerisms, sometimes rough and uncouth, of her associates. The Nativity scene in the little chapel was her inspiration and her encouragement. The charm of her gentleness and zeal soon captivated the hearts of all with whom she lived and whom she served.

Father Dujarié realized with joy that the time had come to give structure to his young community. Accordingly, in 1820 he decreed that the members would in the future take religious vows, adding to those of poverty, chastity, and obedience that of devoting their lives to the instruction of children and the care of the sick poor. The Congregation would be governed by a superior-general elected by the sisters. Mademoiselle du Roscoät, now Sister Marie Madeleine, was unanimously elected first superior. [22]

The entrance of Zoé du Roscoät had inspired an influx of postulants. Among those who followed her from her native Brittany was a young woman from the Ile de Bréhat, who had been an invaluable assistant to Zoé in her works of charity. The gentlewoman of Pléhédel had met the simple working girl of Bréhat at a meeting of the Third Order of St. Francis, of which both were members. Mademoiselle du Roscoät recognized in Perrine-Aimée Lecor [23] a kindred spirit. Impelled by the same love of God and souls, both were spending themselves eagerly in the service of the sick poor, in which apostolate they complemented each other, Zoé better able to supply material means, Perrine adept in the dialect of the Breton peasants, which Zoé understood but did not speak well. She was happy to place Perrine in charge of the little school she had opened in a small house belonging to her family in Pléhédel and she herself departed for Ruillé. As superior-general, she lost no time in writing to remind Perrine that this place awaited her.

When Perrine-Aimée Lecor arrived at Little Providence in 1820 it was to find a community larger than the one, which had greeted Zoé du Roscoät two years earlier and more widespread in its influence. There were now 18 novices in the small house, and the Sisters who had gone out, two by two, to other houses in seven dioceses had to remain always at their posts, for Little Providence had no space at all to give them in which to rest from time to time. Mother du Roscoät did her best to keep in touch with her daughters, writing them, undertaking the long uncomfortable journeys to their separated missions. Meantime, she and the founder pondered means of filling the desperate need for an adequate dwelling, near enough to the church to facilitate consultation with their pastor, large enough to the church to accommodate the increasing number of novices and postulants and to permit the Sisters to return for rest and renewal. In

1821, with what remained of his patrimony, Father Dujarié purchased a site at the entrance to the town, adjoining the presbytery. The cornerstone of the new Providence was laid in March; by the following spring it was almost ready for occupancy. [24]

While the community joyfully anticipated moving into this new Motherhouse in time for Retreat, their Mother made arrangements to spend a few weeks in Brittany, taking care of family affairs, which required her presence and visiting the houses in the region. On her return she would be free to give all her attention to the happy transfer. To soften the temporary parting and to remind them of their uninterrupted union in mind and spirit, the founder offered the Sisters the prayer that would be treasured by all who succeeded them, the "Prayer of Reunion," strongly reminiscent of the "Salutations" of St. John Eudes to the Sacred Hearts of Jesus and Mary, which Jacques-Francois Dujarié would have recited with his fellow students in the Eudist College of Domfront. Father Dujarié wrote: "We unite with all our Sisters to adore you, O divine Heart of Jesus! Heart most holy, most pure, most humble, most wise, most amiable, and most merciful. We give you our hearts, we consecrate them, and we immolate them to you. Deign to receive, possess, purify, enlighten and sanctify them, and render them like to yours!"

If during the weeks which followed Mother du Roscoät'departure the sisters found consolation in this prayer. It served to keep them closely united to each other and to their Lord as they looked forward to her early return; much greater was their need for any encouragement it might provide in the unexpected trial that awaited them. On May 27 the Count Amédée du Roscoät, brother of Mother Marie Madeleine, wrote to impart the news of her dangerous illness. Subsequent letters expressed alternate hope and concern. On June 22 she died, the victim of typhoid, surrounded by her family, but far from her sisters, of whom only one could be with her. When the community moved into the new Providence in time for the Retreat, as they had planned, they were still in mourning for the one who had endeared herself to all, and whom they now needed more than ever. [25]

To fill the place left so achingly empty by her untimely death, the founder turned to the one whom Providence had been preparing to continue the work so well begun, the one who had been Zoé du Roscoät's collaborator in her apostolate in Brittany, who had responded to her invitation to enter the community at Ruillé, and whom she had hoped to have as assistant in her government of the Congregation. To Father Dujarié alone, Mother du Roscoät had confided her hope for Perrnine-Aimée Lecor, since 1820 known as Sister Cecile.

The founder had only to make known to the sisters the desires expressed to him by Mother Marie Madeleine. So devoted to her were they, so confident of her judgment, that they could but accede to her known wishes. In September 1822 at the time of the Retreat conducted by two Jesuit Fathers from Laval, Sister Cecile was unanimously elected to succeed Mother Marie Madeleine.

There could be scarcely have been a greater difference in personalities, in aptitudes, in education, in background. Sister Cecile was the first to recognize this fact. Father Dujarié, entering into her sentiments, consoled her with the reflection that since her unanimous election revealed the will of God for her, she must indeed accept the burden, entrusting its accomplishment to the Blessed Virgin, in whose honor she would change her name to Mother Mary. Unhampered by any illusions about her own competence, the new superior faced her task with indomitable courage. As she was to acknowledge later, "After having prayed and abandoned myself to God, I felt such strength that if I had seen the vault of Heaven fall, I would have inclined my shoulders to receive it." [26]

Under such leadership the Congregation so well launched made steady progress. The founder continued to oversee all the material aspects of the administration, handling the funds, making all arrangements, civil and ecclesiastical, for its welfare. As early as 1820 he had begun negotiations for government authorization of the Congregation, which in fact was granted five years later. [27] Recognizing the similarity of aims and ideals between the community of Ruillé and that directed by Mère Francoise Jamin [28] in nearby La Flèche, he wrote Mère Jamin in November 1822 [29] suggesting that she unite her community to his, now larger that that of La Flèche and firmly established. The superior of La Flèche preferred to retain her autonomy; but Father Dujarié's letter presents a picture of the Sisters of Providence of Ruillé-sur-Loir at that time.

"The principal end of the Sisters, " he wrote, "is the instruction of youth, especially of the poor, the aid of the sick in their homes, especially the poor little children in the towns. The Sisters have a novitiate of two years. After this time, they can be admitted to annual vows of obedience, of poverty, and of chastity, and of the consecration of their talents and energies to the education of youth and the care of the poor. Vows are renewed every year; after a certain time and age, they may be made for several years, or even perpetually. They choose a superior-general every three years, who can be re-elected. This superior appoints to all the employments. Monseigneur is the superior by right."

The founder's formal outline of the congregation assumes a more intimate, human aspect in the glimpse of community life given earlier by Mother du Roscoät: "I am already accustomed to the rule of the house. We help each other and in this way we have the happiness of imitating the life of poverty of our Divine Savior, and I am finding that a life of work, poverty and regularity does more for my weak health than a life which is too dainty." [30]

This simple life of work, poverty and regularity, lived from day to day for the love of God and in total dependence on Divine Providence, was characteristic of the new French congregations, living witnesses to the eternal solicitude of the Father in heaven for his struggling children on earth. Father Dujarié's pastoral concern for the welfare of his flock, reflected in the response of a few parishioners who offered all they had, their willingness to serve, had been encouraged beyond his most ardent expectations by the providential help sent to him from the distant coasts of Brittany. It was a fervent, growing religious Institute for which he was now responsible; and he found himself aided in his administration by women of enthusiasm and dedication, under the able direction of Mother Mary Lecor.

Such was the community, which on August 18, 1823, admitted to its novitiate another daughter of Brittany, Anne-Thérèse Guérin, a postulant from Etables-sur-mer. [31]

Saint Mother Theodore Guerin

1798–1856

Foundress of the Sisters of Providence
of Saint Mary-of-the-Woods

Chapter 3

To 20th century American Sisters of Providence seeking deeper insight into the spirit of their foundress, a French superior thus explained the disappointing scarcity of details: "The Sisters of Providence of Ruillé were not accustomed to commit their thoughts and their feelings to writing. The life of your good Mother in France would have been a simple one, like that of one of us." [1]

This statement, in itself a eulogy, might have been made by thousands of the dedicated laborers called forth by Providence in those early years of the 19th century. Theirs was indeed a life of outward simplicity, complete abnegation; a life lived in the presence of God, humbly taking from his hands daily in order to give to the nearest neighbor in need. Busy days began with hours of mental and vocal prayer; that left no leisure for self-communing, and even the hours of prayer were often filled with the needs of others.

At Ruillé-sur-Loir the community annals chronicle the names of those who entered, the date of their entry, of their vesting, of their profession, their various assignments, and finally the date of death. The very simplicity of the account is awesome and admirable. And so we read that Mademoiselle Anne Thérèse Guérin, daughter of Laurent Guérin and Isabelle Lefevre, born at Etables, Côtes-du-Nord, October 2, 1798, entered August 18, 1823, bringing a dowry of 100 francs. She received the habit September 6, 1825, was professed September 8, 1825, and took perpetual vows September 5, 1831. She was sent from the novitiate to Preuilly in 1825; to Rennes as superior in 1826; to Soulaines in 1834; she left for Vincennes (America) on July 13, 1840. [2] Thus is summarized 17 years of religious life. The few details that may be gathered from personal reminiscences and chance references in letters fail to provide insights that elude the most diligent research.

When Anne-Thérèse entered the novitiate at Ruillé-sur-Loir, she was almost 25 years old. She arrived just in time to take part in the community retreat, given that year by Father Louis Nicholas Petit, S.J.[3] one of the Fathers of the Faith from Laval, to whom Father Dujarié always felt free to turn for advice and direction. Whether or not this was her first Jesuit retreat we have no way of knowing. The diocese in which she had grown up, Saint-Brieuc, was among those in which the Fathers of the Faith, established in Laval in 1816, had preached missions. It is possible that, like Zoé du Roscoät, Anne-Thérèse Guérin had attended one of these missions, and like her had there received her orientation towards the little community at Ruillé, whose founder was known to the Fathers; but this must remain conjecture only, for nowhere does one find a substantiating note. Long years later she was to recall her first retreat as a religious.

Mother Mary recognized in the postulant from Etables a candidate of unusual promise. Already matured by responsibility and acquainted with hard work and sacrifice, gracious and outgoing in manner, adept in the household arts, and above all solidly grounded in the knowledge of her religion and the practice of recollection and prayer, she was well equipped to assume a large share in the works of the Congregation. The life of the novitiate, founded on an uncomplicated spirituality of self-forgetfulness and constant striving to live in the presence of God, represented to her all that she had desired for so many years. This life must, however, have made uncompromising demands on her, both affording opportunities for her energy and generosity and presenting challenges to her lively intelligence and her imperious will. She was of an affectionate disposition, amiable and quick to respond, alive to all she saw around her. There can be no question of her contribution to the life of the novitiate.

During her first year at Ruillé, there were 16 novices and 36 postulants in the newly erected Providence; they were under the direction of Sister St. Charles (Helen Jolle). [4] Sister St. Charles was not yet 25 years old, and had been a member of the community for only two years. She was one of those who had begun religious life in the Little Providence on the Heights of Ruillé. Having entered in 1821, she had known the gentle, amiable Mother Marie Madeleine du Roscoät. Like her superior, she had founded her spiritual life on love of the Blessed Sacrament and the virtues depicted in the humble Bethlehem scene above the altar at Little Providence. Mother Mary had no misgivings about placing this fervent young religious in charge of the novices, some of them, like Anne-Thérèse Guérin, now Sister St. Theodore, a little older than herself.

Sister St. Theodore had, however, no difficulty in showing affectionate respect for her young novice director. The humility which was the counterpart to her ardent, impetuous nature marked her from the beginning of her religious life. Her openness, her spontaneity, her avid search for the will of God in her regard would have made her a consolation to her young mentor.

At that time, it was customary for the postulants to spend a period of time, individually determined, at the motherhouse, in secular attire. Then, having put on the habit, they were sent to complete their novitiate in one of the establishments, under the directions of the local superior. Besides religious formation, they received instruction in preparation for their duties as members of an institute devoted to the teaching of young girls and the care of the sick. In the pharmacy opened at the motherhouse in 1819 they learned the principles of first aid. They also studied the subjects necessary for primary teaching. The length of time of each one's novitiate at Ruillé would be regulated by the calls on the growing community and the qualities of the candidates. As one parish after another made its plea for laborers, young sisters were sent out, sometimes after only a few months of novitiate, some even to take charge of a small establishment. Just two weeks before Anne-Thérèse arrived, for instance, three young women, after less than a year of novitiate, had left Ruillé to take on the responsibility of newly-opened missions, Sister Athanase to Orleans, Sister Marie Ann to Montauban, and Sister St. Elia to Chateaudun. [5] As urgent calls for their devoted service multiplied, the superiors were forced to seek among the postulants those who might most profitably be called upon to leave the peaceful seclusion of the novitiate.

Sister Theodore, capable, mature, fervent, would have been a logical choice. It would seem that no sooner had she made herself at home in the atmosphere of prayer and recollection so long awaited, than she would be called upon to enter the life of dedicated charity to which she had committed herself. But the Providence which had finally removed all obstacles to Anne-Thérèse's vocation had other plans for Sister Theodore. Early in her novitiate, an attack of smallpox, completely disabling her and seriously endangering her life, put an end to all thought of an early mission assignment. Instead, the young woman who had so long been accustomed to minister to others became the recipient of the loving attention of her superiors. During the long months of her illness she experienced at first hand both new aspects of suffering and new expressions of religious charity and devotion. During these months were forged bittersweet links which were in the future to bring her both great happiness and exquisite suffering. She never forgot the hours her superiors had spent at her bedside and the tender affectionate care they lavished on her. Their devotion was evidence not only of their sisterly charity, but also of their esteem for the promising aspirant. Her illness was protracted; in desperation the physicians prescribed very severe remedies, which indeed cured her illness, but which left her a quasi-invalid for life. [6] Never afterward was she able to digest solid food.

Slowly she recovered some semblance of health; but almost a year and a half were to pass before she could be considered physically strong enough to continue her novitiate on mission. Then, in the hope that the change would complete her convalescence, Mother Mary assigned her in January 1825 to the little establishment in the village of Preuilly-sur-Claise. The temporary parting from Ruillé was not easy for Sister Theodore; it demanded of her one of those sacrifices which her affectionate nature would never permit her to make with indifference. Years later she remembered the painful separation. Writing from America to Sister St. Charles, on January 6, 1847, she reminded her former mistress, "Twenty-two years ago today I left you for the first time to go on mission." [7]

The house at Preuilly had been opened just the preceding year, when the village offered lodging and 600 francs for the support of two sisters, one of whom would conduct classes and the other visit the sick. The community assumed the expenses of a third Sister to take charge of a paying class, the proceeds to benefit the Congregation. The records do not indicate the role filled by Sister Theodore; she may well have been the third sister, sent at congregation expense to undertake the paying class, once the free school had been a few months underway. At any rate, the end of the school year found her, to her great joy, back at Ruillé for the annual retreat and the canonical reception of the habit, which took place September 6. Two days later, she pronounced her first vows with her novitiate companions, among them Sisters Marie Anne and St. Emile.

What her first assignment after profession was seems to be somewhat in doubt. According to the community " Register of Transfers" compiled by Sister St. Damian Chalot, community secretary between 1840 and 1846, Sister Theodore was assigned to Preuilly in 1825 and then to Rennes in 1826. The record specifies no definite dates. Those closest to Sister Theodore, however, her niece Sister Mary Theodore and her first biographer, Mother Mary Cecilia Bailley place her appointment to Rennes immediately after her first profession, hence in 1825. Such a move would not have been surprising, given the practice of the community at that time and the qualifications of Sister Theodore. She herself, writing to one of the sisters on January 28, 1851, remarks, "....when I arrived in Rennes twenty-six years ago," [8] which seems to indicate that she had been appointed to Rennes in 1825. The possibility must remain however, that as noted in the community record, she was sent as superior to Rennes in 1826, having spent the preceding year at her post in Preuilly-sur-Claise.

Her brief ministry at Preuilly was outwardly uneventful. This little establishment was itself short-lived. The Revolution of 1830 having put an end to the euphoria induced by the Restoration, found that support was withdrawn and the school closed in 1830. [9]

In the summer of 1826 she was once again at Ruillé, eagerly anticipating the silence and recollection of the retreat. She had benefited from the experience of active apostolate and life in a small community; now she was happy to return to the contemplative atmosphere that she loved. Once again she could open her heart to Mother Mary and to Sister St. Charles with all the humble candor that was one of her most endearing qualities.

As was to be expected, they, too, were frank with her; whereas accounts of her little spiritual and apostolic triumphs might be lightly passed over, no failing was apt to go unnoted. A woman of deep spirituality who never spared herself, Mother Mary was not inclined to deal gently with the souls under her care in whom she discerned great promise combined with great generosity. Sister St. Charles could always be counted on to support her superior's policies, at the same time softening the edges of her exhortations, when softening was indicated. Both superiors were living examples of the principles they taught; both recognized in Sister Theodore unusual promise.

At the close of the retreat Sister Theodore renewed the vows pronounced the previous year. The days of calm reflection and scrupulous self-examination, the precious hours before the Blessed Sacrament, the solitary walks in the little woods, the visits to "Little Providence," where lessons of poverty, humility, and perfect abnegation could still be read in every stone, came all too soon to an end. The last retreat conference was over, the community knelt in prolonged thanksgiving after the general Communion; there followed an afternoon of lively, truly French recreation; and then came the inevitable preparations for the year's assignments. Spiritually renewed, the sisters could now go out once more, to share with their pupils and the poor whom they served their increased store of courage and hope. There was everywhere so great a need of these virtues.

Nowhere, perhaps, was this need greater than in the bustling city of Rennes, to which Sister Theodore's obedience of 1826 assigned her. [10] This city, situated in the valley of the Vilaine River, at the heart of the region of medieval chateaus, bore little resemblance at the time of Sister Theodore's arrival to the Rennes of the past, capital of the ancient province of Brittany, land of fable and romance. The Rennes which Sister Theodore found had been long in preparation. The city, with the entire Province, had known periods of change and strife ever since the Gallo-Roman days. Deplorable conditions prevailed during the 18th. century, when land cultivation was reduced by half, absentee landlords having left their domains to seek fortunes elsewhere. The meager harvests and consequent malnutrition, epidemics and unemployment, together with Breton reaction to the Royal Edicts curtailing the rights of provincial parliaments, had led to bloody riots in the streets of the city even before the Revolution.

Conditions during the Revolution are vividly portrayed in the notes[11] of a native of Rennes, Simon Gabriel Bruté de Rémur, first Bishop of Vincennes in Indiana. These notes, which describe the inhuman depravity of the Terrorists and the persecutions and heroism of the faithful, clergy and laity alike, offer a glimpse of the underlying faith of the Rennais. Bishop Bruté has left a sketch of the Cathedral, the former Benedictine Church of St. Melanie, founded in the sixth century, which during the Revolution served in turn as a prison for priests, a stable for the cavalry, a city hospital and an arsenal, before being finally restored to the diocese as cathedral in 1802. It stands on the site of the old Roman town. Most of the historic town had been destroyed by fire in 1720; what remained, including the ancient walls and ramparts, had been razed in 1783. The rebuilt city presented a few of the external characteristics of antiquity and romance; and the years of persecution and revolt had left large areas socially and morally ravaged. The overcrowded quarter St. Malo, in particular, long one of the poorest and most disturbed sections of the city, seemed to have been abandoned completely to ignorance and immorality.

The school directed by the sisters from Ruillé was located in this miserable and ill-famed quarter, on the rue Haute, in the parish of St. Aubin. This school, the first staffed by the Ruillé congregation in Rennes, had been opened in 1821 at the request of the pastor of St. Aubin, Abbé de Léon, and with the encouragement of the Abbé Garnier, vicar-general of Rennes, to continue the zealous work of pious and charitable parishioners.

A monograph history of the parish [12] published a century later details the inception and progress of this timely endeavor: Moved by the sight of so much misery and the degradation into which the greater number of the young girls of the quarter were falling, the Abbe Le Forestier and the Abbe Hunault, pastor of St. Aubin, resolved to seek a remedy by establishing a free school for the poor young girls of the quarter. But devoted women were needed to take care of these children. Just at this time a charitable woman, Mademoiselle du Jarday, moved into the rue Saint-Malo.

Father Le Forestier asked her to assume the direction of the school. Three teachers were found to take classes and to super-vise the workroom.

It was to be no haphazard undertaking. "The directory of the house, approved by the Lord Bishop, comprises three chapters. The first chapter enumerates, in 16 articles, the duties of the Mistress. The second chapter informs us in fourteen articles of the role of the Mistresses, and the third concerns the regulations for the children."[13] The children were to receive two hours of instruction in the morning, and two hours in the afternoon. They were to be taught their prayers, the Catechism, reading and writing. The rest of the time was to be employed in knitting, spinning, carding wool and sewing. The school day lasted from seven or eight in the morning until noon, and in the afternoon from one until five or seven, according to the seasons. The aim was to make of these children who would have been left to roam the streets or to beg, good Christians, prepared to earn an honest living. The project won the favor of the parents; within a few years the enrollment had increased from 80 to 200 pupils. The death of Mademoiselle du Jarday, however, made it evident that only by entrusting the school to a congregation of teaching sisters could the work become permanent. The pastor, at that time the Abbé de Léon, appealed to the Sisters of Providence, and in 1821 four sisters from Ruillé opened their first school in Rennes, the Providence of the rue Haute.

The pastor was soon describing this school enthusiastically in his appeals for support written to people of prominence, including the Duke of Angoulême, Madame Royale, the Duchess of Berry, King Louis XVIII himself.

There exists in my parish," ran his letter to the Duchess of Berry, "a school directed by the Sisters of Providence for the instruction of girls from poor families. They are taught their catechism, to read, write and work with their hands. Instead of bad example,

37

they are constantly given that of modesty and uprightness. The school has grown so much that the original premises no longer suffice. The house next door, which would suit us perfectly, is at this moment for sale. The price is 1700 francs. The acquisition of this house would put us in a position to form a novitiate for these good Sisters of Providence." [14]

His appeals were successful; the house was acquired. With the help of a grateful municipal council and the alms of charitable parishioners, new classrooms were arranged and provisions made for the maintenance of five sisters, who would devote themselves to the formation of the girls under their charge to habits of industry and virtue.

During the ensuing five years the sisters were to discover the peculiar difficulties and demands of their task. When in 1826 her superiors placed Sister Theodore in charge of the mission, they were confident that she would not be easily discouraged; she possessed that fortunate combination of amiability and firmness required in the challenging circumstances. [15] Although from the beginning she enjoyed the support of the pastor and of benefactors, she soon found that she would have need of a patience and an endurance truly supernatural in her dealings with the children. The classes were large and the little girls exhibited at times such insolence and defiance as made them seem almost incorrigible. Conscious of the power in their very numbers, they seemed to take pride in making the task of their teachers difficult. Like children everywhere who are aware that they have the upper hand, they took advantage of the least sign of discouragement or frustration. When their misconduct resulted in disheartenment, their unruliness increased.

There was speculation, therefore, in the look they fixed on the new superior who appeared before them on the opening day of the 1826 term. Her very appearance – tall, calm, with piercing dark eyes – might portend a challenge which they must at all costs meet. For the superior herself, it was a situation she would not soon forget. Long afterward she could recall the insolent stares and the exchange of knowing glances with which they responded to her first greeting. "She will be crying, too, before long!" they seemed to say. Sister Theodore said a silent prayer to their Guardian Angels. She realized it would take all her considerable courage to face these hostile children; but she knew, too, that their outward belligerence covered deep and vibrant yearnings. They had no personal quarrel with her, she knew, nor with the other sisters, even those whom they had forced by their rude behavior to withdraw. The children would not themselves have been able to express the feelings of their half-savage little souls; so they disguised them. These little beings had human hearts aware in their depths that they were destined for something better than the future their surroundings promised them. Sister Theodore would try to reach them.

So she spoke to them in a soft voice, with an expression at once serious and benign; she invited them to cooperate with her for their own instruction and improvement. The reaction was an impudent shout, "Is she a fool?" Does she think we are going to be like sisters?" In the midst of the raucous laughter which followed, any remonstrance would be lost. There was nothing for her to do except to wait quietly, outwardly composed. The next days she tried again. This time there was at first a pretense at rapt attention; then, at their ringleader's signal, the little girls rose in a body, clasped hands, and began a boisterous dance. Although they pretended to ignore Sister's presence, they were, in fact, acutely conscious of it. Sly glances sought her desk. How was she taking it? Half the fun would be lost if they did not succeed in upsetting her poise.

The new Superior sat quietly, watching them, apparently enjoying their frolic! Finally, tired out, they stopped of their own accord, and dropping into their seats looked somewhat apprehensively towards the front of the room. Their gaze followed sister's gesture as she reached deliberately for the switch that lay at hand. There were stifled little gasps. Anxious eyes watched as, still slowly and deliberately, Sister Theodore began to break the switch into little pieces. Then with a careless flick, she tossed the pieces into the basket beside her desk. Then she began to speak again, and this time they listened. "Now, children," she began, in her quiet voice, her black eyes seeming to probe into each girl's soul, "we shall begin our lessons. I see you have a great deal of energy, and you have many talents, I am sure; and I know you want to make the very most of them. But to succeed in anything so important, one must have order and good conduct. Now to help you, I have prepared rewards which I hope to give to all who behave well. We shall begin today. Those who give satisfaction this morning will each receive one of these tickets (she reached into her capacious pocket and held up a sample). Every day it will be the same. Take good care of these tickets, for with them you will be able to purchase recompenses for yourselves." Amazed, perplexed, they finally settled down. It was worth a trial. Sister Theodore offered another silent prayer, this time of thanksgiving, to their Guardian Angels. Years later she was to advise her Sisters to appeal to the angels of the children they taught, remarking that this was a practice she had found invariably successful.

She kept her promise to the children; each day those who merited them received the precious little tickets, meted out with justice indeed, but a justice tempered with mercy. Often a child might be rewarded for being just a little less mischievous than she had been the day before. Sister Theodore was always careful to take effort into consideration, and she understood how much good will must sometimes go into the slightest curbing of mutinous spirits. She persevered in her program of justice and kindness, virtues she always believed essential for teachers, and saw with gratitude and relief that it was succeeding. The children were not converted overnight, of course, but their gradual and steady improvement was a source of deep satisfaction to the sisters and the benefactors of the school. The priests of the parish and the municipal council could not fail to remark that the changes in the children were leading to a change in their parents, also. Fathers were starting to lift their heads a little higher; mothers were beginning to look to the cleanliness of their wretched homes. Little by little the face of the quarter Saint-Malo was being changed. [16]

"The very populous and ill-famed quarter where the school was located was transformed by the zeal, the enlightened piety, and the outstanding qualities of the young superior, and her Christian influence on the children was not long in communicating itself to the families and changing the face of this sad and miserable quarter," declared a later superior general of Ruillé, summing up the activities of Sister Theodore in Rennes. [17]

Sister Theodore herself recalled this experience at Rennes when, years later, she was training teachers in America. "You must try to invent a means of correcting your children," she told them, "but remember that the most powerful means are rewards: a kind word, an approving glance, a little gesture, is sometimes sufficient to correct what the harshest punishment would not have eradicated." And she reminded them, "If it is necessary to be just, it is especially necessary to be kind. We must be the mothers of our children, have for them maternal attentions and feelings. God confides these young girls to us so that we may form them to virtue." [18] Her own pupils in Rennes recognized that she had indeed a maternal interest in them, an interest at times perhaps far more real than that of their own mothers. Eventually they responded to her to the best of their ability.

But her solicitude was not limited to the children in her classrooms. Her sisters, she realized, were also in need of it. Like, her, they faced the difficulties of the arduous school days, with their recurrent bouts of schoolgirl insubordination. After class hours, they gathered in the little convent, to meet for Community prayer, to prepare for the following day, to seek recreation in each other's company. Sister Theodore exerted every effort to make these few hours spent together a time of relaxation and rest. In the process she learned that for her sisters, as well as for the pupils, it was sometimes necessary and praiseworthy to make allowances. To her, each of the religious was an individual, one of her sisters, and especially dear to her. She was for each one a mother and a friend, and their community life was a happy one. One of their number, Sister Francis Regis, might have felt more than a touch of nostalgia when years later Theodore, her former superior wrote her, "I remember the pleasure you gave me while we were so happy in our old house on the rue Haute." [19]

The superior herself was responsible for much of this happiness, as another member of the household, Sister Emmanuel, [20] could have testified. Sister Emmanuel had been a year at Rennes before Sister Theodore's arrival. The new superior noted, to her surprise and chagrin, that matters were not going well for the young sister, who seemed to be the victim of dislike and ill-will which no one, least of all a fervent, zealous young religious, should have to endure. Sister Theodore lost no time in seeking out the cause. Her findings emphasized for her the importance of fraternal charity and the harm that could be caused by thoughtless and ill-natured speech. In this instance she would do her best to repair the damage, which she had traced to unfair and unkindly criticism. When she heard someone exclaim, "Our Mother must be devoid of common sense! What could she have been thinking of to send such an unprepared person to a city like Rennes?" Sister Theodore's dark eyes glowed, and she determined to justify both Mother Mary and poor Sister Emmanuel, who, it was remarked, "although she was a Norman, was as unlettered and clumsy as a Breton!" The new superior began to call on Sister Emmanuel's experience for help in becoming acquainted with the house and the school; she asked Sister Emmanuel's advice as occasion offered; she found opportunities to praise the young teacher before her sisters and the pupils. Within two months, it almost seemed that the welfare of the establishment depended on Sister Emmanuel. Criticisms were forgotten; Sister Emmanuel basked in a new atmosphere of respect and understanding. [21]

Always quick to penetrate appearances, Sister Theodore soon understood the sister who after a wearying day was inclined to seek solitude rather than the company of the other sisters. When something happened to upset this sister, she would present herself after school to her superior, pleading indisposition. "May I please go to my room?" she would murmur. "I am too ill to come to prayers or supper." Permission was graciously given, and the sister trudged silently upstairs. As soon as her own duties permitted, Sister Theodore would mount to the invalid's room, armed with a cup of tea and her special laughter, and the invalid, recovered from her "blues" would soon feel strong enough to join the other Sisters at recreation. [22]

Sister St. Felix, [23] sent to Rennes to spend her year of novitiate under Sister Theodore's direction, observed and tried to imitate her superior with all the ardor of her 19 years. Sister Theodore was careful to instruct, reprove and encourage her. She was never too busy to listen to the girls earnest projects; she knew how to curb her flights of fancy and tried to instill into her something of her own love for her vocation. Sister St. Felix responded with her whole heart. A letter she addressed years later to her former superior, then in America, bears testimony to the spirit that prevailed in the little household, where the sisters recognized and responded to Sister Theodore's affection as they strove to carry out her precepts and follow her example.

"You are wondering, my good superior, how I am getting on with my interior miseries, for you loved the soul of your Felix, didn't you? Alas! I am always poor in the sight of God. However, I am improved in some respects. First of all, I am very resigned to all that the good God wishes of me. I have with His grace, a love of my duty, and my class is my delight. The things of the world, and what is foreign to my employment, do not touch me. I am still at Rennes, in the midst of my dear children of the Rue Haute, who are filled with good, docile and loving sentiments.

"My paper is almost filled, and my heart is not yet satisfied, there are so many things I would say to you. But I must be reasonable. I am old enough. When I think that I am 30 years old! Goodness, it seems to me that it was only a few years ago that you had to direct my nineteen-year-old head, filled with caprices! Therefore my gratitude to you increases always. If I do not have you anymore, I have your counsels, your advice; since they were for me those of a mother and a friend, they have made my heart the heart of a daughter, a truly grateful daughter. I pray for you and ask prayers for all of you. No, I will never forget you, never! never! May these words tell you all that my heart feels!" After signing herself, "Your daughter, and dear daughter for life, respectful and grateful, "Sister St. Felix notes that she was writing her letter at "five-thirty in the morning." [24]

The "good, docile and loving sentiments" which Sister St. Felix ascribes to the children reflected the attitude of the parish in general, as the change effected in the children, and through them, in the neighborhood, persisted. No longer need the Providence of the rue Haute be a cause of anxiety for the superiors of the Congregation at Ruillé-sur-Loir. When Mother Mary arrived in Rennes during the course of her visitation of the missions of Brittany, she could greet the community with the gentle assurance that she had come to rest for awhile, confident that house and school were in good hands [25] – and the dedicated, forthright Mother Mary was not accustomed to dispense flattery. Praise from her would be well-deserved, and rich encouragement indeed, for she had only one end in view: the welfare of her Congregation and the success of its apostolate.

In the furtherance of this end she had occasion from time to time to make use of the talents and virtue of Sister Theodore, who now, in her capacity as superior of the important establishment at Rennes, was a member of the General Council of the Congregation, established in 1828 with the approval of Monsignor Claude La Myre-Mory, then Bishop of Le Mans. [26] Precisely during the years that Sister Theodore was in Rennes, a situation calling for the utmost tact and forbearance was developing in the Congregation. In her difficult position, Mother Mary relied on the advice and assistance of the Abbé Pierre-Louis Coëdro, [27] Superior of a society of diocesan priests known as the Missionaries of Rennes. The Abbé Coëdro, highly esteemed in his own diocese, was also a close friend of Monsignor Philippe Carron, [28] Bishop of Le Mans, in whose diocese the Motherhouse at Ruillé was located. In a letter dated November 23, 1829, Mother Mary did not hesitate to confide to Abbé Coëdro her difficulties, her scruples, her anxiety in the delicate situation which preoccupied her; nor did she hesitate to assure her trusted counselor that she relied "on the prudence of Sister Theodore" to see that his confidential response would reach her. Again, in a letter to Bishop Carron of Le Mans, December 3, 1830, Mother Mary thanked him "for the advice you have given us through Sister Theodore of Rennes." [29] Sister St. Charles, who replaced Mother Mary in 1831, relied also on the loyalty and good judgment of Sister Theodore. [30]

Sister Theodore's years in Rennes were full and happy years. One event alone would have made this period memorable for her. At that time, the sisters renewed vows annually. Perpetual profession was optional; those who wished to make permanent commitment in the Congregation might seek the permission of the Ecclesiastical Superior, in this case the Bishop of Le Mans. Having obtained the desired permission, Sister Theodore was one of the 20 young religious who pronounced perpetual vows at the close of the retreat, September 5, 1831. [31] The years of preparation added intensity to the fervor with which she pronounced the hallowed formula:

"Eternal and almighty God, my creator and sovereign Lord, animated by the desire of consecrating myself to your service under the special protection of the holy Virgin Mary, mother of God, of my holy Guardian Angel, and of all the holy patrons and protectors of the Community, of my full, free, and deliberate will, I, Sister Theodore make to your divine majesty forever the vows of poverty, of chastity, of obedience, and of devoting myself to the service of the poor, either for the instruction of youth or for the care of the sick, in the union of charity in this society; very humbly begging you, O my God, through the merits of Jesus

Christ crucified, whom I choose for my divine Spouse, that, as it has pleased you to grant me the grace of consecrating myself to you by these vows, you will be pleased to accord me abundant grace to fulfill them faithfully. Grant, Lord, that I may be until my last breath, a perfect image of Jesus crucified, and a victim entirely immolated to your will and your love. Amen."

With renewed dedication she returned to her work in Rennes. Under her direction the school was flourishing. "The Sisters of Providence left their special mark on the school," wrote the parish historian. [32] He gave as a prime example only one instance of Sister Theodore's multi-faceted concern for the welfare of her charges: her enterprise in securing a contract with a manufacturer of the city to supply wool sufficient "to provide occupation for the children for ten years," [33] and to pay for the products of the children's industry.

Constantly occupied with the progress of the pupils and the welfare of her sisters, she nevertheless did not neglect the material upkeep of her establishment. One document still preserved in the parish archives refers to improvements she arranged. While few details remain after the lapse of so many years, Sister Theodore's contemporaries could note that "The people of Rennes did justice to Sister Theodore by the love and esteem they had for her; their admiration for her virtues and talents, and their confidence in her were such as might be expected from their having seen the good she effected where everything seemed hopeless and almost impossible." [34]

Chapter 4

The opening of a new school year in September 1834 brought surprise and disappointment to the parishioners of Saint Aubin. The Sisters who staffed the "Ecole de la Providence" had returned as usual after their retreat at Ruillé-sur-Loir to begin the work of the new year. But Sister Theodore was not among them; another sister[1] was taking the place of the superior they had all learned to love and respect. It seemed to the parishioners, those especially who remembered conditions as they had been before her arrival, impossible to imagine the school on the Rue Haute without the gracious and capable directress of the past eight years. It was to be expected that the children who had learned to love her, the parents whose respect and cooperation she had earned, the parish priests whose efforts she had so ably seconded should regret her going, and ask the reason. Why, they wondered, remove someone obviously so necessary to the success of an important work?

Sister Theodore herself would have been the first to remind her friends that God has no need of anyone in particular to accomplish his designs. The school at Rennes was so evidently his own special work, and the people of the district among those so dear to his Heart that he would certainly continue his solicitude for them.

As for herself, after eight years of tireless, successful labor in the parish of Saint Aubin, she had been assigned to the little village of Soulaines, in the diocese of Angers.[2] From a large and flourishing establishment in the Episcopal city, a city itself gradually becoming a center of intellectual and spiritual renewal, she was going to a modest, recently-formed house in a little village difficult to find on any map. However, she might have tried to stifle the questions arising spontaneously in her own mind, she was powerless to silence those raised around her – the thoughtlessness, all-too-human speculations that could not fail to reach her ears and to afflict her heart.

It would have been possible, of course, to assign a very simple reason for her change. It was entirely within the province of superiors to change subjects freely from one mission to another, as their prudence directed. Those especially who had at heart the spiritual advancement of their sisters, placing it even above their apostolic success, would not have hesitated to make changes considered necessary for such advancement..

There is in Sister Theodore's case a strong probability that her health might have been alleged as reason for her transfer. In one of his fatherly letters to her the bishop of Rennes, Monsignor Claude-Louis de Lesquen,[3] alludes to this possibility:

> I see that the change of environment has not improved your health, and that it was mistakenly that they attributed to the air of Rennes the discomfort from which you were suffering. It seems to me nearly obvious that it is by means of tribulations and discomforts that God wishes to try you in this land of exile. The portion that He gives you is not too sweet, I agree, but He sees that dainties and sweet-meats do not agree with your spiritual constitution.[4]

Sister Theodore's health, it is true, was a recurrent source of trial to her; in this instance, however, it was but a minor part of her cross. She was now entering upon a period of exceptional interior suffering. Her unexpected change would have been difficult enough. All her efforts at adjustment notwithstanding, she would miss those with whom and for whom she had labored at Rennes, but grace and her own good will would soon have prevailed. What was almost unbearable for her was the thought that she might in some way have displeased or saddened the superiors whose confidence was so necessary to her sensitive and affectionate heart.[5] According to the rather obscure accounts we find of her transfer, her fears were not unfounded.

The occasion for her removal from Rennes to Soulaines, tradition reports, "was an event extremely painful and embarrassing for the Community."[6] Both the pain and the embarrassment involved on the one hand one whom she had known from the beginning of her religious life as founder and superior, confessor and counselor, Father Dujarié; and on the other hand the religious superiors who had won not only her filial respect and reverence, but that deep affection which it was part of her very nature to give and to seek. Her suffering was, in fact, her participation in a deeper, somehow inevitable human drama; her Congregation – founder and followers – must, in common with all who set out to accomplish great things, purchase the blessings of growth and fecundity at the price of sorrow and conflict.

During the eight years Sister Theodore had spent in Rennes, years of growth and fulfillment for her, the affairs of the Congregation had been moving through periods of uncertainty and painful anxiety towards a crisis. As time went on, she would have been aware of the increasing tensions. In her position, and with her natural perceptiveness, she could appreciate the difficulties of her superiors; she could observe, also, the suffering of the founder and the growing estrangement between him and the community he had founded. The situation was rooted in the very nature of the work that Father Dujarié had set in motion and the circumstances under which his projects had to take form.

> We have already noted his exertions, begun in 1806, on behalf of the congregation of the sisters which, once established through his zeal, with the blessing of God and the devotedness of its members continued to flourish. Now, scarcely had this Institute been launched, under the leadership of its first superior-general, Mother Marie Madeleine du Roscoät, than the founder was induced by his own zeal and the earnest entreaties of his colleagues to undertake the establishment of a similar Institute dedicated to the education of young boys. In 1820 he began the foundation at Ruillé of a congregation of teaching brothers, called Brothers of St. Joseph.[7]

As he had done for his congregation of sisters, Father Dujarié sought for the brothers also the civil recognition which would assure them a stable future. After long delays he had succeeded in his efforts for the sisters; on November 19, 1826, a royal ordinance conferred on the Sisters of Providence legal personality with the consequent ability to possess and administer property. Father Dujarié then transferred to the congregation property he had acquired for it; the congregation became proprietor likewise of the properties donated to the various establishments. The sisters, therefore, were in possession of a considerable patrimony and the consequent expectation of material stability and growth. Their growth was, in fact, steady and encouraging; by 1829 the congregation counted 200 members, in 52 establishments scattered throughout 12 dioceses.[8]

> Legal and political complications hindered Father Dujarié in his attempts to secure similar assurance for the Brothers of St. Joseph.[9] The early recruits, lodged in a small section of the rectory, began their religious life in circumstances of poverty and abnegation very like those of the first sisters in the "Little Providence." In 1824, with the aid of alms painstakingly solicited from the king, from the bishop and clergy of Le Mans, from

provincial officers, benefactors among the nobility and the meager dowries of the applicants, the founder was able to install the rapidly-growing novitiate in a suitable house in the town.[10] The difficulty of providing for the large household was, however, a constant source of anxiety for the aging founder. No longer hale and vigorous, but subject to frequent prostrating attacks of gout, he was suffering the effects of the hardships and deprivations of his youth and the relentless labors of his early years as cure of Ruillé.

At the same time, despite his growing involvement with the brothers and his heavy parish responsibilities, he continued just as during the first days of "Little Providence" to maintain his role as superior, chaplain, confessor, and director of the sisters he had founded.[12]

The active mentor of those first trying years did not seem to realize that his control was now no longer necessary. The sisters were well equipped to assume to a great extent their own direction. They had in their superior-general, Mother Mary Lecor, a woman of courage, of complete dedication to the interests of her Congregation, a born administrator, prompt and firm in her decisions, undeterred by obstacles from without or by any shadow of self-interest. Had he realized it, the founder might without misgiving have left the ordinary government of the sisters in her prudent care, thus easing at once both his own burden of responsibility and the painful restrictions under which Mother Mary and her council were obliged to work. But this realization, obscured by cherished plans, familiar routine, human nature itself, unfortunately eluded him. Meanwhile, occasions of unrest and misunderstanding arose daily.

Prominent among the sources of uneasiness for the sisters was the question of financial administration. As founder and superior of both the Sisters of Providence and the Brothers of St. Joseph, Father Dujarié considered the resources of both Institutes as forming a common treasury, from which the expenses of both must be met. The expenses of the brothers, unfortunately, by far exceeded their income. As their number and their needs increased, despite his untiring efforts to obtain additional outside help, the superior found himself obliged to borrow. He must borrow, however, in the name of the sisters, who alone were capable in law of contracting debts. With mounting anxiety the superiors of the Sisters of Providence saw their own community and its credit threatened. Repeated pleas to Father Dujarié to separate the accounts of the two Institutes went consistently unheeded. Not perceiving any threat to the sisters, whereas he was convinced that the brothers could not otherwise subsist, the beleaguered founder continued to draw on the common purse, a source dependent chiefly on the sisters' dowries and the fruits of their careful and frugal management. By 1830 the debt, for which the sisters would of course be liable in law, amounted to almost 25,000 francs. [13]

Mother Mary had recourse to the bishop of Le Mans, Monsignor Guy Philippe Carron. In Monsignor's opinion such a situation was not to be tolerated. After the sisters' retreat of 1830 he authorized Mother Mary to assume the administration of the temporal goods of her community, at the same time seeking insofar as possible to lessen the pain he foresaw this would cause to Father Dujarié.[14] Finally, after careful consideration and meticulous discussion with both sides, on April 21, 1831, he issued an Episcopal ordinance declaring the material interests of the two Institutes separate.[15]

Father Dujarié felt keenly the effect of this decision, coming at a time when, in the wake of the Revolution of 1830, he felt the future of the brothers to be extremely precarious. Of the 80 small establishments he had hastily founded as need arose, staffing them with young brothers insufficiently prepared, 50 had been forced by the circumstances of the Revolution to close. The frightened brothers fled, and Father Dujarié saw his Congregation of Brothers in danger of complete collapse, while doubt and misunderstanding clouded his relations with the sisters. Recording events later, one of the brothers recalled:

That separation which had been sought by his daughters, whom he had formed with a tenderness of which God alone knew the depth and the extent, was for him one of the greatest sacrifices of his life, which Providence imposed on him through the order of his bishop, Monsignor Carron; it was for him a mortal blow and from that moment his moral and physical forces suffered keenly.[17]

It is not difficult to imagine the infirm old priest, confused and distressed, seeking for understanding and sympathy from the "daughters whom he had formed." We know that he wrote to the sisters in Brittany. None of his letters are extant, but in a letter to Mother Mary in June 1831 Bishop Carron deplores "the adverse impressions produced by the letters he had the indiscretion to write to the sisters in the establishments in Brittany,"[18] and advises her to exert herself to counteract any influence these letters may have had. There is no indication that Mother Theodore was among the sisters whose loyalty and prudence Mother Mary might have felt inclined to question at this time. On the contrary, a year later her successor, Mother St. Charles, could write to Bishop Carron, "Sister Theodore will tell you where we stand with regard to our superior and how she finds him. I rely more on her judgment than on my own."[19]

It was some time during the following two years, then, that Sister Theodore may have given utterance to the expression of sympathy for the founder which tradition gives us to understand was the cause of her removal from Rennes. Inevitably, the plight of Father Dujarié would be a subject of discussion among the sisters to whom he had communicated his fears and his chagrin. Sister Theodore's lively sympathy and her forthright response to the sufferings of others make it seem unlikely that she could remain unmoved by the woes of one she had known and revered so long. An eminent ecclesiastic who had occasion to observe Father Dujarié during this period, Father Basil Moreau, Founder of the Society of Holy Cross, confided in a letter to Bishop Carron:

> Being worried in mind, thwarted in the execution of his plans, and wounded in his dearest hopes, he shows the weight of his years every- where and in everything, and appears to manifest a certain lack of resignation. It may be that he has not received all the consideration that he deserves. All this is truly heartrending.[20]

What had so distressed Father Moreau could not have failed to affect the loyal and sensitive heart of Sister Theodore. It would have been comparatively easy for anyone so inclined to exaggerate her expression of sympathy. Amplified and distorted, we are told, her words were reported to Ruillé and interpreted as disapproval of measures adopted by the superiors, perhaps even support of contrary plans which Father Dujarié might be projecting.

If her superiors were painfully surprised to learn that one who stood so high in their esteem and affection, and whose position lent weight to her judgments, opposed their decisions in a matter of such importance, Sister Theodore was no less distressed at the thought that they could for an instant credit such a report of her. "The accusation fell heavily on her," records first biographer, Mother Mary Cecilia Bailly, who continues:

> She suffered not only for herself but also for her Superiors. When relating this to us Mother said with a humble simplicity, as if to own a faultpublicly, that she was so imperfect as to try to exculpate herself, that she denied positively the truth of the representation made against her, and she described the distress she showed at such a thing being believed of her.[21]

Despite her grief and her humble protestations, however, when at the close of the retreat of 1834, the sisters received their assignments for the coming year, Sister Theodore was named, not for Rennes in Brittany, but for the little country mission of Soulaines, in the diocese of Angers. For one who had identified herself, as she had during her years in Rennes, with the ideals and the purpose of the congregation she loved, this apparent rejection of her potential contribution was the cause of almost unbearable pain, intensified by the unkind reflections which surfaced around her. Feeling herself somewhat an outcast, suffering from a sense of abandonment and rejection she had never known before, she left Ruillé early in September to carry out her obedience in Soulaines. There she would find a tiny house and school in an unfamiliar setting, where there awaited no familiar smile to welcome her, no sympathetic heart to share the burdens of her own.

She would, then, have found precious understanding and a great measure of encouragement in the letter which Bishop de Lesquen hastened to address to her soon after her arrival in her new mission:

> The time of trials has arrived for you, our very dear daughter, and now a terrible struggle is being engaged between nature and faith. This latter I have no doubt, will be triumphant. She will allow her companion to be saddened, but she will end by imposing silence.[22]

That his fatherly interest did indeed console and encourage her is evident. From his next letter, written a few weeks later in response to one of hers which has not been preserved.

> Your suffering. It is not blameworthy when it is kept within just bounds; it is even meritorious when one offers it to Him Who has promised to reward a glass of water given in His Name. If our life were not crossed by contradictions, what assurance would we have of our resignation and of our submission to the will of God? Would we not have to fear that we had many traits in common with those who will always come to taste the sweets of devotion without participating in the bitterness of the Chalice drunk to the lees by the One Who should be our Model? He might well say to you " If there has been a misunderstanding in the change which has occurred, think that my Providence has permitted it in order to strengthen you in the crucible of tribulations. Pray for your superiors who have been the instruments of which I made use to give you an occasion to suffer for me and with me. They open to you the way to heaven which is the same as that of the cross."[23]

Sister Theodore would have expressed her fervent gratitude to her friends and advisor, and consoled him in her turn by describing her growing appreciation of her new surroundings. Writng to her at the beginning of the new year, Monsignor de Lesquen, after thanking her for her good wishes, offered her his own, which he said had already been heard, since you are beginning to feel at home in your new situation.

How happy I should be to find myself relegated to a little corner of the earth where I might be unknown! It seems to me that I would fervently thank Providence. It knows how much I sigh after such a retreat, and how much I have need of one. Providence refuses me this consolation which would be the sweetest in my life, and refuses me because my sins render me unworthy of such a grace.

It is because you are more pleasing in His sight that God has granted you this favor which you have not asked of Him. It is a new proof of His love for you; it is God's inducement for you to increase and strengthen your love for Him. He even permitted in His mercy that this real benefit would not at first be appreciated, or even recognized by the one who received it and who was its object. He hid it from her eyes in the beginning, because sacrifices made in faith are very meritorious, while natural satisfactions are reserved for beginners.

In showing favor to you, He wished to appear to be the one placed under obligation; this is a kind of delicate consideration which enhances the value of services rendered. He constantly repeats to us that His yoke and His burden are light, and that all things work out to the advantage of those who love Him. He has done everything for His elect, and His crosses, even the heaviest in appearance, are worth more than all those joys which pass so quickly and leave a frightful void in the heart.[24]

Another filial letter from Sister Theodore to Monsignor de Lesquen, written towards the end of her first year in Soulaines, brought her once more an expression of his satisfaction in her adjustment to her changed circumstances:

This poor Claude thanks you cordially, our very dear daughter, for the wishes you express for him and the prayers you say for him. He rejoices that you are becoming little by little accustomed to your solitude, and he would not be surprised if in a short time you would find such charms in it that it would be necessary to snatch you away in order to separate you from it. If the bustle of cities offers certain compensations, it is no less true that in country places one is more recollected, and that everything there is more conducive to meditation. Manners are more pure, scandals fewer, dissipation less common, tastes simpler, and repose of heart and mind easier to obtain.[25]

Sister Theodore's letter must have revealed to him, however, that despite her avowed affinity for the tranquil life of Soulaines, there were still obstacles in the way of the desired repose of mind and heart. Not all of her reflections in her solitude, it seems, were fraught with peace; not all the shadows surrounding her transfer had been dispelled. The bishop continues:

I know that we find ourselves everywhere, and that our miseries accompany us everywhere, that they mount with us when we ride, that they sit beside us when we are in a carriage, and they are our companions when we go modestly on foot. It even seems that they keep us faithful company when we write. In fact you are tormenting yourself about the comments some persons amuse themselves by making on your correspondence with your Superior, and you are tempted for that reason to discontinue it. That does not seem to me to be a sufficient reason, and to follow such a guide with docility is to give it undeserved confidence.

Monsignor's frank and penetrating comments lift a corner of the heavy mantle of darkness under which Sister Theodore had been struggling throughout the year just past, and offer deeper insight into her mental sufferings. Besides her sense of rejection by her superior, to whom in her distress she wrote faithfully and frequently - thereby courting criticism – she had to contend with the tormenting surmise that her former confessor also had advocated her removal from the mission in Rennes.

What motive might have impelled her confessor to such a measure nowhere appears. Her letter expressing her suppositions has not been preserved, and except for the single reference in Monsignor de Lesquen's reply there is no indication that Father Botrel[26] was in fact involved. Shortly after her arrival in Soulaines she had received a letter from him, partly chiding, partly teasing, wholly Breton:

> Have you profited from the good fortune which has come to you entirely unexpected, and contrary to many wills, beginning with your own? How many times I have thought of you before the Lord! I prayed my hardest that He would make you see in all the design of His paternal Providence which loves you too much, my daughter, not to inflict rude blows on your enemy, that wretched nature whose will finds it so hard to submit. I beg you, my child, to ask our Lord often, through His Holy Mother, that you may not judge so humanly the different events of life, but that you try to adore, bless, and love the designs of His paternal goodness.

> I saw recently your worthy Mother Mary, now Assistant to your Superior General. I shall not recount our conversation, in which I perceived that she really wishes only your welfare and to help you become a worthy daughter of Providence.[27]

His reference to the Carmelites opens an avenue of conjecture which must perforce remain simply conjecture. Sister Theodore had at first desired to enter Carmel. When at last she was free to seek entrance into religious life, she had attempted to answer the call of both the contemplative and the apostolic ministry by resorting to an ingenuous compromise; for ten years she would turn to a life of prayer, sacrifice, and deeper union with God in the cloister.[28] As the years passed, it seems only logical to suppose that she would have opened her heart on the subject to her confessor and advisor, in this case Father Jean Botrel, vicar-general for Bishop de Lesquens from 1825 to 1835, hence during the entire time that Sister Theodore was in Rennes.

What his advice to her might have been remains unknown. It will be recalled that she began her active service as a Sister of Providence in 1825; the ten years she had allotted herself were then, in 1834, drawing to a close. Against any speculation set in motion by circumstances, however, there stands the fact that in 1831 she had pronounced perpetual vows as a Sister of Providence. At the time such vows were optional, and permission for them was granted only at a sister's own request. Sister Theodore seems then to have arrived at a decision. She was to remain a Sister of Providence. She remained also always genuinely devoted to the Carmelites, counting on their prayers, visiting them when she was in Le Mans, sending them messages of affection and gratitude through another friend of her apostolate, Canon Lottin,[29] secretary at the chancery, and for 30 years chaplain of the Carmel of Le union of prayer contracted between the Carmelites and the religious community founded in America by Sister Theodore.

Father Botrel himself, after leaving the diocese of Rennes for Paris in 1835, continued his interest in Carmel, particularly in the Carmel of Tours, center of the devotion to the Holy Face. Monsignor de Lesquen had no further need to chide Sister Theodore for her mistaken supposition in his regard. Knowing her, and confident that she would harbor no resentment, he mentions Father Botrel only once again, when in a letter to her in Paris, where she had gone for medical treatment, he requests, "Remember me to Botrel."[30] In the same letter he continues his encouraging reflections on solitude and on trust in God's mercy:

> I am not surprised that you prefer your solitude to the tumult of which one feels, in spite of oneself, the proximity, despite the precautions one takes and the care one exerts to close one's ears. Solitude! It is a delight I long for, towards which all my desires tend. But I must bear the burden of anxieties. Earth is not heaven, as we know by experience. The way that leads there is narrow, but it is not impassable. Grace is a good guide, and it is never refused when we ask for it with confidence. If on the road that

we must travel we happen to take some false steps, why should we be discouraged? A great many saints have done the same. Divine mercy helped them; it will raise us up also, provided we have recourse to it.

Among the illnesses of the body some are incurable; it is not so with maladies of the soul: we have a Doctor who cures them all, Jesus Christ.

Sister Theodore would have understood Monsignor's reference in this letter to illnesses of the body. He had directed it to the convent in Paris where, as we shall see later, she had gone in the summer of 1836 to consult the truly Christian physician, Dr. Joseph Claude Récamier,[31] in the hope of recovering the health and strength which consistently eluded her, even in the relative quiet of her country mission.

It was not, however, bodily suffering only which intruded on the solitude she was learning to love. The unfortunate rumors which had attended her move to Soulaines three years earlier continued to batter at her peace of mind. So we find Monsignor de Lesquen writing in October 1837 to advise her of her duty to herself and her establishment. The bishop expressed his views precisely and emphatically:

Sufferings and crosses are wanting to no one, our very dear Daughter in Jesus Christ, because they enter into the plans of Providence. They are in a way the purgatory of the earth, and give us traits of resemblance to Jesus Christ, who to the title of Redeemer joins that of Model.

That calumny should also arise to try you is a misfortune almost inevitable. Our divine Savior Himself permitted this most odious weapon to be used against Him. One of the greatest and the holiest of bishops, St. Francis de Sales, had that cruel trial to suffer. I could quote many others who instead of becoming distressed or broken up, on the contrary rejoiced that they were judged worthy of being thus nailed to the Cross.

However, that may be, it is a duty to refute calumny when it can do harm to an establishment of which one has the responsibility.

Such is that which your unfortunate companion has launched against you. Not only has she failed in justice and charity, but also in the truth; for I certify and I will certify to all who wish that you have carried away with you the esteem of the Bishop of Rennes and of the Curé of St. Aubin, and that if I did not, as the good of the house seemed to demand, make strong representations to implore your superiors not to snatch you away from the affection of your companions, from the esteem of those who took an interest in your establishment, and from the tears of the children who attended it..

There you have, our very dear Daughter, the exact truth. And if in your present establishment doubts are raised in this regard, ask those who formulate them to write to me and I will give them full and entire satisfaction. I will not give a testimonial of courtesy but a testimonial of conscience.[32]

We have no way of knowing what steps Sister Theodore may have taken to follow the counsels given in this letter, or what measures the bishop himself may have employed to assist her. In his solicitude he did not stop at addressing words of advice to her; he exercised his own ability and influence to bring truth to light and her long trial to an end. It was with real pleasure, then, that he could write her at the beginning of the New Year:

It is a great satisfaction to me, our very dear Daughter, to learn that justice and virtue have carried the day. I like to persuade myself that it was a moment of vertigo which caused your unfortunate companion to tell fables which had not ever the merit of likelihood. You owe me no thanks for having re-established the facts and having attested to the exact truth. Besides, she who has put herself on such dangerous ground is more to be pitied than you. Her conscience must be re-proaching her and her heart must be plunged in bitterness when she thinks of the suffering that she has caused you. God had permitted it, our very dear Daughter, to make you more and more like His Divine Son and to attach you to the cross with Him.[33]

Whatever may have been the source and the substance of the charges alleged against Sister Theodore is nowhere clearly stated. Mother Mary Cecilia suggests in her biography that not only were Sister Theodore's expressions of sympathy for the harassed founder misconstrued, and falsely reported to her superiors, but that "it was even alleged that Sister Theodore was inciting the Bishop of Rennes and the priests of his household to condemnation of Mother Mary's action in regard to Father Dujarié."[34] A note inserted by a later hand into Mary Cecilia's account informs us that "the unfortunate sister who made false accusations did not die in the Community."[35] In her notes, Sister Theodore's niece, Sister Mary Theodore Le Touzé, supplies a name, that of a sister dismissed from Ruillé September 8, 1841, Sister Thaïs.[36] According to records at Ruillé, Sister Thaïs was dismissed "because of her insubordination."[37] Sister Theodore herself has left no name, no details. For her it was sufficient to reflect that, as Bishop de Lesquen assured her, it was God himself who had permitted her trial, God who in his love wished to offer her still another opportunity to grow in resemblance to his son. Neither she nor the bishop could have foreseen at this juncture the full extent of the divine plan for her, or the great work for which her years in Soulaines were destined to prepare her.

After the initial difficulty of adjusting to an environment so different from that which she had left in Rennes, Sister Theodore was not long in learning to savor the attractions of her new situation. The sequestered little village offered a way of life to which, with her temperament, she could not fail to respond. Coming from her strenuous apostolate in Rennes to the still-hidden challenge of her mission in Soulaines there was a blessed interlude, which provided not only precious hours of meditation and quiet prayer, but time also to deepen by diligent reading her knowledge of the Scriptures and the Faith that she loved.

All this she found possible with no diminishment of zeal or loving attention to those around her. Indeed, her natural ability to attract confidence and affectionate cooperation was enhanced as her spiritual gifts developed. The people she loved and taught and cared for in illness and distress soon became and were to remain among her most faithful friends; they would also be among the most generous supporters of her future missionary labors.

The establishment of Soulaines-sur-Aubance, in the department of Maine and Loire, had been opened six years earlier. In 1828 the town's leading citizen, M. Claude Marie Perrault de la Bertaudière, offered to the Sisters of Providence a house and its furnishings, together with an annual income sufficient to support three sisters who would devote themselves to teaching the children of the countryside and visiting the sick poor. The official act of donation was registered February 2, 1829, Sister Dosithee Hardy signing on behalf of Mother Mary.[38] It was the first superior of Soulaines who exchanged missions with Sister Theodore in 1834.

The donor, M. de la Bertaudière, seems to have been the ideal of the traditional country squire, possessed of a large estate and exercising his benevolent influence over all within his range. "Soulaines has lost one of its greatest benefactors,"[39] it was said of him at the time of his death. Claude Marie Perrault de la Bertaudière was born in Angers in 1771, the son of Pierre Claude Perrault de Seigneur de la Bertaudière, and the Lady Laurence Josephine Foulloue du Lys. The ancestral chateau was confiscated during the Revolution, and a great part of the family holdings lost. The remnant which remained, saved by a faithful servant of the émigrés, was enough, however, to enable Claude Marie, Knight of the Royal and Military Order of St. Louis, to establish himself on his estate in Soulaines, "la Contentinière." Unmarried, he devoted his still considerable fortune to procuring the good of the less fortunate around him. Wherever there was need, "Monsieur," as he was known, was sure to be called upon, and never in vain. From 1808 to 1821 he had been mayor of Soulaines, and he never lost his interest in the welfare of his people; his gift of the school was but one instance of his benevolence.[40]

He was pleased to see Sister Theodore in charge. She for her part gave his generosity every opportunity to reach out to God in the needy villagers, she took at once to her heart. Her duties at the school were light and could be shared with her two companions, Sister Sophie and Sister St. Calais; but the mission of the sisters included also the care of the sick poor in the area. Never one to do things by halves, she obtained permission to study medicine and the elements of pharmacy under a physician from nearby Angers, Dr. Honoré Lecacheur,[41] in order to equip herself to fulfill competently this phase of her charge.

An aura of friendly and purposeful activity surrounded the sisters' little establishment, where daily were dispensed not only instruction for the children, but material help in need, sympathy and understanding in difficulties, healing in sickness and sorrow. Those unable to come themselves for help knew that Sister Theodore, undeterred by inclement weather or muddy roads, would find her way to them. Nor did she limit her ministrations to the inhabitants of Soulaines; all within her reach, on foot or if need be on horseback, benefited from her maternal vigilance and concern.

Long years later, as the sisters who succeeded her were to testify, these grateful friends remembered her untiring devotedness. "She had a special gift for teaching catechism and Holy Scripture well," reported Sister Xavier-Joseph. "Actually the most solidly Christian families of the parish are those of her former pupils."[42] And another, Sister Joseph Alphonse recalled, "I have heard it said that the intelligent care which Sister Theodore lavished on the sick, as well as her reputation for goodness and sanctity, inspired these poor people with such confidence in her that they preferred her visit to that of the doctor."[43]

The wholehearted cooperation of the sisters in the work his charity had initiated was highly gratifying to M. de la Bertaudière. Nothing escaped his paternal regard, and his alms were there to meet every emergency. It is very likely safe to assume, therefore, that when it became apparent that Sister Theodore's generous efforts were taking too much toll on her fragile health, it was he who made possible a visit to Paris to consult an eminent physician. Sister Theodore's letter to him after her arrival was the occasion of a response which affords appealing insight into the relations between the sisters and the kindly patriarch, father and adviser to his co-laborers as well as to their common protégés. No detail seems to have escaped his observation. On June 30, 1836, he wrote her:

Good and respectable Sister:

It was with the greatest pleasure that I received from Sister Sophie yesterday your charming letter, and that I see that your situation in Paris is as pleasant as you could have hoped. I like these good Ladies of St. Thomas very much, and all that they do for you gives me as much pleasure as it would if they were doing it for me. If ever I return to Paris, I will certainly go to express my thanks to them. I suppose that you will have made arrangements for your board; one must not give the impression of living on the love of God, but do all money in hand. You will be better off that way, without however affecting a haughtiness which could bless. You have enough intelligence and knowledge of the proprieties to follow the golden mean in this respect, and I rely on you for it.

You have made, I believe, a very good choice in Doctor Reccamier (sic) (and not Recabien); he is considered one of the finest doctors in Paris. It is with doctors as with confessors; when one has put one's confidence in them, one must absolutely follow their advice; and you will certainly do well to follow his prescriptions scrupulously, even if you have to let him know their effect on you, for if the regimen which he prescribes for you should weaken you too much, I think that he would make some modifications. What you tell me of the near certitude he has of improving your health and even perhaps of curing you completely was music to my ears, and I will have the pleasure of seeing our good Sister Theodore able to do all the good she has done in the past for the relief of the poor sick and unfortunate.

Goodbye, very respected Sister! Always preserve for me the sentiments of friendship that you are kind enough to express to me, and be assured of all that I feel for you in return.

Your very devoted and respectful Servant,

de la Bertaudière[44]

Sister Theodore returned from Paris not, indeed, completely cured, but sufficiently restored to give her benefactor the pleasure he desired of seeing her able once more to continue her work with his poor. With renewed energy she resumed her tasks, assisted by Sister St. Edmond, who had come as a new novice the previous year, replacing Sister St. Calais, and Sister St. Jacques who replaced Sister Sophie after the 1836 retreat. Her devotion to her charges and the respect and affection they gave her in return increased as the months passed.

The retreat of 1837 was the occasion of the regular community elections. At this time, Mother Mary and Mother St. Charles once more exchanged roles; Mother Mary was elected to her former office of superior general, to which Sister St. Charles had succeeded her in 1831, and Mother St. Charles again took up her post as First assistant. Sister Theodore was one of the five general councilors whose term expired at this time.[45]

Since it was after this summer of 1837 that Bishop de Lesquen declared himself ready to testify to the "exact truth" concerning the unjust charges brought against Sister Theodore, it is very likely that during her stay at the motherhouse these charges had been revived. It was only, as we have seen, as a result of the Bishop's firm and indignant protest, that they had at last been silenced, and that he was able to reflect with satisfaction in his letter of January 2, 1838, "justice and charity have carried the day."

Back in Soulaines for the new term, encouraged by Monsignor de Lesquen's support, Sister Theodore immersed herself once again in her daily round of spiritual and corporal works of mercy, and in her quiet hours of prayer. Those hours, passed alone before the Blessed Sacrament in the old parish church, were to remain her most cherished memories. There it was that when later circumstances kept her from the tabernacle, her imagination was most apt to place her; there she might make her spiritual visits. "I am more frequently at Soulaines than anywhere else," she would write in her first <u>Journal of Travel.</u> "It is in the poor barn there that I transport myself in order to pray where, so often, I was alone with God."[46] Certainly there was nothing about it to distract one's attention from the Lord who made it his home. Yet, overcome with distress at her first sight of the cathedral of Vincennes a few years later, she would comment, "Our barn at Soulaines is better ornamented and more neatly kept!"[47] There is no need, incidentally, to wonder at whose hands the dilapidated little edifice was kept thus piously and properly.

It could not be denied, however, that the parish was in need of a suitable church to replace the pitiful survival of revolutionary days. The difficulty, as is usual, lay in the total lack of funds. Neither the pastor, Father Francois Brillouet,[48] nor the parishioners had any means to contribute, and so inevitably all thoughts turned to the one person who possessed such means and who could always be depended upon to respond to real need. "Monsieur" was approached.

His fellow-parishioners were not disappointed. M. de la Bertaudière took the matter under consideration. He approached the pastor with his offer and his suggestions, and Father Brillouet, delighted and grateful, entered with understandable enthusiasm into the project. All Soulaines breathed in happy anticipation.

The euphoria was short-lived. Suddenly Father Brillouet and Monsieur found their views diverging, and the prospects of mutual understanding rapidly diminishing. The priest with his concept of the ideal setting for divine worship, and the pious benefactor with the funds necessary to make it a reality, were unable to agree on important details and procedures.

Father Brillouet was left helpless in the matter when M. de la Bertaudière, offended, withdrew his interest and support.

The pastor confided his distress and embarrassment to the one member of his disappointed congregation whose influence, he believed, would prevail with their disgruntled benefactor. Like his parishioners, Father Brillouet had the utmost confidence in the abilities and the good will of Sister Theodore; like his parishioners knew, too, the reverent esteem in which "Monsieur" held her. If anyone could succeed in reversing his decision, it would be Sister Theodore.

It was not an easy task, even for her. It took all of her persuasive eloquence, fired by her own intense zeal for the adornment of the Lord's house; all her deep concern for the spiritual growth of the people too poor to provide a fitting sanctuary where they might gather for divine services; her most earnest and humble appeals to his piety and well-known generosity. It took, besides, the cooperation of his guardian angel, whom according to her custom, she did not fail to invoke, before at long last she succeeded in overcoming his injured sensibilities and assumed indifference. Once persuaded, he spared himself no effort or expense in order to furnish the parish with a church of which its members might be justly proud.[49] Sister Theodore would not be there to follow its progress. She is not mentioned in the tribute unanimously voted by the Municipal Council of Soulaines in 1845:

> In the year 1842 the church of Soulaines was completed, rebuilt almost entirely at the expense of a pious man, M. Claude Marie Perrault de la Bertaudière. May this name, today covered with gratitude and love, recall to our children his inexhaustible benevolence, and may it be intermingled with their prayers in this temple raised through his piety.[50]

Mother Mary Cecilia, who saw the church after its completion, describes it as a "gem of beauty," and tells us that Sister Theodore is mentioned in a cornerstone manuscript in commemoration of the fact that it was through her influence that M. de la Bertaudière undertook to defray the expenses of the building.[51] In a letter addressed to Sister Theodore as the church reconstruction neared completion, six months after her arrival in the New World, Father Brillouet gave expression to his own sentiments and those of his people. In almost lyrical terms he described their affection and their gratitude to Sister Theodore, not only for her part in making possible their beautiful new church, but for the self-sacrificing devotion she had shown in all their needs. On January 15, 1841, he wrote:

I will not speak to you, my good Theodore, of the extreme affliction that your departure caused. We were crushed to the center of our deepest feelings; our hearts I can say, were grieved. It is impossible for me to describe the impression made at Soulaines by the sad news that you would never return. How many tears you have caused! If you had been witness, you would no longer say that our good people of Soulaines do not know friendship and have no heart! Yes, everyone regrets you and will regret you always at Soulaines. I wish you could have heard all our inhabitants express their regrets and their love for you, each one in his own manner. "It is she," says this one, "it is she who used to give us bread." "It is she," says that one, "it is she who used to give us clothing." "It is she who was so zealous for our children." "It is she," says another, "It is she who used to visit us in our illness so frequently and who did not fear either mud or rain." "It is to her," we all say with one voice, "it is to her that we owe our being able to see with a holy pride rise in our midst this beautiful monument to the glory of God which all our neighbors envy us."

But how painful it is for sensitive hearts, and for mine in particular, to be obliged to compare your situation with ours, your destitution with our abundance, your poverty with our riches, your stable with our cathedral!

Yes, my good Theodore, it is truly painful for grateful hearts to know and to think that she to whom we would be happy to render this just testimony, to whom we owe our magnificence, our riches, is in a strange land two thousand some hundred leagues from us, deprived of all conveniences or rather reduced to all privations and subjected to all rigors. With what pain, with what interest, we have read your journals and your accounts of your voyage which we literally snatched from one another's hands and which we devoured.

Goodbye, goodbye, my dear sister, until we see each other as soon as possible at Soulaines.

Your entirely devoted servant,

F. Brillouet, priest[52]

The pastor's delight at Sister Theodore's success in obtaining Monsieur's gift of the new church, together with his observation of the good she was accomplishing among the sick fired his enthusiasm for another cherished project. Sister Theodore, he reflected, took such good care of the sick and suffering in her little dispensary and on her visits to their homes. How much more might she and her sisters be able to accomplish if only the village had a hospital.

Sister Theodore, in the meantime, had in mind her own projects not only for the spiritual and physical welfare of the people of Soulaines, but also for their intellectual advancement. Herself an outstanding teacher, she was thorough in her training of the novices who like Sister St. Edmond were sent to help in the little school. The children of Soulaines were receiving an education excellent for the times. There were, however, other little girls on the surrounding farms, in the families she visited on her rounds of mercy. The school was too far for them to attend daily. If the Sisters were permitted to receive boarding pupils, these children, too, might have the benefits of a Christian formation.

The school laws of 1833 required that for the opening of a boarding school, the local school board, headed by the mayor, be consulted; this body in turn must seek permission of the district Committee for Instruction, over which presided the Rector of the Royal Academy in the area – in this

70

case the Academy of Angers. There would, of course, be no doubt about Sister Theodore's receiving the approval of the local committee, or about the willingness of this committee to request permission from the proper higher authority. The decision rested, then, with the Rector of Angers. As the school year 1838-39 drew to a close, Sister Theodore received notification of the decision, with the recommendation that she approach the Prefect of the district of Maine and Loire, who had already been informed of the approval of the rector, M. Collet Dubignon. It was the prerogative of the local authorities to determine the number of boarding pupils who might be received.[53]

She shared the good news with the pastor, always concerned for the instruction of his children; with "Monsieur," who contemplated with satisfaction the success of the little school which ten years before he had confided to the Sisters of Providence, and especially with her sisters, who began with her to plan for the broadened scope of their apostolate. Their summer was a busy one, filled with glowing prospects for the coming year.

Then, towards the end of July, the three sisters having said their farewells to Father Brillouet and "Monsieur," – both deeply involved in their plans for the church, to their pupils and friends, and to the sick whom they were leaving well provided for in their absence, closed their little house and set out for the annual retreat at Ruillé.

With light baggage and lighter hearts, they mounted the stagecoach which was soon rattling northward over the dusty road, leaving behind the familiar countryside, and hurrying Sister Theodore towards the undreamed-of paths into which Providence was even then preparing to direct her.

Chapter 5

While Sister Theodore was spending herself in her works of charity at Soulaines, and profiting by the opportunity for meditation and study afforded by the relatively quiet atmosphere of the little country town, Providence was preparing a more far-reaching outlet for her zeal and for the spiritual riches being confided to her. The same year which saw the unfolding of the painful circumstances which caused her transfer from Rennes to Soulaines witnessed also the first steps taken in preparation of what was to be for her a distant and undreamed-of mission. In 1834 the Diocese of Vincennes, Indiana, in the United States of America, was established, with Simon Gabriel Bruté de Rémur, a native of Rennes, as its first bishop.

At this period in history, the United States of America, an independent republic for the past 50 years, was still a missionary territory. Before England recognized the independence of her former colonies by the Treaty of Versailles in 1783, the missions of America were dependent on the Congregation for the Propagation of the Faith, under the jurisdiction of the vicar-apostolic of London.[1]

In June 1784 however, John Carroll was appointed "Superior of the Mission in the thirteen United States of North America."[2] In his letter naming Father Carroll to this appointment, Cardinal Antonelli, Prefect of the Propaganda, asked that the new vicar-apostolic furnish a "correct report" of the state of the Catholic religion in the 13 states.

Carroll's report to the Congregation of the Propaganda in 1785 revealed the poverty of the church in America. To minister to 25,000 Catholics, he could count on only 24 priests, of whom 19 were in Maryland, five in Pennsylvania, and not one in the other 11 states.

Cardinal Antonelli had concluded his letter with the expression of his confidence that Father Carroll would discharge the office committed to him with zeal, solicitude and fidelity. This confidence was indeed well-founded. Father Carroll was untiring in his devotion to his duties, wise in the comments and recommendations he made to the Holy See, fraternal in his relations with his brother-priests, and deeply understanding of the American character and needs. The arrangement under which he was working had been intended as temporary, and in fact, in 1789 Pope Pius VI, after careful consideration of the American situation, accorded to the priests of the United States, for one time only, the privilege of electing a bishop from their own number, and of naming the city they considered most suitable for the erection of a See. On March 25, 1789, accordingly, Father John Carroll was elected bishop of the first American diocese; and because it was located in the state which counted among its inhabitants the largest number of Catholics, Baltimore was chosen as the site of the first See.

By one of those strange dispensations of history, the signing in November 1789 of the Bull which erected the first Episcopal See in the United States of America, youngest in the family of the Church, coincided almost perfectly with the promulgation of the infamous decree against the clergy of the Church's eldest daughter, France. In the era of outrage which followed that decree a great many French priests turned their eyes towards America.[3] Thus, out of evil there emerged a source of great good for the new bishop of Baltimore, charged as he was with a vast diocese in a country huge, uncultivated, lacking the means of communication; a country whose inhabitants, often without instruction, and many of them poor, struggling pioneers, had great need of priestly ministry.

Among the French priests who directed their zeal and their talents to the service of the Church in America were the future bishops Dave, Le Maréchal, Dubois, Dubourg, and Flaget. Benedict Joseph Flaget, a Sulpician priest having arrived in Philadelphia in 1792, spent six months on the road to Vincennes, where he ministered for two and a half years before being called to the seminary at Baltimore.

When in 1808 the vast American diocese was divided, and four suffragan bishops appointed, the learned and saintly Flaget was named bishop of the diocese of Bardstown, Kentucky. His jurisdiction, extending throughout all the country northwest of the Ohio River to the Great Lakes, comprised eight states and covered an area three times as large as all of France. Inevitably, he turned to France for help, seeking out his former friends at Saint-Sulpice. It was there that he met the young priest Simon Gabriel Bruté de Rémur, of Rennes, who accompanied him back to the United States in 1810.[4]

Father Bruté was not, however, destined to labor in the Kentucky diocese. He began his missionary life at Baltimore, in the Sulpician seminary at St. Mary's. Two years later he was sent to the new seminary of Mount St. Mary's at Emmitsburg, Maryland where he remained until 1834, when he was appointed bishop of the newly-erected diocese of Vincennes, the 13th in a country where 20 years before there had been but one, as he himself recalled:

> When I arrived at Baltimore, in 1819, there was only one single bishop for the United States, Msgr. John Carroll, bishop of that city; little by little Sees were created; that of Bardstown, that of New York, of Louisville, of St. Louis, of Cincinnati; that of Detroit, erected in 1833 was the twelfth; and that of Vincennes

to which I have just been named is then the thirteenth. I had no resources, for this diocese, in priests or money....My cathedral was a brick building, 115 ft. long and 60 wide; it had four walls and a roof; the walls were without plaster and whitewash; there was no sanctuary; a simple wooden altar with a pretty gilded tabernacle, a cross and six beautiful candlesticks, a gift from France, which highlighted the poverty and the bareness of the place. There was no sacristy, not the least little place to keep the priestly vestments. My episcopal <u>palace</u> consisted of a comfortable enough little room and an office; no other room, no attic above, no shed beside it.

Among the inhabitants, I found Germans, Irish, and many French, all poor, unlettered, but with frank, open, happy dispositions which revealed their origins. They had kept their faith, they loved their priests, but they are ignorant and negligent in fulfilling their religious duties. How can one establish a clergy? How call together for the instruction of the children? How build them a decent house to lodge them? How, finally, without money and without priests, extend the Catholic religion in a diocese? Lord, for your glory, we need priests and religious![5]

Msgr. Bruté, then, in his turn, made a voyage to Europe in 1835, to seek co-laborers. In Rome he gave to the Congregation of the Propaganda his report on the Church in America, not only in his diocese, but in the whole country, a very important report, because of his experience and his competence.[6] He noted that the diocese of Vincennes was composed of the state of Indiana and the eastern third of Illinois; it was 330 miles long and the same in width, with a population of almost 600,000, of whom 50,000 were Catholics, very widely dispersed. He indicated also the extent, the needs, the great interest for the church of the American missions. "Nearly the whole surface of the United States," he said, "is of land and climate favorable to population growth. It can in a century find itself equal to that of Europe. What immense interest for the activation and the development of the Church!"[7]

In his native city of Rennes, Monsignor Bruté asked the bishop,

Monsignor Claude de Lesquen, to suggest to him a priest whom he might take as his vicar-general, and later his coadjutor. Monsignor de Lesquen recommended to him the young Father Célestine de la Hailandière, then serving in the parish of St. Germaine. Two years later, himself too ill to travel, it was this vicar-general that Monsignor Bruté sent to Europe in search of additional results. At Strasbourg, Father de la Hailandière found five seminarians willing to devote themselves to the Vincennes mission. There he found also the community of Sisters of Providence of Ribeauvillé, who promised to send Sisters to found a school; their chaplain, the Abbé Ignace Mertian, offered the sum of 50,000 francs for the American foundation.[8] At Le Mans, Father Basil Moreau, superior of the Brothers of the Holy Cross, promised a colony of brothers.

While Father de la Hailandière was still in France, he received the Bulls appointing him coadjutor to the Bishop of Vincennes with right of succession. This was followed almost immediately by the news of the death of Monsignor Bruté. Father de la Hailandière was now himself Bishop of Vincennes. He was consecrated by Bishop Forbin-Janson, August 18, 1839,[9] and continued his quest for the aid so desperately needed in a diocese of which he was now not merely the agent, but the responsible head.

He had already met with some disappointment. For a reason never made known, the community of Ribeauvillé had withdrawn its offer of sisters for Vincennes. The Abbé Mertian, however, persevered in his promise of financial means[10] but the new bishop was obliged to seek the concurrence of other sisters for the foundation. At this point he made known his needs to the bishop of Le Mans, Monsignor Jean-Baptiste Bouvier,[11] a prelate noted for his piety and his zeal.

Monsignor Bouvier exposed the plight of the American bishop to the superiors of the Sisters of Providence of Ruillé-sur-Loir. As ecclesiastical superior, he himself presided at a meeting of the sisters' Particular Council on August 19, 1839. What occurred at that meeting is best told in the official minutes:

> Today the nineteenth of August, one thousand eight hundred thirty-nine, the Particular Council of the Superior-General of the Sisters of Providence of Ruillé-sur-Loir met in its ordinary place under the presidency of Monsignor the Bishop of Le Mans, who informed the Council of the ardent desire expressed to him by Monsignor de la Hailandière, Bishop of Vincennes in America, to have some Sisters of Providence to found an establishment at Vincennes suitable for forming subjects who would have a vocation to the religious life; in addition, the sisters would devote themselves, comfortably to the end of their Institute, to the education of youth and to the care of the sick; but since there was question of going out of France, into a foreign and distant country, Monsignor stated formally that he had no intention of obliging us to accept this proposal, however excellent the work might be in itself.
>
> Furthermore, Monsignor de la Hailandière can offer no endowment; consequently, the sisters will have for their support only the resources of Divine Providence.
>
> Having considered the good which would be accomplished in a country deprived of spiritual assistance, there being only a very few priests in this vast diocese, the Council decided to enter into the benevolent designs of Monsignor de la Hailandière, since this would enable us to procure the glory of God and to multiply the benefits which our holy vocation obliges us to spread everywhere. Monsignor the Bishop of Le Mans approved this decision, the work being in the interest of Religion.[12]

The superiors had agreed to respond to the needs of the distant mission; they would not, however, command any of the sisters to take part in a venture whose demands went so far beyond anything they might have anticipated in consecrating themselves to the works of the Congregation. It should be left to each sister's personal decision. As the sisters were at that season nearly all assembled at the motherhouse for the annual retreat, no more propitious circumstances could be desired for prayerful discernment among them – and for the emergence of the desired volunteers.

Volunteers there were, despite the unprecedented call on the generosity of these simple servants of the poor. Meantime, according to her custom, Mother Mary had in her own mind been reviewing her community, almost unconsciously compiling her mission list. One of her most serious problems, even for the smallest missions, was always that of finding a superior endowed with the prudence, firmness and administrative capacity required. For this new mission, she must indeed select with care. In this case, no common prudence, virtue or talent would suffice; no common courage would be required. Drawing on her knowledge of her daughters, Mother Mary invariably found her choice resting on one sister alone – and that sister was not among the volunteers.

Sister Theodore had not volunteered for the American mission; it had seemed an honor too great for her humility. Besides, common sense told her that her precarious health could be only an obstacle and a drain on such a mission. One can readily imagine, then, her astonishment when Mother Mary appealed to her, asking her to go, not only as one member of the missionary band, but as its leader. Her deep and sincere distrust of her own virtues and abilities made it difficult for her to accept the decision that unless she consented to take charge, the community would be obliged to refuse Monsignor de la Hailandière's request. We have no record of her interviews with her superior. It is easy to imagine her startled protests of her own incapacity, her fervent proposal of sisters she honestly believed to be much more capable, much more virtuous than herself. Sister Theodore was by nature spontaneous and frank, and she had been trained to be open with her superiors. When she had said all that she felt she must, however, she was always disposed to submit to the judgment of those who held the place of God for her. And now, judgment was that she was the only one at present capable of directing such an enterprise, and that she should prayerfully consider her response.

But for her, of course, there could now be but one response. As she recalled the point of Rule which told her, "The Sisters will be disposed to go to any part of the world where obedience calls them, to work according to the spirit of their Institute,"[13] she recognized the will of God, which it was always her desire to fulfill perfectly. Her decision might have been made in the shadow of Gethsemane, but it was made. Plans could now go forward for the new mission, and in the meantime Sister Theodore would return to her house at Soulaines, where there was still a work to be done even while she prepared for the great, unknown work of the future.

The Bishop of Vincennes, consoled and encouraged by the response of the Sisters of Ruillé, found time in the midst of his hasty preparations for departure for his diocese, to make a brief visit to Ruillé, a visit all too brief indeed to satisfy his desires and to arrive at any satisfactory regulation of the terms of the agreement into which he and the Congregation were entering. Before leaving Le Havre, he wrote, on August 31:

> The very brief time that was given me to spend at Ruillé permitted me to observe for only an instant what was taking place in your house, but that instant sufficed to fill me with joy and edification. "Yes, God blesses this house," I said to myself. "O, when will it be given to the poor diocese of Vincennes to see realized for itself something similar?" Up to that point it was, however, still only a feeling of joy, an impression of happiness which filled my soul at the sight of what was transpiring around me; later, I read your Constitutions, and I found them so wise, so filled with the spirit of God, that I was not astonished at the success they obtain and that God reserves for them as long as they are faithfully observed.

Then, noting that he counts now more than ever on what has been decided, he offers some comments and suggestions:

> I hear about this good Sister Theodore and the four others well chosen to help her with their lights, their counsels, and

their devotion in the work of the foundation that we are going to undertake at Vincennes.

Since you have had the kindness to permit me to offer you some postulants, I must tell you that I have written to Mlle. Irma Le Fer de la Motte, of St. Servan (Ille and Vilaine). She is a subject I consider singularly precious.

He then mentions several other young women, of whom he gives short descriptions, none of whom ever realized his hopes for her. He asks about dowries, wondering whether a part could not be left for Vincennes; he comments that since:

Sister Theodore must become the head of our Establishment, it would seem to me desirable that she be formed with particular care to the responsibilities and duties of superior, assistant, mistress of novices, that she know how to keep books, and has a knowledge of business.

It is quite possible that Mother Mary and her council smiled as they read this; obviously Msgr. de la Hailandière did not know Sister Theodore, her experience, and her gifts, as they did. They felt that she would not have to take time out from her work at Soulaines to perfect herself in any of the prerequisites he mentioned.

Then Monsignor went on to urge the early departure of the missionaries:

This dear colony that you are going to form for me, when will you send it?

As soon as possible, is that not so? Yes, but to speak more precisely, what do you think of the month of March or April of next year? That seems to me personally the most favorable season; the end of the year would not permit them to take up a suitable position before the winter.

After a few further tentative details, and a declaration of his submission in all to the judgment of Monsignor of Le Mans, the Bishop concludes with touching humility and deference:

> If there be in this first letter or those which follow some words which might seem out of harmony with your Constitutions or your customs, disregard them. Please, above all, do not forget our interests. There is perhaps no diocese which has greater need than that of Vincennes. I have the honor of being, with the most profound respect, my dear Mother,
>
> Your humble servant,
>
> Celestine, Bishop of Vincennes
>
> United States of America[14]

The missionary bishop is conscious of being a mendicant, and of the vastness of the area in whose behalf he must beg.

Monsignor's mention in this letter of having "heard of this good Sister Theodore" would seem to suggest that he had not met her personally. She might have been only one of the sisters in the chapel, in the cloisters, in the garden, when the stately prelate passed through during the course of his short visit. We do know that the sisters destined for his mission observed him and were impressed by his fine appearance and his dignified bearing. The remembrance of his "episcopal grandeur" on that day was to linger with them, to be contrasted with his humble appearance at the scene of his labors in the New World.[15]

It is to the postulant he mentions, Mademoiselle Le Fer de la Motte, that we owe those delightfully intimate glimpses of Sister Theodore on her last mission in France which reveal the qualities which were the source of her ascendancy over the souls of all who really knew her.

The family of Irma Le Fer de la Motte, of St. Servan, and that of Monsignor de la Hailandière, near Combourg, were long-time neighbors and friends. When he arrived in France as the emissary of Bishop Bruté in 1839, Father de la Hailandière visited his family and renewed old friendships in Brittany; and no one with whom he conversed could fail to be influenced by his enthusiasm for the missions of America, where the need was so great, the opportunity for spreading the Faith unrivaled.

Among the listeners carried away by his earnest eloquence was the young Irma Le Fer de la Motte, fourth of the 12 children of Charles Le Fer de la Motte and Eugénie de Ginguené. The family estate bordered the River Rance. Life in this delightful and truly Christian family has been described by one of the younger daughters, Clementine, in her biography of her sister Irma. At the time of Father de la Hailandière's visit, Irma, a young woman of 23, carefully educated, pious, lively and gracious, was already devoting much of her time to works of zeal: teaching catechism, visiting the sick, encouraging retreats, helping the poor around her with all the means at her disposal. She was an independent young person, who for all her devotion to prayer and selfless service, had no desire whatever to enter Religion. Even as a very young girl she had felt convinced that God must be all, that "for Him one should be willing to leave country, family, all, even oneself." This leaving of all, for her, however, never connoted becoming a religious, even though the first time she heard from a visiting missionary of the souls to be gathered beyond the seas, she had cherished the hope of one day becoming a part of such an apostolic endeavor.

It was with avid attention, then, that she listened to Father de la Hailandière's details of his missionary labors; when he returned to Brittany after his consecration as bishop of Vincennes, her decision was almost made. "We had a visit yesterday from Bishop de la Hailandière, who spoke of his diocese and great labors," she wrote to a friend. " Cecile wished to set out with him immediately. I did not say anything, but I thought it is there that God calls me."[16] And then again,

> I have just been to hear Bishop de la Hailandière. He preached nothing but America. It was a conversation rather than a sermon. On leaving the church I went to Madame B's where I again saw him and also Abbé Cardonnet. His pressing exhortations to follow

him to America were not mere jests, and I did not laugh while listening to them. An hour later I saw the two of them in the garden, and I went up to them. They were talking to me. Oh, what a moment! What! leave all I love, and so suddenly! How shall I ever ask my father! How speak of it to my mother! And he would take me away in three months. Abbé Martin and twenty priests are going with him…I am happy here, perfectly happy; so it would be only for God that I would abandon my happiness in France. God! Oh He is well worth a few tears, a few heartbreaks![17]

Irma's plan to accompany Monsignor de la Hailandière and his missionaries to America had to be abandoned when it was learned that the sisters of Ribeauvillé, whom she would have joined, had withdrawn their proffered assistance. After his successful appeal to Ruillé, however, Bishop de la Hailandière again approached Irma. He advised her to go to Soulaines, where Sister Theodore, the superior appointed for the American foundation would help her prepare for her new lifework. So completely was Irma won over to the American apostolate, that she was willing to give up even the independence she cherished, in order to go to Vincennes as a religious; and so she made plans to begin her novitiate with Sister Theodore at Soulaines. With her brother Charles, she left St. Servan on November 15.

Sister Theodore, meanwhile, had returned to Soulaines in September to take up again the routine of her days among her beloved children and her poor, with what inexpressible emotions one can only imagine. She would put all the love and tenderness of her heart into these last ministrations. As she looked into the eager faces of her little pupils, or each time the different smile of a bedridden patient turned to one of gratitude and renewed confidence, she had to struggle against the thought that this was really her last year among them. In the convent she could speak of the coming separation with her two young companions, Sister St. Edmond and the novice Sister Olympiade. The young sisters listened, filled with wonder and even fantastic conjecture, and almost envious of her lot.

Still, now that she was away from Ruillé, back in the quiet round of duty, sometimes the future seemed like a dream, and there was no one to whom she could look for understanding when that dream became a frightening one. For there were times when the thought of leaving forever all that she knew and cherished insinuated itself into the midst of her most ardent longings for the great work of evangelization that awaited her.[18] She looked forward, then, to Irma's coming. Now she would have some opportunity to plan for the work of Vincennes with someone who would be sharing it and they could strengthen, console, inspire each other.

Sister Theodore, who loved to share whatever she had of good news with her companions, happily informed them early in November of the treat in store for them: they were to have a visitor – a charming, beautiful young lady, talented in drawing and painting, proficient in Latin and history, and above all in sacred scripture and Christian doctrine. She was amiable and gracious in manner and conversation, and most remarkably pious and charitable. And she, too, was going to Vincennes. Sister Theodore's black eyes glowed as she pointed out to them the treasure that her mission in Vincennes was to possess.

Her two young listeners knew her better than to protest that she herself had even more to offer to Vincennes. Such a thought would never have occurred to her, and they knew her well enough not to risk offending her humility. But surely she was exaggerating! Could there be such a person as she described? She always made allowances. There must be a flaw somewhere!

Nevertheless, they were inclined to be courteous and more than kind to the young visitor, to whom on her arrival they frankly revealed their reservations. "They declared that it was impossible that her description was complete; I must have some 'ifs' or 'buts' and doubtless I was blind in one eye, or humpbacked,"[19] she wrote to her sister. The sisters assured her, however, that they had been wrong, and they unaffectedly took her to their hearts and made her feel at home with them.

In her description for her family of their kindness to her, we find homely little details of her surroundings which would otherwise not have been known. Sister Theodore had gone to meet her at Angers, the nearest city, where she said "Goodbye" to her brother Charles. The Loire, along which they traveled, was a beautiful sight; but the roads by which they journeyed were inadequate beyond description. "There was so much mud that more than twenty-five times I thought we should be upset before reaching Soulaines!"[20]

The little village of Soulaines was indeed in an out-of-the-way place, difficult of access. The two would have found the journeying together a delightful and consoling experience. Irma had never met Sister Theodore, of whom she had heard enthusiastic reports from sister's cousin, Marie Heurtel.[21] Now, meeting her personally, she was charmed. "Sister Theodore is as good, amiable, and gracious as I expected. She is tall and well-formed," she wrote. But she adds with perfect frankness, "Her beautiful black eyes do not make her the beauty that her cousin described her to be."[22] But she could not fail to recognize the beauty from within, and upon closer acquaintance, she could write, "Sister Theodore is broadminded, though austere; she is charming without knowing it, lively without being tiresome. One cannot help loving her."[23]

This was, it seems, the opinion of all who knew Sister Theodore, as Irma was not long in discovering. They went to greet M. de la Bertaudière, the little community's greatest benefactor, whose regard for Sister Theodore had induced him to consent to replace the parish church fallen into ruins and neglected since the Revolution. They met the curé, Abbé Brillouet, whose gratitude to the superior at Soulaines knew no bounds, and whom, Irma reported, she and Sister Theodore were begging to come to Vincennes with them.

But Sister Theodore's chief concern for her young recruit was to initiate her into the practice of religious life, to fashion the ardent soul and the lively imagination into instruments for the good she was destined to accomplish for God. She began at once to provide for her newest daughter from the resources of her own deep spirituality.

"I am beginning my religious education," wrote Irma. "I do not know the ABC's of community life." And again, "How clearsighted Sister Theodore is! Her revelations concerning my vanity are astounding. My dear ones, how blind you were in my regard, how you spoiled me!" She adds, "I have found with Sister Theodore two very sweet and good young sisters; they have informed me of the days of labor and especially of humiliation that await me at Ruillé. Sister Theodore planned that Irma have the advantage of novitiate training at Ruillé, but in the meantime she began in all earnest the formation of this privileged soul. "Imagine Sister Theodore taking me aside last evening," wrote Irma after a few days in Soulaines, "and after a few words concerning my appearance, saying to me, 'My dear child, I believe you are not vain of your exterior, but you have too much consideration for your intellect.' Think of it! At the first glance she had guessed my weakness."[24]

Superior and postulant spent an hour each day studying English. At recreation, as may well be imagined, the conversation constantly turned to Vincennes. Irma found the two young sisters very good, very friendly, but "nothing compared to Sister Theodore," even though Sister Theodore was not disposed to spare her postulant where spiritual values were involved. "Last evening," Irma related, "I wanted to dress as a religious, and we asked Sister Theodore's permission, but she looked at me and said, 'What! you would make sport of the vesture which should be the price of your efforts, the object of your desires?' A shudder passed over me, and I felt that to obtain this simple costume I would henceforth have courage to suffer everything."

Given food for thought, Irma found her appreciation of her vocation increasing. "Pray for me, my cherished Cecile," she begged. "Now I must leave myself. This last sacrifice is absolutely necessary, or there will be no America for your Irma. At Ruillé they refused to accept two young girls whom Bishop de la Hailandière wished to take with him to Vincennes. You see I shall have to comport myself well, for this Order is very strict."[25]

A few days after her unfortunate project of "dressing-up" Irma came to experience another facet of her superior's generous character. Thursday had arrived, the end of Irma's stay at Soulaines; Sister Theodore planned to leave with her Monday morning, November 30, to conduct her to the novitiate at Ruillé. During dinner, Irma had occasion to mention her dear friend Elvire Payan, who lived at Tours; Sister Theodore was immediately interested, and before the sisters left the tables, she had made her plans. "We will leave tomorrow," she declared. "That will give you a week-end at Tours, which is quite near Ruillé; your friends shall have the consolation of a visit with you." Once more Irma could not resist the reflection "How good Sister Theodore is!" She was so quick to see what would give pleasure, and so ingenious in finding ways to satisfy even one's secret desires.

Sister Theodore did, indeed, do all she could to make Irma's week-end happy. They went to Angers, where they took the steamer for the beautiful ride along the Loire; Irma had an opportunity to visit with her friends, the Paysons, and also her aunt, Madame de la Valette. They assisted at Mass in the magnificent cathedral, and on Monday morning, took breakfast with Madame de la Valette. "She found dear Sister Theodore perfectly charming," wrote Irma with delight. "This caused me great joy."[26]

Then at last they were on the way to Ruillé, where Irma would remain until the time approached for the departure for America; then she would return to Soulaines, to make her preparations with Sister Theodore. It was late Monday night when they reached the motherhouse at the entrance to Ruillé; all was somber and still, safely locked for the night. They waited in the December chill until the heavy doors were unbolted and the portress, her happy welcoming smile over-riding the demands of the place and the hour, admitted them and preceded them with her light to the chapel, always Sister Theodore's first stop, and then to the little rooms assigned them. By the light of their candles, in the hush of the sleeping house, they very quietly prepared for bed.

It was nine o'clock the next morning when Sister Theodore gently knocked on Irma's door. "Come now. I will take you to Mother."

The familiar voice, the encouraging smile were welcome to the young girl in her strange new surroundings. Not so welcome was Sister Theodore's plan of procedure. "I will take you to Mother's room where you shall be first to enter and receive her loving welcome. Do not feel uneasy about staying as long as she can give you time. She will reserve some for me later in the day."

Approach the superior-general alone! Irma could not imagine it. Not surprised, after all, Sister Theodore herself knocked, and in response to the firm and quiet "Come!" she entered with her postulant at her side. Irma found Mother Mary "just as Abbé Coedro described her; she has a severe spiritual look, but after some moments of embarrassment one feels quite at ease with her."[27] as soon as the moments of embarrassment had passed, Sister Theodore quietly took her leave, and Irma remained for a long chat which was to be the first stage in an enduring friendship between two supremely dedicated souls.

And Sister Theodore, having thus left her postulant in excellent hands, returned to her work at Soulaines while she awaited more definite instructions about her American assignment. She had received no further information from her superiors, and had as yet received no reply to a letter she had written to Monsignor de la Hailandière. Unfortunately her letter has not been preserved; but we learn from the bishop's reply, which reached her early in the new year, that it had brought great consolation to the priests laboring in the destitute mission. All were eagerly awaiting the sisters, whom they expected to leave France in the early spring. The bishop's anxiety only served to increase that of Sister Theodore, whose ardent spirit suffered from her inability to make any definite plans for the tremendous undertaking awaiting her. Eager and uneasy, in December Monsignor wrote:

> I addressed a rather long letter to Madame the Superior of Ruille, in which I tried to reply to a part of the questions that would have to be put to me. I also asked emphatically above all that this dear colony of Sisters be sent as soon as possible. They are so eagerly desired, the need is so great, and then inconvenience of the voyage would be lessened.

> If one could, for example, leave soon enough to be at New Orleans at the beginning of May, from there to Vincennes one could come in the same boat, in a few days only. Leaving later, one could no longer think of coming by New Orleans; it would be necessary to go directly to New York. From there, the journey to Vincennes is longer, more difficult, more expensive, etc. However, if I am informed in time, I shall send someone to New York to direct the trip.

> In any case arrange to come so that there will be time to get settled before winter. And by the word "settled" I mean to select the place where the house will be located, begin to build it in part so as to lodge there. O, how much work, how many difficulties await these good religious, difficulties however which the missionary priests and bishop will share with them.[28]

It was to real apostolic dedication that the new bishop of Vincennes was calling the sisters he so eagerly awaited. His attempt to communicate his own sense of urgency revealed the extent of his dedication and that of his priest associates, most of them, like himself, laboring in a land far from home.

Chapter 6

Sister Theodore, having no control over arrangements for departure or circumstances of arrival in the New World, could only embrace in advance whatever difficulties might await her and her companions. Any truly apostolic work, she knew, must of necessity be founded on the Cross. The thought that this Cross would not be wanting in Vincennes was an encouragement to her zeal.

Yet the poignancy of the sacrifice being asked of her must not be underestimated. There seems, indeed, to have been an aura of Gethsemane surrounding her vocation to the missions. It was truly a "vocation," a calling which did not emanate from natural inclinations, but transcended them.[1] Her response was not less wholehearted and sincere because it was the response of an earnest and diffident soul in honest confrontation with reality.

There was the reality, first, of her physical condition. From the days of her novitiate, as we have seen, Sister Theodore was never free from needing to take careful precautions against the debilitating attacks to which her illness had left her subject. And she was no longer young; at 41 years of age she might well question her ability to make the inevitable adjustments. Was it zeal or temerity, she might have wondered, which motivated her consent to undertake this mission. Was it desire to fulfill the will of God, or a secret longing to satisfy the latent thirst for achievement hidden in every human heart? Would she be an asset to the missionary venture, or a heavy liability?

> It was true that God was accustomed to make use of nothing to perform his works. But could she remain in her nothingness, so as to place no obstacle in his way? Her own experience, despite the joys it had brought and the apparent success of her labors thus far gave her no encouragement to trust in her own abilities and virtues. Her clearsighted superior had, besides, taken care of that contingency. Mother Mary feared above all things for her daughters any giving way to pride or self-satisfaction. Sister Theodore had learned her lesson well.[1]

She had learned, also, to her grief, that even with the best intentions and the highest motives, one can be misunderstood by those whose trust is absolutely necessary and whose confidence must never be deceived. Was her superior deceived now in placing so much confidence in her? Might she, despite herself, abuse that confidence? Further – she knew herself well enough to face the question – would she be able to carry on so far from all whose affection and esteem her very nature seemed to demand?

Writing to her former bishop and director, Monsignor de Lesquen, for the new year, she confided to him some of her feelings, her hopes and her apprehensions. Bishop de Lesquen had been her staunch supporter in the trial which clouded her early days at Soulaines. He now saw no reason for her to turn aside from the beautiful opportunity God was offering her; she could still, as always, count on his grace. "The sentiments with which you are animated," he assured her, "cannot fail to draw down on you abundant grace, since you are still determined to undertake the great voyage; since it is only obedience which directs you, he for whom you are acting will take it into consideration." There was always, of course, the question of her health; but "Even if your health should compel you to ask for your return, God will reward you just the same for your good will."[2]

Despite appearances, those responsible for the American mission were not, of course, indifferent or forgetful. While Sister Theodore in Soulaines struggled with the questions always hovering beyond her resolute absorption in her ordinary duties, and Monsignor de la Hailandière, across the Atlantic, watched daily for news of the promised missionaries, the superiors at Ruillé and the bishop of Le Mans consulted together. Both superiors and prelate hesitated to proceed without further information from the bishop of Vincennes, who at the same time awaited a response to communications unaccountably delayed. Monsignor Bouvier undertook to write himself to the American bishop in the interest of mutual understanding.

"The superior-general of the Sisters of Ruillé and the mistress of novices were here yesterday," he wrote on February 27, 1840. After expressing the surprise of the sisters at the lack of news from Vincennes, he went on to raise practical questions based on his own understanding and experience of the prudent conduct of religious foundations: "They are preparing good sisters for you, as they promised, and are disposed to send them, in spite of the need that they have of them, for they are far from being able to supply all the demands addressed to them. But when will these sisters go? By what route, and how will they go? How will they be lodged? What will they do?

The general officers intend to yield them to you gratuitously, and even to give each one a fine wardrobe and even some money so that they may not be entirely without means on arriving in that far-off country. But they have always thought that the expenses of the voyage, of lodgings and furniture would be paid by you.

On what footing will this new establishment be placed? If there is a deficit, who will be responsible for it? If there is a benefice, who will profit from it?

I have the honor of informing you, Monsignor, that in my opinion, it would be better if this community would depend only on you and your successors, because we could not, because of the distance, exercise a real supervision over it. That would not prevent me from rendering you, when I could, all the services in my power.

Nothing has been settled on these different points; it is essential that everything be foreseen and, insofar as possible, decided and written, in order that in the future there may not be any misunderstanding."[3]

In these observations, the bishop of Le Mans, ecclesiastical superior of the Sisters of Providence of Ruillé, voiced his concern for the observance of their Rule, for which in its final form he himself had been largely responsible. The Rule was explicit in its provisions for the opening of new establishments. No new house was to be opened without the guarantee of suitable lodgings and sufficient income to provide a respectable livelihood for the sisters. In all cases a contract was to be drawn up in duplicate, specifying mutual responsibilities, "so as to avoid as much as possible the inconveniences which time and circumstances could cause to arise." And, finally, all the required formalities must be carried out in order to have the new establishment approved and give it legal existence.[4] It was unfortunate, although perhaps inevitable in the circumstances, that these wise prescriptions did not receive greater consideration, on both sides, before the American foundation was made.

In his reply to Bishop Bouvier, Monsignor de la Hailandière expressed his own surprise that his benefactors in France had received no word from him. "I had the honor of accomplishing this duty in your regard," he wrote on April 21.[5] He had written, he said, several letters both to monsignor and to the superior, long letters, filled with important details. He hastened now to reply to Monsignor's questions. When should the sisters leave? "As soon as they can. Certainly they will not be here as soon as we would like and as they will be needed." How will they travel, and how will they be lodged? "They should embark at Havre for New York; from there the way is easier. Arrived here, we will take care of them. For a long time we have been busy building them a house. Unfortunately, the chapel which was to have been theirs just burned down completely. We must now seek means to rebuild it or rather to make another, for nothing remains of the first." What will they do here? "What they do in Ruillé and in the different establishments that they direct in France, with the sole difference that here the people are more exacting with regard to education than in France and that therefore it is necessary to teach more subjects.

Monsignor de la Hailandière's letter to Mother Mary, written a few days later, was the eloquent appeal of a missionary bishop for his flock's needs.

Not having received since my departure any letter from Ruillé, it is only natural that I feel some inquietude, even some fears concerning this community that you have had the goodness to promise me, and which, announced here, is so ardently desired and awaited.

It is not, Reverend Mother, that I doubt the least in the world the sincerity of your views, and their constancy in what concerns us; but I reproach myself with not having sufficiently exposed you to our needs, and also of having left you ignorant of the powerful attraction there is for souls pure and free from attachment to the earth in the position in which Providence has placed us. My silence in that regard is explained by the fact that, arriving at Ruillé, I found all things disposed and arranged beyond my hopes by the special direction, as I like to consider it, of the divine Spirit who had influenced hearts in our favor to such an extent that to try to meddle myself in the situation, beyond blessing God and praying to Him, appeared to me then as a failure in confidence in the holy Providence which was serving us so well. Today, in the same interest of the work and to second divine Providence which demands that we second His views, I ask permission to submit to you some considerations which, I do not doubt, cannot fail, if one has the goodness to mediate on them a little before God, to arouse a great interest in our mission.

These considerations included the immensity of the diocese of Vincennes, the rapidly-growing population, the opportunity opening before the Church in America and the need for schools to second the evangelical labors of the missionary priests.

> There are conversions even in this poor diocese of Vincennes. One priest, in eight months, converted fifty-four Protestants. What would happen if we had schools? Schools for the people especially. O, dear Sisters of Providence, why are you not here? It seems to me personally, Reverend Mother, that there are many souls whose salvation is reserved to your daughters.

He returned to the important matter of jurisdiction over the foundation, still, unfortunately, not clearly defined:

> We have discussed, Monsignor of Le Mans and I, the question of whether our House would be or not a branch of the House of Ruillé. In the interest of the members that Ruillé will send us, and in the fear that it might be too painful for them to be separated from their Motherhouse, I desired that for a longer or shorter time our House would not cease to be part of that of Ruillé. Today, after much reflection, I am perfectly indifferent in that regard. I leave you then to regulate all that with Msgr. Bouvier as you wish, and I submit in advance to what will be decided.

A paragraph toward the end of the bishop's letter could not have failed to awaken certain misgivings not apt to forward the cause he was so ardently pleading. In his desire to present a perfectly honest and convincing view of his needs, Monsignor mentioned details better calculated to arouse in Mother Mary a feeling of relief that the departure of the sisters, despite the need, had not been precipitous. What would they have done in the circumstances which he proceeded to describe:

> Some time ago construction was begun for the reception of your Sisters on their arrival. That puts us in difficulties, because the person who pledged himself to help in the foundation has so far given only one-fifth. Nothing could have saved it; after two hours, there remained only ashes. They are beginning a new one, so much do they fear that the Sisters will not come.[6]

It is in the light of reflections stirred by such letters, so urgent in their appeal, yet so long in reaching their destination and hence in receiving a response, that one must assess the risks inherent in the venture to which the sisters were committing themselves. Such risks demanded, indeed, complete self-surrender and unbounded trust in Providence. This same confidence also was required of those who in the New World awaited and prepared for their promised co-workers.

Part of the price of the conquest of the New World for Christ may well have lain hidden in the difficulty and the sometimes heartbreaking delay in communication with the Old. Monsignor de le Hailandière's letter to Mother Mary, written in April, would in all likelihood not reach Ruillé until early June. Meanwhile, he was expecting from day to day news that the sisters had set out for Vincennes.

A month before writing to Mother Mary the bishop had written to Sister Theodore, answering a letter she had addressed to him early in January, which unfortunately has not been preserved. Judging from his response, one might infer that she had expressed some inquietude. Monsignor played down his own anxiety in an attempt to reassure and encourage her. "What I feared so much has happened," he wrote. "They are losing interest in our mission. On the other hand, your devotion increases, and that gives me great joy in our Lord, and in spite of the difficulties, hope remains and is stronger than the uneasiness."[7]

Sister Theodore, it seems, was preoccupied with the possibility of separation from Ruillé. Just as he had assured her superiors, Monsignor de la Hailandière told her also that he would accept whatever decision Ruillé made on this matter. Indeed, on consideration he could see certain advantages in autonomy; but he himself would not make the decision. He gave her what information he could; one of his priests was looking after the building of a house, which should be ready in the summer; their chapel had burned down, but another would be built. "We are preparing some novices, and if you come this spring, you will have a good number before the end of the year. But if you delay too much, some will lose patience, for we have given them the hope that you will arrive at the end of spring. Ah, if you knew how much you are desired here! What sorrow if you did not come! What misfortune! God will not permit it. He has till this very hour been so good to us!"

Did Sister Theodore wonder a little that this letter, which reached her some time in May, spoke at once of arrival at the end of spring, and completion of a house by the summer? Whatever the seeming inconsistency, however, there could be no doubt of the bishop's eagerness to receive the sisters. His interest included even minute details, which would indeed have been superfluous if, as he really hoped, the sisters were already on the way:

> You must yourself judge what is useful to bring with you – models for writing, drawing, embroidery, silk for embroidery, chenille – these things can be found here, but less beautiful and more expensive. One can bring many things without paying freight and without import tariff, when one ships them as part of one's baggage. It is very cold here in the winter; you must bring clothing suitable for this season. I believe that you will have to procure simple little hats and black shawls to wear outside. You will see that there is no one here dressed like our French peasants; every woman wears a hat and shawl, and in the winter a coat.[8]

He concluded with an exhortation certain to find an echo in Sister Theodore's soul, "Pray, Sister, pray much. Our mission is henceforth yours; and on the missions nothing is done except through prayer. I will pray for you without fail, and our hearts will find each other in God."

A postscript typical of Bishop de la Hailandière furnished postal instructions surprisingly simple considering the distance and the size of his adopted country:

"Write me simply and without envelope: The Right Rev. Dr. C. de la Hailandière, Bishop of Vincennes, United States of America. Stamp and mail to Havre; a courier leaves the 1, 8, 16, and 24 of each month."

However imperative the call of the mission as yet only vaguely defined, Sister Theodore still directed her best efforts to the mission of the moment, her work at Soulaines. Years later she would warn her sisters against neglecting the real good at hand while meditating immense projects for the future.[9] She herself, with good reason for distraction, had overcome that temptation. She was surprised by both a reward and an incentive late that April.

She and Sister St. Edmond had been, of course, neither surprised nor alarmed by a visit the preceding year from the inspector of schools, an official from the Royal Academy at Angers. They were not surprised, for the School Law of 1833 had provided for such supervision; and they had in reality no reason to be alarmed. Sister Theodore was an excellent teacher, and she had trained Sister St. Edmond well. Their little girls were industrious and well-behaved. On this occasion, as usual, they recited admirably. Sister Theodore's class shone particularly in mathematics.

The surprise came in a communication from the Inspector, M. Névo-Degouy, dated April 15, 1840, informing Sister Theodore that on the recommendation of the Academic Council, the minister of education was awarding her a bronze medal, to be presented in the future. "Receive my sincere congratulations," he wrote, "and be assured that I am happy to have been delegated to announce this decision, in which I pray you to be persuaded I take part."[10]

The date and manner of the actual presentation have nowhere been clearly recorded. In her biography, based on Sister Theodore's own recollections and those of sisters who knew her, Mother Mary Cecilia relates that the gentlemen who came to make the presentation found Sister Theodore occupied in household tasks. However, the presentation address which has survived suggests a ceremony more formal, an occasion of rejoicing for the entire village. The call at the convent may then have been one of courtesy and congratulations, during which they discussed arrangements for an official gathering.

The discourse pronounced on that occasion, for all its 19th century rhetoric, is worthy of reproduction in its entirety. It provides an insight into the attitude of the French government toward religious education at that time. In its own way, it presents a summary of Sister Theodore's mission in Soulaines; and it gives voice to the grateful sentiments of all those whom she served.[11] Its effect on its hearers can readily be imagined. For the villagers there was unaffected delight. For those who shared the knowledge of her impending change, Father Brillouet, M. de la Bertaudière, M. and Mme. Marie, there would have been a touch of irony, an intensification of regret. Sister St. Edmond, the "modest fellow-laborer" honored in the speaker's closing words, struggled to resign herself to the loss of the one who had been her daily guide and inspiration.

Sister Theodore's own reactions remain a secret, but inevitably the affectionate pride of those who surrounded her brought into painful relief the realization that she would soon be leaving them. Certainly the circumstances added to the doubts and misgivings which so frequently assailed her. She seemed to be doing well the work that she was prepared to do; was that not, perhaps the sign that God wished her to continue as she was, leaving the more glorious mission for one more worthy? In her distress, she sought the advice of the ecclesiastical superior of the community, the bishop of Le Mans.

Bishop Bouvier, whose long experience in the guidance of souls had taught him to trust where the works of God are concerned, answered her in terms he knew she could understand and embrace. "The sentiments you express, my dear Daughter, are not without foundation. If you counted only on your worthiness and your capacity, you would not be a suitable instrument for the work of God."[12]

He recalled to her the Gospel example which was certain to call forth a response from one steeped in the lessons of self-depreciation and abnegation which characterized the spirituality which had nurtured her religious life:

When Jesus Christ established the ministry of sanctification to which you must now be associated still more than you are by your first vocation, you know that He chose for His disciples not the princes, the powerful ones of the times, the learned; but poor and humble fishermen, in order that the divine workings be more striking. He always acts in the same way; He confounds the proud and exalts the humble. Let us count ourselves as nothing, but nevertheless let us be ready for everything. If one sets us aside as objects of rejection, let us not murmur, but if one employs us in great affairs, let us not take glory in it any more than the chisel which is used to make a beautiful statue.

Since you have been chosen for the foundation, think only of preparing yourself to the best of your ability, and take with you a good will which does not waver. Great matters will be in your hands; fear to compromise them, and hence do not cease to rely on help from above.[13]

The former seminary director, Bishop de Lesquen, was more demanding in his recommendations than the sympathetic counselor of her early years in Soulaines; but if there is in his advice no note that resembles Bishop de Lesquen's gentle promise of the rewards of God's grace, there is a challenge that would be certain to appeal to Sister Theodore's courageous heart and reinforce her own opinion of herself. Her acceptance would help her to entrench herself still more profoundly in the "nothingness" which could not fail to attract the aid of God's omnipotence. Her whole future course would carry out the program outlined for her during these days of tremulous waiting to plunge into the unknown.

The word for which she had been waiting came at last. On June 12, 1840, the Particular Council of the Sisters of Providence at Ruillé met in formal session to make definite arrangements for the voyage of "three or four Sisters of our Congregation designated to take part in the expedition of Vincennes in America in order to form novices and to try to establish in the diocese of Vincennes a teaching Congregation on the model of Ruillé-sur-Loir."[14]

In compliance with the desire of the bishop of Vincennes, and with the advice of the bishop of Le Mans, the Council determined that the sisters would leave France July 14, 1840. Named for the mission besides Sister Theodore Guerin, the Superior, were Sister St. Vincent Ferrer Gagé and Sister St. Dominique Châtel. With them there would be two novices, Sister Marie Xavier Lerée and Sister St. Liguori Tiercin, young women who had entered at Ruillé solely with the Vincennes mission in mind. It was decided also that the Congregation, "in view of the greater glory of God, would be responsible for the trousseau of the five Sisters and for the expense of the journey to America."

Mother Mary was at last in a position to send Monsignor de la Hailandière some definite information, which she hastened to do in a letter written the day of the Council decision:

> We have received three letters which you have done us the honor to write to us, dated February 27, April 22 and 29. I answered the first, which you have no doubt received, and which will have reassured you on our continuing intention to enter into your plans and to do all within our power to establish a Congregation of Sisters of Providence in your diocese.
>
> In this respect, neither our thoughts nor our wishes have varied an instant since we had the honor of seeing you at Ruillé last August. We only regret that various circumstances have not permitted us to realize our promise sooner. But Monsignor, I hope that you will readily excuse us when you know that the three religious whom we are sending were each at the head of an establishment that they could not have abandoned in the middle of the scholastic year and that it was necessary to leave them at least till the First Communion of the children, in order not to do too great an evil in France by wanting to do good at Vincennes.
>
> Today, Monsignor, I am writing to advise you that the

departure of our Sisters for America has been settled for July 15; they will be at Le Havre the 18th, whence they will leave, no doubt, at the first opportunity, for New York where we trust they will find the Guardian Angel and conductor whom you will have the extreme courtesy to send to meet them to direct them to the place to which Heaven destines them.

We thought, Monsignor, that we should send at present only six persons: three religious capable, pious, and all very well equipped to help your work succeed insofar as one can count on human capacities, two novices, and a lay Sister. This number seems to us sufficient for the beginning.

You will pay to our Sisters, Monsignor, the money that we have advanced for their voyage to New York. If it were possible, we would make further sacrifices, both for them and for you. At least we have the consolation of being able to assure you that we are doing even more than we can. Two of the Novices had no dowry; one only 600 francs, which we are giving in its entirety to Sister Theodore. We would be very sorry to keep a centime against the poverty of these poor daughters.

We recommend our Sisters to your solicitude and to your charity for the spiritual and the temporal. Be their father, their consolation, their guide and their support.[15]

Four days later, on June 16, Mother Mary addressed to Sister Theodore her invitation to come to Ruillé to prepare for her departure. It was a bittersweet message. Mother Mary, by nature so reserved, seemed to give way to unusual emotion; yet not even the event which occasioned this excess of feeling was to divert the superior from the regular round of her duties. She would not be at Ruillé to greet her daughter returning for the last time, nor would she be there to bestow a farewell embrace on the daughters about to be separated from her, she regretfully announced, for the rest of their lives. Sister Theodore had difficulty, through her own tears, in reading the missive so touching and at the same time so uncompromising. It was her letter of obedience, informing her of God's will for her:

It is from Ruillé, my Theodore, that I bid you goodbye, for it is probable that I shall be deprived of the pleasure of embracing you at your departure, which has been fixed, in concert with our venerable Prelate, for the fifteenth of next July. Consequently, you may come to Ruillé to make your preparations for the great journey which will probably separate us for the rest of our lives, until we see each other again in the Bosom of the God who has acquired an eternal kingdom for us at the price of His blood. My hand trembles, my dear Theodore, my heart beats, and my tears flow as I write you these words which may be the last I shall say to you; I hope they impress you as they do me, for in spite of the war that I have incessantly waged with your self-love, with the desire of destroying it, God is my witness that I have always loved you from the bottom of my heart, and I will always love you. Whether you be at Vincennes, whether you be in China, everywhere my love will follow you, even to heaven or purgatory. Go then, my dear daughter, with the assurance of our sincere and cordial friendship, with the good wishes and the blessings that I can make or give. In one word, my daughter, let God alone be the object of all your undertakings, and the end of all the actions you will perform for His glory. Only, remember us for the love of Him.

Now, my daughter, in spite of your latest representations, it is determined that you will go to Vincennes and that you will be the superior of the house of Novitiate which they wish to establish there, and the superior general of all those which will be established in the future, until the two prelates of Le Mans and of Vincennes decide otherwise.

Two statements in this important letter forecast problems for the future. As she had indicated to Bishop de la Hailandière, Mother Mary gives Sister Theodore the hope to look forward to additional recruits. Sister Theodore was to count on this promise more than future circumstances would warrant:

Here, my daughter, is how we wish to begin this work for the greatest glory of God, in order not to tempt Providence, nor yet to distrust the goodness of God. Together with our venerable and learned Prelate, we have decided to send for the time being only three of our Sisters: you, Sister St. Vincent Ferrer and Sister St. Dominic, with two novices and a lay Sister. You will begin by getting settled, and moving into the house destined for you, which is not yet finished. There you will judge your needs, the good there is to be done, and the help you must request. You will open schools in a little congregation of Catholics. Sister St. Dominic will visit the sick. You will begin by getting things as well organized as possible, with the help of God, and next summer the Congregation engages itself to send you other help if there is need. We have thought that considering the poverty of the diocese, of the bishop and his clergy, who live on alms, it was necessary to proceed with prudence in order not to overburden them.

One of your Novices is a beautiful writer. The other is a good seamstress. The lay Sister will do all the heavy work. The Americans, they say, like talents which stand out: drawing, music. The French also, you know very well, especially at this time; however, during the forty years that our Congregation has existed we have not been able to teach these branches ourselves. At present, three of our Sisters are studying, but they will still need two years of study in order to be able to teach others. In France, at the Sacred Heart even, where most of the religious are of high estate, all the ornamental branches are taught by masters in the boarding schools. Then how can you expect that we, poor little country girls, can possess these talents for Vincennes or for France. So, my daughter, say to God that it is not for all that that you are going to Vincennes, but to make Him known, loved, and served, and to teach these people the "one thing necessary."[16]

Another harbinger of future difficulties was the hesitancy of the bishops to conclude definite arrangements in advance. Thus the way was opened to a period of uncertainty as to jurisdiction and accountability, painful and prolonged.

Monsignor cannot, he says, decide anything for the moment with respect to the agreement to be made between Monsignor of Vincennes and him. He wishes that you look over things before concluding anything definitely, because he cannot found his agreement on anything until you are at Vincennes. You will tell your good Bishop that we have given you all that the Novices brought us, that we are even adding the religious habit to their modest trousseau at the expense of Providence, which has no desire to be reimbursed.

Bring everything you have, and try to obtain something from M. de la Bertaudière for your Mission. He is so good that I do not think he will refuse you. Sister St. Vincent will be your Assistant, Sister St. Dominic will be able to take care of temporalities, as econome.

They both have intelligence, piety, devotedness, joined to a great facility in learning. Sister St. Dominic knows how to care for the sick, and both have gentle and pure manners, and are of good character.

It is agreed that the voyage will be at the expense of Monsignor of Vincennes. He has asked us to advance what will be required as far as New York; there you will find money in the keeping of his correspondent, and a priest sent to meet you and direct you on the rest of your journey. You will be reimbursed for what you will have spent. To that point, we substitute you as creditor in place of the Congregation, and you will apply this money for the voyage, instead of the Congregation, which waives it. But I advise you to take it, for certainly you will need it.

Goodbye, my dear Theodore! May the grace and peace of our Lord be with you, everywhere and in all things![17]

After signing herself, "Your friend," Mother Mary adds a little homey advice: "Come to pack your trunks and packages so that you will know where everything is when you disembark." Then touchingly she takes Sister Theodore into her confidence: "I am leaving for Brittany very tired and very much worried.

The life of a superior, my dear Daughter, is full of crosses and solicitude. But since victims are required, it is better that they be ourselves than others. We will soon have rest."

Information about the route, together with a list of Monsignor de la

Hailandière's correspondents in the various cities through which the sisters will pass, is followed by the poignant valedictory:

There you have, my dear Theodore, all the information I can give you. Pay close attention, and take notes during your voyage, so that you will be able to guide those who will go to seek you in your New World. Send the information that you gather to the superiors of the congregation to help them in their efforts to serve you.

Goodbye, my dear daughter! May Jesus our Savior give you his blessing. May his divine mother take you under her protection! May the Angels guide and protect you!

Goodbye, Goodbye again![18]

Sister Theodore slowly folded the letter. She was to read and re-read it frequently during the next few months. Now at last she was assured of God's designs for her, but her summons left her very little time. She had, indeed, less than a month in which to round out the year's program at Soulaines, make what provision she could for the voyage into the unknown, and bid a definitive farewell to the people and the places she had known in France.

Chapter 7

The date set for the departure of the missionaries for Vincennes was mid-July. Unusual as the mission to America undoubtedly was, and unforeseen in the plans of the Congregation of Ruillé-sur-Loir, there was nothing to indicate, during the few weeks between the announcement and the departure date, that any special and far-reaching project was actually under way. All of the circumstances surrounding the new apostolic venture conspired to cloak it in simplicity and hiddenness.

There was to be no formal farewell ceremony such as customarily marks the sending forth of missionaries. These missionaries were, after all, Sisters of Providence, called always to remember their littleness, dedicated to God's service wherever obedience might appoint, prepared to accept any sacrifice. And the sacrifices entailed were, indeed, many, and such as might well demand heroism on the part of ardent, sensitive Frenchwomen, fervent and devoted religious.

The missionaries would be leaving the motherhouse before most of the sisters from the establishments had gathered there for the annual retreat. They would miss this last visit with those who had been their companions in the novitiate and their friends during the ensuing years of community life. The inevitable heartbreak of final departure would, besides, be intensified by the absence of the mother whose embrace and blessing would have eased the parting.[1]

For Sister Theodore there was added the anguished conviction that she was leaving all, not only without the support of her superior's encouraging farewell, but under the cloud of her disapproval. She was facing again, in even more poignant circumstances, such a situation as in the past had led to much soul-searching, resignation, and ultimate self-abandonment.

What could have occasioned a manifestation of disapproval at the very time she was preparing to leave all she had held dear in order to undertake in the New World a work so well directed toward the glory of God?

Once again, her forthrightness had betrayed her. As she pondered her new responsibilities and the companions assigned her, she had felt impelled to present an observation for her superior's consideration. Sister St. Dominique had been ill; would she not perhaps find it difficult to sustain the hardships and privations of mission life? Would it not be preferable to assign to such a laborious post a younger, more robust sister?

Mother Mary, having written to the bishop of Vincennes and to the three professed sisters who were to respond to his hopes for his diocese, had set out June 22 for her scheduled visitation of the missions in Brittany. She was not without concern for the daughters she was sending so far away, but she was confident that in her letters she had satisfactorily covered every phase of the new undertaking.

Whether this representation reached Mother Mary in a letter from Sister Theodore, or whether it was transmitted by one of the council members with whom, in the superior's absence, she would have discussed it, remains impossible to determine.[2]

The realization that her candid representation had occasioned displeasure on the part of Mother Mary and disappointment for Sister St. Dominique clouded Sister Theodore's harried days of preparation. Already she had been obliged to resign herself to the fact that the one on whom she and Bishop de la Hailandière had counted most, Irma Le Fer de la Motte, would not be among her companions. The enthusiastic projects which she and Irma had shared when she brought the postulant to Ruillé to prepare for the Indiana mission would have to be deferred, as Irma's delicate health precluded her early departure from France. For the present she would follow the missionaries only in desire and in prayer. On Sister Theodore's arrival at Ruillé late in July, Irma had written to her mother, "I have had the pleasure of seeing my dear Sister Theodore again. I cannot tell you the feelings that moved us. We are very reasonable, however, hoping that we shall see each other next year."[3]

Another young woman who had caught the missionary spirit since the announcement of the American foundation was, indeed, to accompany Sister Theodore to America. This was Sister Olympiade Boyer, whose association with the mission was destined to contribute to the sufferings which attended Sister Theodore's last days in France.

Sister Olympiade had entered the Ruillé Community in November 1837. After reception of the habit in September 1838 she had passed her first year of novitiate at the hospital in Orleans, her second at Soulaines under Sister Theodore. Although a lay sister had been promised to the American mission, none had as yet been named. When Sister Olympiade offered her services, Sister Theodore, aware of her generosity, ability, and capacity for hard work, had transmitted her offer to Sister St. Charles and the councilors arranging the mission in Mother Mary's absence.

With Sister St. Charles' approval and that of Bishop Bouvier, to whom Sister Olympiade had appealed, Sister Theodore accepted the new recruit, who set out to pay a farewell visit to her family and to make her preparations for departure. During her own visit to Le Mans early in July, Sister Theodore consulted with Canon Lottin, who was handling arrangements for the journey and who added Sister Olympiade's name to the five others for whom provision must be made.

It was at this point that Sister St. Charles, who had in the meantime informed Mother Mary of the decision, learned that the superior was emphatically opposed. Mother Mary had not intended to admit Sister Olympiade to vows; she declared that if the novice accompanied the mission, it would be as a lay member for whose expenses the community would not be responsible. Sister St. Charles communicated this information to Canon Lottin in two letters well calculated to shift the responsibility for the difficult and embarrassing situation to Sister Theodore.[4]

It was the devoted Canon Lottin who found a means of supplementing the funds allotted by the community in order to cover Sister Olympiade's passage. Sister Theodore was later to express her gratitude to him as well as to Bishop Bouvier. "It is to you, dear Father, that we owe this treasure," she wrote Canon Lottin on December 6, 1842, when Sister Olympiade was proving her worth in America. In the meantime, just when she most needed the approval and the support of the superior to whom she was so sincerely devoted, she was feeling the full effects of that superior's displeasure.

Sister St. Vincent alluded to the suffering her companion was undergoing when she wrote to Mother Mary before setting out for America, "I returned to Ruillé without seeing my family, and on the fourth I began my retreat. Impossible, however, to devote myself to it as I would have wished, because of the host of distractions incident upon our approaching voyage, the trouble and care of our trunks, which I had to share with Sister Theodore, and still more because of the sorrow that she feels for having displeased you."[5]

Sister St. Vincent's description allows a glimpse of the duties and distractions of those last days at Ruillé. Even attended only by a sense of blessed purpose and inner satisfaction, the travelers would have found in the preparation of the trunks a challenge to their ingenuity, their patience and their physical endurance.

There were needs to be filled which must be imagined before they could be anticipated, needs of all kinds. Bishop de la Hailandière had impressed upon the sisters both the poverty of the diocese of Vincennes and his fervent hopes for its future. The missionaries must arrive prepared with the bare essentials of convent living; with chapel and catechetical supplies; with materials for whatever subjects they might be expected to teach; with remedies for the sick to whom they would minister; with all, in fine, that foresight could suggest. Their friends in Soulaines had been more than generous. Sister Theodore had brought with her to Ruillé books and school supplies and remedies. The sisters in the lingerie at Ruillé had been busy preparing clothing, table and chapel linens. Nothing was overlooked which sisterly love and thoughtfulness could devise.

And all must be ready before July 12, the date set for departure from Ruillé. All must be carefully packed, securely roped and labeled, so that there could be no danger of its going astray. What moments of recollection Sister Theodore and Sister St. Vincent could achieve in the interludes of their labors must substitute for the private retreat that they had hoped to make.

They must pay a visit to Le Mans, also, for a final interview with Bishop Bouvier. This they did early in July. The bishop received the sisters with characteristic fatherly kindness. He offered them words of prudent direction founded on his own deep spirituality and wise experience. He gave them his blessing, and had prepared for them the all-important document which authorized their missionary journey. This letter, written on the most official Episcopal stationery, read:

To all who may see these letters, greetings!

We certify that Sister St. Theodore and her companions, of the Congregation of Providence of Ruillé-sur-Loir, in our Diocese, recognized legally by Royal Ordinance of November 19, 1826, are leaving to found, with our consent, an establishment of their

Congregation in the Diocese of Vincennes, in the United States of America.

We recommend these Sisters to the benevolence of their Lordships the Bishops and of the pious persons with whom they will come in contact during their voyage.

Given at Le Mans, in our Episcopal palace, under our seal, the seal of our arms and the countersignature of the Secretary of our Diocese, July 4, 1984.

SEAL Jean-Baptiste, Bishop of Le Mans

By Monsignor Lecottier, honorary Canon, Secretary[6]

Some months later, in a cabin in the Indiana woods, Sister Theodore's hand would tremble a little with the emotion which possessed her as she wrote on the back of this document, so formally signed and sealed, the legend, "Passport of Monsignor the Bishop of Le Mans to the foundresses of our house of St. Mary-of-the-Woods." Returned from Le Mans, only a week before leaving Ruillé, she meditated on its challenge. There was a certain reassurance in its statement of their destiny; there was encouragement in the approval it expressed.

And Sister Theodore had need of approval and encouragement. During her absence Sister St. Charles had received a letter reiterating Mother Mary's attitude toward the acceptance of Sister Olympiade. There was no letter from her Superior for Sister Theodore, no reply to her own written appeal.

A little time remained, when the greater part of the packing had been completed, for Sister St. Vincent to gather together a few personal necessities and set out to spend her last few days with her family. Sister Basilide, too, having said her "goodbyes" to her pupils at Argentré-du-Plessis and to her sisters at Ruillé, had gone to take leave of her family. Sister Olympiade had parted from the friends she had made during her year at Soulaines, and, having left Ruillé happy with Monsignor Bouvier's permission to dedicate her services to the American mission, was paying her farewell visit to her home.

Of Sister Theodore's immediate family only her sister, Marie-Jeanne, remained. Madame Guérin, who had found the first parting from her elder daughter so very difficult, had died in May 1839 before any thought of this greater separation had arisen. Marie-Jeanne had married in 1826 Louis Bartholémy le Touzé. The young family still lived at Etables, too far for Sister Theodore to venture at such a time, when last moment details which only she could arrange kept her occupied at Ruillé.[7]

There was so much she still had to learn, in order to carry out her formidable mission. Everything must be done, she had decided, just as it was done at Ruillé, if the establishment in Vincennes were to be truly "after the model of that of Ruillé." Having been a general councilor, she was familiar with the proceeding of the meetings of this body. Carefully she made copies of some of the records, to serve as models for the new foundation. She copied carefully, too, the minutes of the particular council meetings which had established the mission and named the first members. With Mother Mary's letter of obedience and directions and Bishop Bouvier's formal authorization, these would be in a way their charter in the New World.

She met, as often as they could make themselves available, with the assistants, Sisters St. Charles and Marie Lepinay, and with the novice mistress, Sister Eudoxie. She consulted with Sister St. Vincent Levillain, the econome, and with the secretary, Sister Augustine; and she sought the advice and the suggestions of the sisters in charge of the various departments.

Nor did she forget the three young women in the novitiate who had a special claim on her time and her attention. Irma Le Fer, now thoroughly at home after over seven months at Ruillé, was trying to hide her disappointment at the deferment of her departure under enthusiastic dreams for the future. She availed herself of every opportunity for conversation with Sister Theodore, as did the two other young Bretonnes, Francoise Lerée and Louise Tiercin, who, like Irma, had heard the appeal of the Church in America.

There had been a great deal for them to learn in the few weeks since their arrival in May. Between their studies and the exercises of the novitiate, timidly at first, then with more and more confidence, they responded to Sister Theodore's own desire really to know them, that she might encourage and assist them. They had endless questions to put to her about that remote and beckoning land, where, dressed like her, they would be among the first Sisters of Providence to help evangelize what they visualized as a pagan people. Clearsighted and discerning, Sister Theodore applied herself to direct their zeal, to fortify them against disillusionment, and to help them begin to become humble, worthy instruments of Providence.

The momentous day, July 12, arrived. The novitiate wore that special air of breathless anticipation which always marked Reception Day, but this time there was the added excitement of last-minute preparations for an unprecedented event. In the lovely chapel, still new – it had been completed in 1836 – everything was festive. The altar beneath the painting of the Holy Family was bright with candles and flowers. There were more tear-drenched smiles than usual as the postulants entered the chapel clad in simple white dresses, mantles, and net veils and left after the ceremony happily self-conscious in their new habits. For Francoise Lerée, now Sister Marie Xavier, and Louise Tiercin, the new Sister Marie Liguori, the exchange was symbolic of a double renunciation; they had elected to leave not only their father's house, but also their native land.

Irma, still in postulant attire, joined her novitiate companions in showering congratulations and good wishes on the new missionary novices. Amid the happy and unaccustomed bustle, the two took part in their last novitiate recreation and devotions, then scurried about, elated even though faintly apprehensive, gathering together their last few belongings and tucking away the little tokens of affectionate remembrance lavished on them by the sisters they were leaving.

Sister Theodore made one last pilgrimage to the places grown precious over the past 17 years. She walked the long bright corridors, pausing in chapel, refectory, novitiate and infirmary. She climbed the wooden stairs to the dim gallery overlooking the chapel; through it she passed to the hall which housed the superiors' offices. She went out through the garden into the little woods, and took the path past the presbytery and the village church. Back in the chapel, she gathered and offered her memories.

Then finally it was time to say goodbye. The evening meal was over. They attended community recreation, and made their last visit to the chapel. Outside the carriage waited; in the midst of tears and promises of prayer and undying affection, the travelers entered. It was 9PM o'clock as they drove out of the courtyard into the narrow, silent streets.

The carriage clattered into the Episcopal city of Le Mans towards dawn the following morning, and the sisters dismounted at the convent of Notre Dame du Pre. Here their sisters of Le Mans waited to offer them welcome and refreshment, and here their fellow-travelers were to join them. Here, too, Sister Theodore was to spend three busy days under Canon Lottin's guidance, concluding arrangements for the voyage.

The canon had been untiring in his efforts to smooth the way for the missionaries. He was wise in his provisions for them, paternal and understanding in his attitude toward them. "How much we owe to the unparalleled kindness of M. Lottin," noted Sister Theodore at the beginning of her journal of travel. "Without his wise counsels we would have committed a host of blunders, results of our inexperience .[8]

She was to rejoice also in the company and the assistance of the mayor of Soulaines, M. Louis Marie, who arrived in Le Mans accompanied by his wife and laden with gifts and letters from their friends in Soulaines.

There were letters and packages, too, from Rennes and from Orleans; these, added to the supplies assembled in Le Mans for the mission, called for further labor with the trunks.

It was midnight on July 15 before every piece was at last ready to be dispatched. At four o'clock Thursday morning, feast of Our Lady of Mount Carmel, Canon Lottin met them in the cathedral, where he offered Mass for their safety and success and gave them his farewell blessing. Among his gifts to the mission was a relic of the true Cross. "In this sign you shall conquer," he said impressively, seeming, Sister Theodore felt, to read her inmost soul.

After Mass, in the coaches which were to carry them northward to the sea, the sisters turned their attention to the precious bundles of mail which had reached them during those tense and crowded days. There were some for Sister Theodore from Soulaines, of course. She opened Sister St. Edmond's first.

"Oh!" It was a cry of bafflement and distress which drew all tear-washed eyes toward her. Her expression incredulous, Sister Theodore was reading the letter which Sister St. Edmond had enclosed in hers.

"It is from M. Legros, the ship's agent, telling us not to start out until he notifies us. The ship on which we are to sail is not yet ready!"

Bewilderment and dismay brought back to her companions' cheeks half-banished tears. How could this have happened, after all Canon Lottin's careful planning? Why had the letter been addressed to Soulaines? What were they to do? Even while they filled the coach with their anxious queries, it was carrying them relentlessly forward.

Sister Theodore was the first to recover. "We need not be afraid," she told them. "The choice is no longer ours. As we are already on the way, we must continue, trusting that Providence will make all arrangements for us."

And Providence did so admirably, as Sister Theodore gratefully recorded.

"We traveled on without any trouble whatever, M. Marie providing for all our needs like a most devoted brother."

Confidence restored, they could even take note of the countryside through which they were passing. "France seemed to wish to make us regret her even more than we did," Sister Theodore continues in her travel journal, "by displaying before our eyes all her loveliness, for this part of Normandy is singularly charming. The exquisite steeple of the Cathedral of Seez. One would imagine it was lace-work, so delicate is the tracery."[9]

It was ten o'clock that Thursday night when the travelers reached Lisieux, to leave at five the next morning for Honfleur, where they were to take the boat to Havre. Providence continued to take care of them; a Sister of Mercy whom they met on the boat was its agent in Havre. She accompanied Sister Theodore and M. Marie to the office of the agent, M. Legros.

"He was sick in bed; we could not see him," relates Sister Theodore. "He had us informed that we had arrived too soon and that he had made no arrangements for us. From there I sent poor M. Marie to see what had become of his wife and our Sisters whom we had left on the boat with our baggage, and I went with the good Sister of Mercy to look for M. Franque, a man of good will and devoted to the missions. He was in the country, I was in the street, and our Sisters on the quay with our trunks. Judge of our embarrassment in a city like Le Havre!"[10]

Since the kindly Sister of Mercy was unable to accommodate so many in her little convent, Sister Theodore found lodgings with the Sisters of St. Thomas of Villanova, who received them "with that tender charity which characterizes them." While Sister Theodore was seeking lodgings, M. Marie was looking for an available ship. He learned of an American merchant ship, the <u>Cincinnati</u>, scheduled to sail Wednesday, July 22. Always prudent, Sister Theodore consulted the agents Legros and Franque before making definite reservations. To her relief, those gentlemen pronounced the deal excellent. In the meantime, M. Marie had succeeded, "by dint of bargaining," in obtaining a decrease in fare of 100 francs per person, no small saving in their limited circumstances.

Further unexpected assistance came to light amid the delicacies and medicines sent by their generous benefactress, the Countess de Marescot. In a box from the Countess, marked "Confections," carefully-wrapped medicinal orange flowers surrounded a little packet of 3000 francs in gold – one more endearing expression of the solicitude of their friends.

Meantime the date of departure had been deferred until July 26. In the time that still remained the sisters read (with what emotion can be imagined!) the packets of farewell letters they had received. They had time also to write their own letters, the last they were to address from French soil. Sister Theodore's first letter, written as soon as she was settled the evening of their arrival, had been addressed to Canon Lottin:

> My first duty on arriving at Le Havre is also the greatest need of my heart, that of witnessing to you my gratitude, which is inexpressible. Could it be otherwise after the care and paternal solicitude which you have had for us? Yes, dear Father, we will always cherish the remembrance of it; on the immensity of the ocean it will come to refresh our souls and to tell us that Providence is watching over us.[11]

Having described for him in detail all the events of that momentous day, Sister Theodore confided, "I must tell you further for your consolation, that I believe that charity will reign among us; everything begins well. My soul is also tranquil and fortified, and above all perfectly submissive to all that the good God may please to ordain."

Yet she could not conclude without a further confidence: "The remembrance of our Mother ill-disposed towards me follows me everywhere like a phantom. I am going to write, but help me, I beg you!" [12]

She wrote to Mother Mary the day before they were to embark, after she had said farewell to M. and Mme. Marie, her last links with the incomparable friends she had known in Soulaines. Her letter reveals a part of the anguish of soul which shadowed her last days in her homeland.

It is accomplished, Mother, my great sacrifice! I have said Goodbye to my tenderly loved Mother St. Charles, I have left behind the dear Providence which was everything to me, the dear Sisters who bear us so much affection! I could never express to you all that my heart suffered on leaving Ruillé, all the sorrow that poor heart held; for, O, Mother, I did not see you, I did not see sparkling in your eyes the tears of love that you would have shed, seeing your children leave, perhaps never to see them again until Eternity. I did not feel your hand on my head to draw down more potently the blessing of the Lord; I was deprived of the salutary counsels that your maternal tenderness would have given me, and which would have been so priceless to me! If you knew how painful all these privations have been for me, you would be moved.

Many times I went to the door of your room, to your place in the chapel, to your place in the refectory; it seemed to me these places would give me what I was seeking; finding them empty made me weep. O, yes, Mother, I wept, I still weep, and I will continue to weep, for I have a great bitterness to add to all my others, and I will have it until the day I receive from your hand the favor that I solicit so earnestly; this great, this profound sorrow was, is, and will be, to know that you were displeased with me, to the point that you did not wish to write me a line in reply to the letter I sent you. I confess, my Mother, that I had to a certain point merited it by refusing to take to America a Sister of your choice; I assure you, however, that I thought I was acting for the best. It is possible that I was deceived, but it was impossible for me to decide otherwise; perhaps you might have convinced me if I had had the happiness of seeing you, for God is my witness that I wished nothing but to do His will.

As for the departure of Sister Olympiade for America, I can protest to you in the face of the death which I am going to risk this evening in exposing myself to the furies of the sea, that I was impelled, forced, even, by a series of circumstances absolutely independent of my will, to act contrary to yours in that affair; I hope that the truth of this will be made known to you and that you will adopt other sentiments in my regard, and give back to me the affection of a mother, which you told me ten days before had never been changed. I beg you, then, my Mother, pardon me, it is to your heart that I call. It is the very day that I am leaving my country to obey you; it is in the presence of that immense ocean which may be my grave. O, yes, my Mother, you will pardon me, you will bless me, I carry away the consoling hope. Perhaps, alas! when you read these lines, the hand which traces them will have become the prey of ocean monsters! If this is so, you will at least be able to tell yourself that the heart which animates it was to the end filled with love for you, that it has no thought of bitterness, and that it asks you in return to forget the wrongs in which it never had part.

More poignant, however, than her own imperative need of understanding was her fear lest any of her companions be deprived of it. She was fervid and pathetic in her appeal for them:

Permit me, my Mother, to ask one further favor of your generosity. It is perhaps the last, the last prayer of your daughter, which is like her testament. Grant it to me, I beg you, dear Mother. It will cost little to your generous heart: love all my companions of exile, confound them in your love as I unite them in my heart. See these poor children cross, while trembling, the insecure plank which takes them aboard the ship, and thus deprives them forever of their dear country; see them turn their tear-filled eyes toward their dear Mother and say to her, "Love us always as we will love you. Be always our Mother as we will always be your submissive daughters; pray for us, and we, on the abyss of the ocean as in the wilds of America, we will invoke Heaven in your favor."

Goodbye, my Mother, since this is the divine will. If you soon receive word of my death, be assured that if the good God grants me mercy, I will intercede in your favor, for in time and I hope even in eternity, I will always be your very humble servant and very submissive daughter.

After having signed her letter, she appended one further plea, "O my Mother, write to me at Vincennes; let me find my pardon on arriving!"[13]

It was not, then, on the crest of a beautiful exaltation, which might have smoothed the way and made every hardship welcome, that Sister Theodore was departing on her mission of mercy. Rather, it was from the depths of painful desolation that she faced the unknown, as though her Lord wished to render her fully conscious of her own weakness in order that she might with more complete abandonment and confidence follow wherever He might lead her.

Their farewell letters written, the sisters had only to wait for the morning of July 26, when they were to embark. They were up very early that morning. At five o'clock, having said goodbye to their "dear Ladies of St. Thomas," they set out for the wharf where, they thought, they would board ship. But, as Sister Theodore relates, "as we walked through the silent streets of Havre, we met an old sailor from the hospital, who had gone an hour ahead of us and was returning to say that the vessel would not sail that day!"[14]

There was nothing to do but return to the hospice, but they were glad of the delay. They would spend St. Anne's Day in France, happy to be able to assist at Sunday Mass, even though deprived of Holy Communion because they had broken their fast. The following morning, July 27, they boarded the Cincinnati.

Chapter 8

One by one the <u>Cincinnati's</u> sails billowed in the wind. Around the little group of sisters huddled at the rail the air vibrated with commands, directives, and exclamations, all in a foreign tongue. Even as the travelers looked back on the land they were leaving, its shores seemed to flee from them. Their long sea voyage had begun.

In the journal which she kept during the voyage[1] and her detailed letters to her superiors in France, Sister Theodore has left her own inimitable account of the journey which began that Monday morning in July of 1840. As soon as she was able after the first few days at sea, she opened her long, ruled notebook, carefully wrote the dedication, "To the greatest glory of God," and commenced her "Notes on our voyage to America." She was ill during much of the voyage, but every day that she was able she wrote a little.[2]

She wrote for her sisters and her friends in France, in response to their request[3] and in the conviction that they would be interested in every detail of the momentous voyage. She wrote, too, to satisfy the need of her own ardent temperament to share all that she could with those she loved. Under her pen conditions of travel and companions on the way take life, providing insight into the heroism of early missionaries to the American Middle West and the circumstances of their difficult apostolate. Her account therefore constitutes a precious source for the historian of 19th century America.

It affords also a glimpse of her own sensitive, generous nature, outgoing and affectionate, open and eager to respond to all the world around her. Her response was first of all one of gratitude to the Providence which watched over their journey with unfailing solicitude. Aboard an American ship, whose captain and crew spoke only English, the French Sisters were treated with a courtesy and consideration truly admirable. The <u>Cincinnati</u> was a merchant vessel, not a passenger steamship, which would have been beyond their means; yet they were in a position to fulfill all the prescriptions of the Rule for travelers. "We were like queens on the ship," she reported gratefully to Mother Mary.[4] We were free as in our own houses. We performed all our exercises in common; our room was perfectly private, reserved for us alone."

Sister Theodore's notes present an appealing sketch of Captain Barstow, "our little captain," – the versatile master skillfully guiding the <u>Cincinnati</u> amid the churning waters of the Atlantic, yet showing himself on every occasion the thoughtful host. "The captain did everything he could think of to give us pleasure," she summed up for Mother Mary.[5] "If he saw a fish, a boat, an extraordinary phenomenon, he called us quickly to point it out to us, explaining by signs what we did not understand, for he knew no French except 'oui'."

The genial captain was well rewarded by Sister Theodore's appreciation of the marvels he pointed out. Every aspect of the sea and sky was to her an object of wonder and admiration. She had the true Breton's love of the sea. The time she could spend on the deck was to her a continual source of joy. She loved especially to contemplate what she termed the ravishing spectacle presented as evening closed, "that pure sky, the majestic sun which seemed to descend so proudly into the waters, as if to refresh itself;

that luminous ray darting from it, reaching even to us, and gilding the waves lightly stirred by the evening breeze."

As often as she reveled in this sight, it always seemed new to her, and always drew her to its Creator:

I felt happy in belonging to Him and said within myself, "What will our good God be in our True Country, since even in our exile, he is so great, so powerful, so magnificent.

Moved by the contemplation of this imposing beauty, she reports, the sisters "went down to our cabin to mingle our voices with nature's majestic voice in blessing and praising its Creator."

Thus the universe of sea and sky in which the sisters passed their days was a never-failing source of interest and delight, always to be shared with those who were never far from Sister Theodore's thoughts. Between the Old World and the New, Sister Theodore found much to ponder and to describe.

In those days of slow and hazardous travel, the journey from France to Vincennes was long. Six weeks passed at sea; it was not until September 4 that the <u>Cincinnati</u> entered New York harbor. The preceding days had been stormy, but at last on September 3 the sea was calm; the voyage approached its end in beauty and tranquility. After supper the sisters went on deck to watch for the last time as the sun set over the waters. They found the scene "ravishingly beautiful." During the night the ship left the open sea to enter the channel leading to the harbor. As dawn broke, the Sisters looked out upon the American shore.

With indescribable fervor, excitement, and trepidation, too, they said their prayers and hurried up to the deck, to kneel and give tearful thanks to God. Sister Theodore's next impulse was, characteristically, to share their overwhelming emotion with her sisters in France:

Rejoice, my Mother and my very dear Sisters, rejoice, bless the Lord our God with us. He has guided your daughters over the immense abyss of the sea; yes, those whom you have followed, accompanied with your good wishes with so much love, at last see the foreign land. There is that America, so feared and so desired! We see its coasts; they form our horizon![6]

She let her pen run over the paper, trying to keep pace with the thoughts and emotions she would crowd into her first letter from America. "We are approaching very fast. How fast my heart is beating! If you only knew what feelings one experiences at a moment like this! My God, you are our only support! Come to our aid!" Very close to land at last, her excitement overflows:

> I am coming back to you, my Mothers, after having been to see the American shore; we are in a channel between two stretches of land, and in two hours the ship will cast anchor. Everything here has the appearance of activity; a crowd of ships, schooners, sloops, which look like moving cathedrals, the shore which changes its appearance every instant, all that has a magical effect which leaves our hearts so moved, our Sisters, let us pray that we be not a stumbling block for this American people!

While the ship rode at anchor, she tried to summarize for Mother Mary the sisters' situation:

> All that we see here turns us towards God, and consequently toward you. All that we see here is charming. We cast anchor last evening about five o'clock, and find ourselves between two truly admirable coasts. Our voyage has been uneventful. We had four storms which frightened our companions, and our sisters a little, especially dear Sister St. Vincent; but we were not in real danger a single instant. The good God no doubt charged one of His angels to guide our ship.[7]

There was a busy, breathtaking interlude, filled with the tremulous excitement of putting into port. Returning Americans were thrilled with anticipation; new arrivals looked around with mingled hope and anxiety. For the sisters, the anxiety threatened to prevail. No word had come for them, no messenger, no instructions or welcome from Vincennes. Did the bishop still expect them? If not, where would they go? Gratitude for their safe arrival and amazement at the first glimpse of shores they had expected to find wild and uninhabited could not completely override their disquietude. No one, it seemed, would be there to direct them to their destination. During the voyage the captain's kindness and the companionship of other travelers had eased for a time the sense of isolation; now in port at last they were beset with the fear of being once more strangers, friendless in a foreign land.

Their forebodings were happily unfounded. Before they had even disembarked, their adopted country reached out with exquisite courtesy and hospitality to receive them. The Customs Officers who boarded the Cincinnati the afternoon of September 4 were both friendly and sympathetic; and scarcely had they departed when the Quarantine Officer, Dr. Sidney Doane,[8] arrived and outdid them in kindness. His greeting, spoken in their own language, lifted the hearts of French religious. "How happy I am to see Sisters of Providence" he exclaimed. "Many will be glad at your coming. There is no reason why you cannot disembark now."

When the Sisters hesitated to leave the ship for uncertain lodgings in a strange city, Dr. Doane offered to seek out for them one of Monsignor de la Hailandière's New York correspondents and to inform the bishop of their arrival. They knew a moment of regret, Sister Theodore relates, when they saw him leave the ship accompanied by the captain. But she adds:

> How sorry I should now be if we had followed him, for something happened to restore our spirits, and which you will not read without being touched. I was occupied looking at the beautiful scenes which surrounded us when I saw a little launch detach itself from the shore. I paid no attention, but when it was near us I recognized with pleasure the doctor who had spoken to us with so much kindness. He was carrying a covered basket. He came to me, hat in hand, and asked me to step into the room for a moment. We entered with him. Would you believe that this admirable man had come expressly to bring us a bottle of warm

milk, an excellent melon which he had picked in his garden, with a dozen peaches, some pears, and a fine dozen of oranges, saying to us, "My ladies, you will enjoy these fruits.

After a long crossing you have need of refreshment." So saying, he slipped away from our thanks and went back home, leaving us penetrated with gratitude for this delicate attention on the part of a stranger.[9]

Besides the refreshments for which he evaded their thanks, Dr. Doane had left with them words of consolation and encouragement. "Soon you will be surrounded by numerous friends who will be happy to see you. The Bishop of New York will be pleased to make your acquaintance. You will find in his Vicar General, Father Varela,[10] a real father. He is a Spanish priest who speaks French, and an excellent man whose life is spent in doing good."

"Scarcely had he vanished," Sister Theodore's account continues, "when we began to share his gifts with our poor traveling companions. The Rabbi had given me a fine orange when I was sick. I now gave him one in return and, for interest, added a pear of enormous size. The other Jew also received his portion, and our old lady was not forgotten. Finally, half an hour after the doctor's departure, many a heart was blessing him while partaking with a keen appetite of the provisions he had brought." That was not all. The next morning, by putting the milk he had brought into the coffee, the sisters had the pleasure of "giving our Americans a breakfast a la francaise."

The sea was high that day, and rain fell in torrents; there appeared no possibility of landing. Then, in mid-afternoon, the sisters saw a small boat approach, struggling through the waves. With joy they recognized their captain. With him was the Spanish priest of whom Dr. Doane had spoken, the Vicar General, Father Varela, come to welcome them on behalf of the Bishop of New York and to give them Monsignor's assurance that they need have no uneasiness. The captain, Sister Theodore records,

appeared happy to see us in such good hands. He showed us a thousand courtesies, and was full of attention for Father

Varela. Everybody gathered around us and envied our lot, for they were still to remain on board for another whole day before being permitted to land. A pretty little green rowboat awaited at the foot of a ladder, but the sea was frightful.

I whispered to the Sisters, "Come, if we have to die, let us die but say nothing!" With these words I descended first by the rope ladder, without experiencing the least uneasiness; the others followed…. Water poured in on all sides. The rain continued to fall. We were rocked as we had never been before, but I paid no attention to this, my eyes being fixed on the vessel we had just left. We exchanged farewells with our friends whom we should probably never see again.

Before knowing it we were at the dock. The sea was no longer beneath our feet, we were on the soil of America! It is impossible to describe what passed within our hearts at that moment.

From the moment they stepped on American soil they were to find shelter and warmth and encouraging friendships. Dr. Doane was awaiting them on the dock to conduct them to his home, where in a short time they dried their damp clothing before a blazing fire. Father Varela then conducted them to the Brooklyn home of Mrs. Andrew Parmentier,[11] widow of a noted Belgian horticulturist. Mrs. Parmentier and her two daughters, Adele and little Rosine, received the sisters "like angels from heaven." Indeed, they were quite overwhelmed by the courtesy and solicitude of this charming family.

Mrs. Parmentier secured also the services of a friend, Mr. Samuel Byerley,[12] a New York merchant, who assumed complete responsibility for their baggage, even to having their trunks, passed without Customs inspection, forwarded at his own expense to Vincennes. "The customs officer was very obliging," Mr. Byerley reported in a note to Mrs. Parmentier:

Captain Barstow told him that Doctor Doane had said that he had visited hospitals in Paris, and that he had witnessed the incomparable conduct of the Sisters, and that it was his opinion that it would be a blessing for anyone who would render them the least service. Consequently he does not expect any thanks for his attentions, and would be mortified to receive any.[13]

It was not in Sister Theodore's nature, however, to neglect expressing her gratitude to the friends to whom she felt indebted, and she begged her superiors in France to do the same. "You would give me great pleasure if you would write them a little word of thanks" she wrote to Sister St. Charles.[14]

Her letter to Sister St. Charles touches upon another cause for thanksgiving:

> It was in New York, Mother, that we had the happiness of communicating on the feast of the Nativity of the Blessed Virgin; it was there that we consecrated ourselves more especially to the good God, with an abundance of tears and singular consolation. What happiness we tasted that day!
>
> We did not buy it too dearly with fifty days of penance. That day I gave myself to the Lord to do and suffer all that it will please Him in America, where there is so much to do.

Their greatest privation during the long sea voyage had been that of Mass. Sister Theodore had confided in her journal:

> How can I express the sadness that filled our souls on the first Sunday that we had to pass on the ocean! Retired within our room, we read the Ordinary of the Mass aloud and united our intentions with that of the priests who were celebrating and with the faithful who had the happiness of assisting at the Holy Sacrifice.....

Now she could joyfully exclaim, "How sweet for us the moment when we had the happiness of uniting ourselves to Our Lord in the Holy Sacrament, after having been so long deprived of this inestimable favor!"

After five days in New York, having still received no word from their bishop, the Sisters set out on the long journey overland, leaving on September 10 by train for Philadelphia. There, as in New York, they were welcomed by the bishop who sent his agent, Mr. Marc Frenaye,[15] to meet their train.

The sisters were fortunate in the prelates whom they met during their first weeks in America – learned and devoted men, unsparing of themselves in their efforts to evangelize their vast mission field. Sister Theodore's account unfortunately contains no record of an actual meeting with the bishop of New York. The bishop for whom Vicar General Varela spoke would have been either the aged Bishop John Dubois,[16] or Monsignor John Hughes,[17] his dynamic coadjutor, later intrepid Ordinary in his own right.

The "good bishop" who welcomed the sisters to Philadelphia on September 10 was Monsignor Francis Patrick Kenrick,[18] coadjutor to the aged and infirm Bishop Henry Conwell, whom, a decade earlier, he had replaced in the administration of the diocese. Bishop Kenrick (1796-1863), born in Ireland, educated and ordained in Rome, was the foremost American theological scholar. He was to govern the diocese of Philadelphia until 1852, when he would succeed Monsignor Samuel Eccleston as Archbishop of Baltimore, and in that capacity preside over the First Plenary Council of Baltimore. During the sisters' stay in Philadelphia, Sister Theodore relates, Bishop Kenrick was "like a father" to them.

After welcoming the sisters, the bishop had them conducted to the house of the Sisters of Charity. Sister Theodore's journal account glows with details of this first experience in an American convent:

> We were accommodated by the Sisters of Charity, who showed us the kindest hospitality. We remarked virtues in these good sisters which excited our admiration. They are model religious, so perfect that we cannot aspire to their virtue....Not one of them knows a word of French; yet they found the means of making us spend very pleasant recreations.

This same hospitality and edification greeted them in the convent of these sisters of Baltimore, and again in Frederick. Here they were greeted by the former superior general, Mother Rose White, "a model of religious, filled with the virtues of her state, especially humility and charity."

The Sisters of Providence had set out from Philadelphia for Baltimore on September 18, after learning definitely that their bishop did not intend to send an escort for them, partly because he had been assured by Mr. Frenaye himself that it would not be necessary. With Bishop Kenrick's approval,[19] the Sisters set out under the guidance of a Canadian priest, Father William Chartier,[20] who was also bound for Vincennes.

At Frederick, the Jesuits also commanded the Sisters' admiration. The superior, showed his visitors through the beautiful church and surrounding buildings, buildings, Sister Theodore noted, "all erected to the glory of God and the benefit of humanity."

The travelers left Frederick on September 22 and four days later arrived in Cincinnati, after a breath-taking crossing of the Allegheny Mountains and a long and difficult voyage by riverboat on the Ohio. They were now venturing into an area quite different from the cultured, opulent America of the Eastern states, of which Sister Theodore had written:

> How very much mistaken we were, Mother, in thinking we would find here an uncivilized people! We have no idea in France of the affluence of the houses and the politeness of the inhabitants and their manners. We have the appearance of rustics beside our Sisters of Charity.

The difference, however, was in appearance only. In the midst of more primitive surroundings, the inhabitants were as polite and hospitable as their more prosperous fellow-citizens of the East. They shared the little they could command with all the graciousness with which the former lavished their abundance; they offered their services with a humility and simplicity which amazed the Europeans.

In Cincinnati, for instance, it was the bishop himself, Monsignor John Purcell,[21] who came to the boat to meet them. As was the custom of the country, Monsignor Purcell wore secular clothing; he introduced himself and welcomed the sisters, who then watched, speechless with embarrassment, as he set to work helping to remove their baggage. He had hired a carriage to take them to the convent, where once again they experienced the charming hospitality of the Sisters of Charity. "A very nice room had been prepared," Sister Theodore recorded. "Dinner was served, but the need of food was not the most imperative; it was rest we needed above all; so, after saying prayers, we hastened to our beds. It was seven days since we had undressed."

The next morning between early Mass in the convent and the High Mass in the cathedral, the Sisters visited, at his invitation, with Bishop Purcell. John Baptist Purcell was yet another of the zealous and self-sacrificing prelates with whose service the Church in America was blessed. Like Bishop Kenrick, Monsignor Purcell was a native of Ireland; like him, he was a serious scholar. He had come to the United States at 18; after preparation at Mount St. Mary's Seminary in Emmitsburg, Maryland. He had completed his studies at Saint-Sulpice and been ordained at Notre Dame in Paris. For the next seven years he served as president and professor at Mount St. Mary's, where in 1833 he was appointed second bishop of the young and struggling diocese of Cincinnati. Bishop Purcell was an ardent advocate of Catholic education, and was happy to welcome teaching Sisters bound for the diocese of his neighbor and confrere, Bishop de la Hailandière.

When the hour for High Mass brought an end to the cordial and encouraging interview, the sisters proceeded to the "cathedral." Sister Theodore had praised, with some reserve, the churches of New York and Philadelphia, of Baltimore and Frederick. In the cathedral of Cincinnati she could only weep, "seeing the poverty and destitution of this church. Never in all my life had I seen such a miserable one." It was a foretaste of what was to come. They were now indeed nearing that "new world within the New World" to which they had been called.

In Cincinnati they were at its threshold. The remainder of their journey was to be through a countryside ever more rugged, its untamed natural beauty forming at rare intervals the background for pioneer homesteads, mere huts for the most part, surrounded by patches of land cleared for rude farming and husbandry.

An early and perceptive traveler in America, Alexis de Tocqueville, deeply impressed by what he observed, described these homesteads and their inhabitants:

> As soon as the pioneer arrives upon the spot which is to serve him for a retreat, he fells a few trees and builds a log house. Nothing can offer a more miserable aspect than these isolated dwellings. The traveler who approaches one of them towards nightfall sees the flicker of the hearth flame through the chinks in the walls; and at night, if the wind rises, he hears the roof of boughs shake to and fro in the midst of the great forest trees. Who would not suppose that this poor hut is the asylum of rudeness and ignorance? Yet no sort of comparison can be drawn between the pioneer and the dwelling which shelters him.[22]

The sisters were to pass many such dwellings before arriving at the one destined for them in the midst of the immense Indiana forest.

They left Cincinnati on September 28, continuing by steamboat down the Ohio. The following morning they were at Madison, Indiana, where, having heard that the Bishop of Vincennes was making his pastoral visit in the area, they went ashore, eagerly anticipating a meeting with their bishop at last. After so many long weeks they were nearing their goal!

Their lively expectancy made the disappointment that awaited them all the harder to bear. Monsignor was not at Madison to greet them; he had gone on to another mission. There was nothing for the sisters to do but wait, weary and anxious, in the little inn where Sister Theodore confessed, they "nearly died of lonesomeness." Not until the evening of October 1 did the bishop finally arrive, and his coming was for the sisters a further indication of the adjustments awaiting them. They found it hard to recognize in the bronzed, weary, and weather beaten traveler, in spattered garments and "mud to the knees,"[23] the stately prelate whom some of them had met at Ruille. In his ecclesiastical garb he had seemed to them the very personification of princely dignity and courtly manners.

Even now, Monsignor had time only to greet the sisters briefly. It was good to see him at last, however, even for such a short time, and even though he told them to go on to Vincennes without him. "I will see you there in two weeks," he promised them. "The Sisters of Charity there expect you. You will have the time to rest a little and begin preparations for your work."

Any attempt to open their hearts on the part of Monsignor's newly-arrived co-laborers would have been useless in the circumstances. Polite, but preoccupied with that larger area of responsibility of which they were to be but a part, Monsignor blessed them and accompanied them to the steamboat landing.[24] The two weeks which would seem so long to the newcomers would pass all too quickly for him, absorbed as he would be in other details of his charge.

A few more hours on the river brought the Sisters to the city of Louisville, Kentucky, 45 miles from Madison. Here they were in the diocese of Monsignor Benedict Joseph Flaget, the venerable "Patriarch of the West," bishop of Bardstown, Kentucky, since 1808. They were received by the Sisters of Charity founded some years earlier in the diocese,[25] who like other American religious she had met along the way, inspired Sister Theodore's respect.

"They are admirable in their poverty," she wrote. "These Sisters have no boarders. They could not provide their fare." Having described the simple fare which they shared with the Kentucky sisters, she concludes, "We were simply compensated for the absence of bodily comforts, however, by the extraordinary kindness met with. The American Catholics here have the spirit of the Christians of the primitive Church: great charity, the love of hospitality which St. Paul recommended so strongly to the faithful of the time, an ardent zeal for the cause of the Gospel, in fine, all the virtues of the Fathers of the Faith."

They had also at Louisville the happiness of meeting the "Apostle of Kentucky," the veteran missionary Father Stephen Badin, a cousin of Sister Olympiade and like her a native of Orleans. Father Badin, the first priest ordained in the United States by Bishop Carroll in 1793, had been laboring for almost fifty years in the missions of Kentucky and its neighboring states, often alone, always amid challenging hardships. The day the Sisters spent in his company, October 2, beginning with the Sacraments and Mass, and lasting until time for the boat at three in the afternoon, was for the travelers a refreshing interlude, for, commented Sister Theodore, "though he has suffered unheard of trials and fatiguing labors, he still retains all his French gaiety and joviality."

The boat scheduled to leave at 3 that afternoon was delayed in its departure until 10 the next morning, October 3. Then, at the end of a long day on the river, heavy fog prevented the passengers from going ashore. Not until the following morning could they step on land at Evansville, Indiana. The journey by water was over, the end of their voyage at last in sight. In grateful relief, Sister Theodore noted:

> We were now only fifty-five miles from Vincennes. This was a great joy to us and filled us with gratitude to God, who had protected us in His goodness during the long and perilous voyage.

Before they set out by stagecoach for Vincennes, however, the Sisters witnessed a touching example of apostolic life in the diocese to which they had been called. In the person of a missionary priest in Evansville,[26] they glimpsed the depths of poverty, destitution and self-sacrifice which the work of evangelization in that diocese sometimes demanded. To their expressions of surprise and sympathy at the sight of the missionary's pitiful garb and humble lodging, he gave the simple explanation:

My companion and I eat only cornbread, which is brought to us every day by a baker. We have only a log hut for our church, house, and school. At night we spread a mattress on a bench and there, wrapped in our coverings, we take a little rest. When we are away on mission duties, and one or the other always is, we sleep on hay or straw or sometimes under a tree.

This was missionary life in the diocese of Vincennes! For the sisters it was another insight into their future on the American frontier. It was an experience to ponder as their carriage bore them into the midst of a thick forest, over one of the famous "corduroy" roads, made of logs bound together somewhat in the manner of a raft.

At nightfall, battered and bruised by the jogging of the coach over the bumpy road, they welcomed the experience of another aspect of pioneer life – that cordial hospitality upon which Sister Theodore had already remarked. They stopped at a farmhouse in the woods, where "the kind people gave up to us a room containing three beds," and provided a lodging also for Father Chartier.

Finally, at 2 o'clock in the afternoon of October 6, as the carriage jolted through the woods, Father Chartier exclaimed, "Look! There is Vincennes!"

Vincennes! What images the sound of this word had aroused during the past months! How far they had journeyed to reach this goal of so much desire, so much prayer, so much planning! And now here they were: in a backward little town on the Wabash River, a town that boasted only a few residents, and only one paved street.

Again it was Sisters of Charity who welcomed the travelers; like the religious who had received them along the way, from Philadelphia to Cincinnati, these sisters were daughters of Mother Seton. There were four of them in Vincennes, occupied in conducting a boarding and day school and free schools for boys and girls until the bishop could secure another community for his diocese.[27] Meantime their schools were prospering and their excellent teaching and exemplary religious life endeared them to the people. Their establishment, called "St. Mary's Female School," was conveniently located opposite the cathedral.

The cathedral! If Sister Theodore had wept at the sight of the cathedral of Cincinnati, she was completely overcome at the cathedral of Vincennes. She reported:

> It is a brick building with large windows without curtains; most of the panes of glass are broken; on the roof there is something like the beginning of a steeple, which resembles rather a large chimney fallen into ruins. The interior corresponds perfectly to the exterior – a poor wooden altar, a railing unfinished and yet seemingly decaying from age. The bishop's seat is an old red chair which even our peasants would not have in what they consider a nice room. To conclude, I have seen nothing to equal the poverty of the cathedral of Vincennes.

The bishop's little house next to the cathedral was in a similar state of neglect and disrepair; nevertheless, the sisters learned, it was the storehouse to which all his priests might have recourse when they were in need. They did not, unfortunately, always find what they sought. All that Monsignor possessed was at the disposal of his priests; often, however, both he and they lacked the barest necessities. The meager resources of the diocese did not, of course, extend to repairs on the episcopal dwelling or embellishment of the cathedral.

The two weeks the Sisters spent in Vincennes awaiting the bishop's arrival may well have been among the most difficult and painful of their long course. They had crossed an ocean to answer the call of the diocese of Vincennes. By ship and stage, railroad and riverboat, they had persevered under the impulse of dedicated zeal, always looking forward to the mission which awaited them. To the travel-weary sisters the Vincennes they found at last must have seemed an anticlimax.

They had come in response to a call to share in the evangelization of a neglected people. Upon arrival in Vincennes, they found sisters familiar with the language and culture, successful in their work, beloved by the people, esteemed by the bishop. There seemed to be no need for their services.

The presence of the Sisters of Charity was not, it is true, a complete surprise. They had learned of it in New York, where they had been edified by reports of the brilliant education these sisters offered in their many establishments;[28] they were disposed to learn from their example how to succeed with the American people. In their brief interview at Madison, the bishop had informed them that they themselves would be located, not in Vincennes, but "near Terre Haute," some 60 miles from the Episcopal city, in a house still under construction. Beset by vague misgivings, and suffering inevitable emotional and physical reactions, they could only wait, clinging to the confidence in Providence which had carried them thus far, until the bishop's arrival should bring further enlightenment.

The atmosphere in which they had to wait was not conducive to tranquil reflection. Their experience even in country towns in France in no way prepared them for what they encountered in this "cathedral city." Vincennes was a noisy little town. The house in which the Sisters of Charity did their best to entertain their guests echoed from early morning until evening with the comings and goings of pupils of all ages, to the ceaseless accompaniment of two pianos provided for the indispensable music classes. Outside all was clamorous movement; swine thronged the rutted lanes of the town; nearly every family had its cow, badly cared for, left to forage in the woods, where the horses also sought shelter and food. Sister Theodore could only note, "One might think she is in Noah's ark."

It is not surprising that, surrounded by such confusion, the sisters should rejoice to hear a familiar tongue and to meet with fellow-countrymen to whom their coming, too, was a breath from home. Sister Theodore had lived for 8 years almost next door to the Eudist College in Rennes. To find some of these "good Bretons" here in Vincennes delighted her. And the fathers of St. Gabriel College welcomed the French religious as only true Bretons could. Amid good wishes, news from France, and information about the American mission, many confidences were certain to be exchanged in the beloved mother-tongue.

As barriers went down before eager and sympathetic listeners, reserve gave way. For the priests there was relief and consolation in recounting to compatriots the difficulties of their ill-starred establishment and the difficulties had been many. The first four Eudists had come from Rennes with Bishop Bruté in 1836; a second contingent, gifted and enthusiastic, had arrived at Bishop de la Hailandière's invitation in 1839. Despite all their well-intentioned efforts, lack of means and differences in outlook had continually plagued the undertaking.

But these missionaries were true Bretons, not too long away from Rennes to have lost their native wit and friendliness, their vivacity and their conversational skills. Visiting with them did much to brighten for the sisters the lowering skies of Vincennes. Unfortunately, however, their story of frustrated hopes and uncertain prospects could offer little encouragement to the newcomers. Although Sister Theodore and her companions welcomed the opportunity of conversing with their French brothers, the lively exchanges left them increasingly apprehensive about their own future.

Monsignor's arrival on Friday, October 16, brought the answer to some of their questions. He gave them his reasons for locating them in the country, far from the center of the diocese. He explained the arrangements he had made for their reception. He had appointed Father

Stanislas Buteux, pastor in the Terre Haute area, to be their chaplain. Father was seeing to the erection of their house and had found lodgings for them with the local farmer. Four postulants already awaited them. Father Buteux would himself conduct them to their mission; their departure from Vincennes had been set for Sunday evening. He gave them his blessing, and they left him with their zeal rekindled, their courage restored.

Monsignor could not, of course, have foreseen the violent storm which was to delay the journey for two days and multiply tenfold its discomforts and its dangers. It was ten o'clock on the evening of October 20 before the carriage bearing the sisters could set off to brave the pitfalls of the rain-swept roads. And then so deep were the mud holes along the way that the travelers were obliged to stop during the night in a farmhouse, to dry and warm themselves beside a hospitable fire and wait until daybreak to proceed. When they reached Terre Haute in the afternoon, bruised, drenched, and exhausted, it was too late to attempt to cross the swollen Wabash River. They had to spend the night in one of the town's little hotels.

Morning, October 22, brought Mass in Father Buteux' new brick church, dedicated only three months earlier to St. Joseph. They were too eager for the end of their journey to delay in Terre Haute, which they had only time to notice was "larger and finer than Vincennes." After breakfast they hurried to mount the large wagon sent from St. Mary's to transport them to the ferry, and once across the river, over the rough "bottom" lands.

They were only little more than four miles from their destination; yet hours were to pass before they could reach it. Other wagons had preceded them to the water's edge. As the river was high and the current strong, it took a long time to ferry each one across. The sisters' turn came late in the afternoon.[29]

Across at last, they found the bottom lands beyond the river so inundated that the road disappeared; and, as Sister Theodore was to record:

> At every moment we were in danger of being overturned, although Father Buteux went ahead with a pole to sound the road. Once the carriage struck a stumbling horse, and a wheel went over the trunk of a tree, and lo! the carriage was once again thrown on its side. The water entered the coach and the horses were swimming rather than walking. It was like being in the middle of a sea, but in a sea surmounted by a thick forest, for the trees are so close together that it required all the experience of the American driver to get through.

But his skill prevailed, and when the worst was over, at the sight of land the horses broke into a gallop. Off they sped, the water passing over their backs and flowing into the carriage, until they reached firm ground. Then suddenly the carriage stopped and Father Buteux was calling out, "Come down, Sisters. We have arrived!"

It was already dusk as they clambered from their sodden conveyance and looked in awe around them. They were at the edge of a dense forest. Before them lay a deep ravine. There was no sign of human habitation.

A little stream ran through the ravine. Descending, they crossed the stream by the log which spanned it. Then they looked up and saw, through the trees on the opposite bank, the outline of a small frame house. It was a tremulous moment for all of them – the sisters who had come so far, and still knew not what to expect; the priest whose task it had been to prepare for the long awaited community, now here at last. With an understandable thrill of relief and gratitude, Father Buteux pointed to the farmhouse and announced, "There is the house where your postulants are waiting, and where you will reside until your house is ready."

Beyond it, a little to the west, there stood a rude log cabin. It was to this cabin that Father Buteux directed the sisters, for they had agreed among themselves that upon their arrival no word should be spoken until they had first saluted their Lord in the Blessed Sacrament. The priest led the way through the trees, along a path already carpeted with leaves and the cones of pine and spruce and fir. In silence Sister Theodore and her companions followed him into the rude shelter where their Lord awaited them.

First Church at Saint Mary-of-the-Woods
Log Chapel 1840

First Convent at Saint Mary-of-the-Woods
The Thrall's House

Celestine-René-Laurent
Guynemer de la Hailandière,
1798-1882,
Bishop of Vincennes, Indiana,
1839-1847

James Marie Maurice de Saint-Palais,
1811-1877,
Bishop of Vincennes, Indiana
1849-1877

John Stephen Bazin,
1796-1848
Bishop of Vincennes, Indiana,
1847-1848

Father John Corbe, chaplin at
Saint Mary-of-the-Woods,
1842-1872, and ecclesiastical
superior of the Sisters of Providence from
1844 until his death in 1872

Chapter 9

The cabin toward which the sisters directed their steps at the end of their long journey lay hidden in the depths of an immense forest, in a state whose very name evokes the thought of regions inhabited by a primitive and exotic people. Indeed, until the beginning of the 19th century all of Indiana was Indian territory; its roads followed the old trails of Indian tribes, beside those of the hundreds of buffalo which roamed its plains.

It was by these trails, along the Wabash River, that the trappers and fur dealers of Canada arrived. American pioneers also followed these routes on their way from the eastern states to the Midwest, where the United States Government was making available huge tracts of land purchased from the Indians. The purchase in 1809 by General Harrison, governor of the Indiana Territory, included the region where Saint Mary-of-the-Woods now lies.

In 1816 plans were drawn up for the little city of Terre Haute, some 60 miles north of Vincennes, on the eastern bank of the Wabash. This city, soon settled by colonists from Kentucky and Ohio, was destined to surpass Vincennes in size and importance. The opposite bank of the river, however, near the Illinois border, remained virtually wasteland. Only in 1833 did the first permanent residents settle near the future Saint Mary-of-the-Woods – a family of Catholic farmers from Kentucky, named Thralls. Because of their extensive holdings, the region became known as "Thralls Station." In the vicinity, and in nearby Illinois, other Kentucky families formed a settlement known as "North Arm."[1]

The first bishop of Vincennes, Simon Gabriel Bruté, confided to Father Stanislas Buteux, a Eudist who had accompanied him from Paris in 1836, the care of the Catholics dispersed in the three missions of Terre Haute, Thralls Station and North Arm. Until then these stations had been visited only occasionally by one of the few Indiana missionaries. Early in January 1837 Monsignor Bruté, making the visitation of his immense diocese, accompanied Father Buteux to the Thralls farmhouse and the little cabin nearby where the priest would lodge. On that occasion, Monsignor Bruté, impressed by the poverty and the isolation of the mission, addressed a plea for aid to the Leopoldine Society. He wrote:

> I send you this letter written in the mission station on the banks of the Wabash, where I live in the huts of the mission-station Thralls… You would certainly be interested in an exact description of the little log cabin which serves Father Buteux as a home and also as a chapel; but lest I ramble too far, suffice it to say that his cabin is a perfect image of the holy stable of Bethlehem, and for this reason consoling both for him and for me. We hope that such a beginning may in time expect greater blessings.[2]

The sisters who on that October evening in 1840 knelt with Father Buteux in what was his parish church and his home, and now also their community chapel, were likewise accustomed to find consolation in the thought of Bethlehem. The image of the Nativity above the altar in the first "Little Providence" had encouraged Mother du Roscoät to make the adjustment from a chateau in Pléhédel to the crowded little stone house on the Heights of Ruillé. The sisters had often meditated before the picture of the Holy Family in the chapel of their larger Providence of Ruillé; and were they not, as a Congregation, under the patronage of the Holy Family?

They could easily find themselves at home in the stable where their Lord was pleased to dwell.

Sister Theodore could not, however, avoid the reflection that the rural stables she had known in France were palaces in comparison with the chapel in which she here found her God. It was a typical pioneer hut, small, rough, fashioned of logs daubed with clay. The uneven board floor wobbled under their feet.[3] There was no tabernacle. A few planks supported by stakes driven into the ground held a small pyx with its "custode" – or covering. This, with the chalice, was hidden except during Mass beneath a cloth of dark blue calico. In addition to the makeshift altar, the cabin, measuring only13 by 15 feet, contained the pastor's narrow bed, his books and writing desk, a couple of old trunks, a bench, a chair.[4]

Sister Theodore did not take inventory at that first visit. Her first impression, as she afterward confided, was so completely overwhelming that she could only kneel there, lost in adoration and gratitude. Despite the tears which flowed so freely, she felt all her courage revive and a whole new life open before her in which she would be ready to endure any privation, after the example of the one who was content to inhabit so poor and humble an abode.[5] The very circumstances in which she found him were a source of enduring confidence and hope. Years later she would remind the sisters:

> You know, my dear Sisters, that when we had left our country and all that was dear to us, we found beyond the sea a Friend, a Father. We found waiting for us in a poor log cabin our God and our ALL. Yes, it was near Him that we consoled ourselves for all our privations.[6]

Having found relief in tears of gratitude and begged their Lord's continued blessing on their work and on all those near and dear to them, the Sisters solemnly placed themselves under the protection of the Blessed Virgin Mary, to whom the new foundation at Saint Mary-of-the-Woods would always in a special way belong. Bishop Bruté himself, captivated by the setting of the little mission at "Thralls Station," had given it this name, saying, as tradition relates, "You will see what great things will be accomplished here."[7]

That October evening the Lord by whom alone all great things are accomplished was gathering around him willing instruments already a world away from all that they might have loved or possessed, already dedicated heart and soul to his great work, whatever sacrifice it might entail.

From the chapel, Father Buteux led the sisters to the farmhouse and the four postulants awaiting them. To these young women that day must have seemed longer than all the weeks which had preceded it. As hour succeeded hour, and the dinner prepared for midday was set back until a little later, and then a little later still, their joyous suspense gradually gave way to anxiety and disappointment.

They were just about to resign themselves to another day's waiting when there came a sound of snapping twigs, and crackling leaves. Hurrying out of the house they glimpsed through the trees the little group making its way first toward the chapel, then at last toward the house. Still too much moved to speak among themselves, the missionaries recovered their voices as they approached their new recruits. Father Buteux hovered nearby, watching for their reaction to the provision he had made for them. He was anxious to reassure himself and them in the face of its obvious inadequacy by the reminder that it was after all only temporary. Daylight, he explained, would reveal to them another, larger dwelling under way, although still far from completion.

The postulants had made what presentations they could to welcome the sisters, whom they now led into one of the two small rooms which, with a corn loft above and an open porch on one side, made up the Thralls family home. The generous owners had, in fact, turned one half of their already crowded dwelling over to the use of the community. The room allotted the sisters would serve as community room, refectory, bakery, infirmary. The loft above provided dormitory space, one side for the ten members of the community, the other for the family, Joseph and Sarah and the six boys and two girls still at home.[8] In such tight accommodations, incredible as it may seem, the French religious were to begin the foundation of a community.

With her accustomed warmth and graciousness, Sister Theodore welcomed the four who had waited so long for them, and who now introduced themselves:

Josephine Yvonne Pardeillan, arrived in America the previous year from Alsace; Mary Doyle, until two months ago a Sister of Charity in Vincennes; Frances Thériaque and Genevieve Dakent, both of Vincennes. Then the postulants brought out the oft-heated dinner, hiding their disappointment at not having been able to present at their succulent best the various little items of feast-day fare which they had so carefully prepared. The sisters, weary, drenched, bedraggled as they were after their long day's ordeal, and more in need of rest than of refreshment, sat down gratefully to try to do justice to this first community meal. The conversation which accompanied it was animated, for all the postulants understood French and two at least spoke it fluently, Mlle Pardeillan as her native tongue, Miss Doyle as an acquired skill.

Not so, of course, the members of the Thralls family, who gathered around to welcome their guests; but the sisters understood the greetings offered in mingled awe, diffidence, wonder, and on the part of the younger members, undisguised curiosity. Once again, strangers to the sisters, Americans, were tendering New World hospitality. The farmer's house had been opened to them. His provisions had helped supply the welcoming feast and his family would be just as crowded on their side of the house as were their guests on theirs.

How very crowded their quarters were became evident when they mounted to their "dormitory" in the loft. The sisters might well have been disheartened, did not the recollection of a similar dormitory dear to the first Sisters of Providence give them reason to rejoice that the new Providence in Indiana was having its beginning under circumstances not unlike those of Father Dujarié's first "Little Providence." Eight straw ticks completely covered the floor, so that the sisters had to dress on their beds, which must be made up one by one. The shingle roof directly above them was very badly joined, an invitation to rain and snow, wind and cold.[9] Somehow they succeeded in disposing themselves for the night. On the other side of a flimsy partition, the family made the most of their own limited sleeping accommodations.

Daylight brought them a glimpse of the house that was to have been theirs, had it only been begun in time. They went from the chapel across a deep ravine, then some distance into the forest. There, behind its barricade of trees, they could discern the edifice which Sister Theodore thus whimsically described:

> Like the castles of old, it is so deeply hidden in the woods that you cannot see it until you come up to it. Do not think, however, that it is built on the model of Father Buteux's. No indeed! It is a pretty two-story brick house, fifty feet wide by twenty-six feet deep. There are five large openings in front....As to our garden and yard, we have all the woods. And the wilderness is our only cloister, for our house is like an oak tree planted there.[10]

The new building occupied land purchased by Bishop Bruté from Joseph Thralls in 1837, as the site of the first church of the region he had just named Saint Mary-of-the-Woods. The small frame church erected by Father Buteux and his parishioners had served the settlers for three years. When, in February 1840 it burned to the ground, Father Buteux's little cabin became once more the parish church. In May Bishop de la Hailandière had purchased 22 additional acres from Mr. Thralls, authorizing the pastor to build a new church, a convent for the expected sisters, and a house for the priest. The added acreage would, when cleared, afford ample space for buildings and gardens.

The convent was now under roof, but as yet only a shell. There was no possibility of its being ready before winter. Possibly Monsignor had waited to hear from the community in France before commencing to build a house for the promised sisters; Mother Mary's letter mailed in June would have reached him in August. At any rate, work on the house had not begun until August 22, as Father Buteux reports in an interesting letter to a friend in Terre Haute, Mrs. Susan Williams. Writing on September 23, he says:

> The reason why I delayed my answer one month is that it was precisely on the 22nd of August that I commenced putting up a house which I candidly believe will be some day your home, and this day, we have got pretty nearly through it; and a house for the clergyman has been undertaken which it will take about 15 days to build. After which we intend erecting a brick church in place of that which has been destroyed by the flames in February last.......
> There are already four Ladies here boarding at Joseph Thralls'. One of them.....is Sister Gabriella, the best teacher they had at Vincennes, whom divine Providence directed to give herself to the Bishop to belong to our Institution. The Sisters are called "Sisters of Providence." What an enrapturing name! Has it not got any charm for you, Madam? And is it not here that Providence will openly discover himself to you and to your very dear children?[11]

The "house for the clergyman" of which Father Buteux wrote had in fact just been completed; the church would wait until later. Sister Theodore might well have wondered, as she admired their "castle hidden in the woods" what would have been their plight had they not found haven in the nearby farmhouse. Yet the Providence of God in this very emergency was all too evident; she preferred to express her gratitude, exclaiming, "Are we not already in our own little nook? Besides, did we not come here to suffer, we who were so well provided for in France?"[12]

Her courageous efforts to keep up the spirits of her sisters increased with her solicitude for them and her appreciation of their own magnificent abnegation. Sister Basilide had been very ill with fever all during the trip from Vincennes. So ill was she before they set out, in fact, that it was only at her insistence that they had left for Terre Haute. Since she was getting no better, her sisters brought her down from the loft, and their room began its service as infirmary. "She is still quite ill," wrote Sister Theodore, "and God only knows whether she will ever recover. Sister Mary Xavier is also ill, but she does not suffer so much and has not constant fever. We take the best care of them we can...."[13]

This care was unremitting, and included the calling of a physician three days later. The first notation in Sister Theodore's diary, after that of their arrival on October 22, tells that on October 26 they had the first visit of a doctor, for Sister Basilide. While awaiting the arrival of their baggage, the sisters could make time for all of them to rest a little, to care for the sick, and for Sister Theodore to become acquainted with the postulants who were to be the first members of the American community.

Josephine Yvonne Pardeillan was a mature and gentle woman, 44 years old, capable and well-educated, the daughter of a prosperous lawyer. When reverses in the family fortunes compelled her to seek employment, she had served first as a governess in a noble family, then as employee in the commercial establishment of Joseph Picquet in Strasbourg. Although she was successful in her work, loved and esteemed by those who knew her, she still longed for a more dedicated life. When she learned that the Sisters of Providence of Ribeauvillé in Alsace had promised a colony of sisters for the diocese of Vincennes in America, she entered that community as a postulant to prepare herself for the mission.

Arrived at Havre in July 1839 after a farewell visit to her family, she learned that the Ribeauvillé community had withdrawn its commitment to the American mission. Her own desire was still strong; consequently, since an aunt of Joseph Picquet was sailing on the same vessel, the <u>Republican</u>, on which the Abbé Martin and his group of priests were leaving, she embarked also and accompanied Mlle Mertian to Sainte-Marie, Illinois, to await the arrival of another Community. At Sainte-Marie she continued the deeply spiritual life she had begun in France. "I can fulfill all my exercises of piety," she wrote to Father Martin, continuing:

> I rise very early and make my meditation quite at my ease before anyone else except M. le Curé has risen. We assist at Mass about eight o'clock and breakfast afterward.....Mlle Mertian is also with me, and we have a good deal of work, which will last some time until everything is in order. .....I have not even time to study English, but I begin to understand a little of what is said to me and much of what I read.[14]

Although she enjoyed this idyllic life, she felt some uneasiness about the affection and consideration shown her. When Bishop de la Hailandière, home from France at last, called her to Vincennes and informed her that within the year other Sisters of Providence, those of Ruillé-sur-Loir, would be arriving, her joy was complete:

> With the grace of God I shall have the happiness to be a Sister of Providence. How sweet and agreeable this thought is! At every moment I say to myself with renewed happiness. "You will be a religious. You will be placed in the care of good and wise Sisters who will teach you to love and serve God well."[15]

She feared only lest her eagerness savor of ingratitude toward her kind friends at Sainte-Marie. Sister Theodore had no difficulty in recognizing the missionary spirit in this first postulant for the convent in the Woods.

At the bishop's request, Mlle Pardeillan had spent the winter of 1839-1840 with the Sisters of Charity in Vincennes. There she lived with another young woman destined to accompany her to St. Mary-of-the-Woods. Sister Gabriella Doyle had been a Sister of Charity for seven years. She was a convert, 25 years old, well-educated, and especially proficient in English, French and music. An excellent teacher, the one in fact whom Father Buteux in writing to Mrs. Williams had called "the best teacher they had at Vincennes," she was well acquainted with and highly appreciated by the people of that town.

And now she was speaking of leaving her Congregation to join the new foundation. How much she may have been influenced by the example of the devout and dedicated Mlle Pardeillan, how much encouraged by the bishop's obvious interest in the projected community, cannot be determined. In any case, while in May Mlle Pardeillan was informing Father Martin, "Perhaps before long I shall go to Terre Haute," Bishop de la Hailandière was writing to Mother Mary Xavier Clark, superior-general of the Sisters of Charity, in Sister Gabriella's behalf:

> I must first thank you for the very special interest you show for the diocese of Vincennes, and for the confidence which you place in me in the affair of Sister Gabriella. In return for that confidence, whatever repugnance I might feel for expressing my opinion in this difficult circumstance, to which I should regret your giving too much importance, I shall tell you quite simply that at this moment, to recall Sister Gabriella or to change her would in my opinion be to force her to take openly a step which is now only in her mind, and which could be modified or abandoned with time. It would also deprive the Vincennes Academy of an excellent teacher… I think it would be more useful to leave her to her reflections. Besides, the Sisters of Providence will not come until the end of the year, if they come at all…..
>
> For myself, I will be content with whatever you decide in this matter, and to speak my thought, the less I mix myself in it, the more I have confidence that the good God Himself will conduct her.[16]

Sister Gabriella's impulse was not modified or abandoned; she persisted in her desire to join the Sisters from France, and took the contemplated step with the approval of the Bishop of Vincennes, who wrote again to Mother Mary Xavier, on August 17:

> This very day I have had to come to a decision. I have had Sister Gabriella conducted to Terre Haute, and to give an appearance

of propriety to what I felt myself obliged to go, I sent with her three good girls who like her wish to become part of our future Community. Nothing had been prepared for all that, and so I acted in spite of myself. They will await together the arrival of the Sisters of Providence.

However, I have examined Sister Gabriella's vocation with care. I did not find anything to find fault with, and were it not that you had said to me that rarely did such vocations succeed, I would have been inclined to think that the good God had arranged all to help us, for what would our poor French Sisters do alone, not knowing how to speak two words of English?[17]

Evidently, although Monsignor acknowledged Mother Mary Xavier's prudent advice on vocations, he did not permit it to influence his own direction of Sister Gabriella. Sister Theodore would have readily concurred in the opinion of the experienced superior, especially since the Sisters of Providence did not ordinarily accept candidates who had spent some time in another community. In the circumstances, however, she had perforce to accept the bishop's arrangements.

"All agree in speaking well of this young person," she wrote to Mother Mary. She is a convert from Protestantism who wished to enter a more perfect order and whose design was approved by Monsignor who was her director." Her own first observations inclined her to share the general opinion, for she added, "She seems truly to seek God alone and His greater glory."[18]

The Foundress was more uneasy about Miss Thériaque, who had previously tried her vocation with the Sisters of Charity of Kentucky, and whose delicate health raised serious doubts about her ability to withstand the privations of a mission foundation. Genevieve Dukent, also from Vincennes, came to her new life eager and untried. Under Father Buteux's enthusiastic direction, the four postulants had been trying to lead a religious life.

A week after the Sisters had left Vincennes for Saint Mary's, Bishop de la Hailandière had written to Mother Mary to express his satisfaction and gratitude.[19] "Your six Sisters and novices have arrived at their destination," he told her. He admitted that they had many trials to support, but offered in explanation the entirely credible excuse that the letter announcing their coming, and the one which stated the time of their leaving France had reached him too late for him to make more suitable arrangements. Consequently, he confessed, many things were wanting. The sisters were admirable in their acceptance of the difficulties involved, and Monsignor comforted himself with the thought that the bounty shown toward them by Providence, even in the least details, more than recompensed them for what he was unable to do himself.

He then attempted an exposition of his intentions with regard to the sisters, in the hope of dissipating what he considered certain misconceptions. The first was that, as he expressed it: having two religious houses in the diocese, I would not have enough interest in the Sisters of Providence, and they, placed in the country, would lack many things and could not succeed. This placing in the country seemed to disconcert your Council. Permit me to respond. I have not two religious houses in the diocese. At Vincennes there are a few Sisters of Charity sent from Baltimore who are keeping a free school and trying to operate a boarding school, which the poverty and lack of resources of the country and of our Catholics in particular scarcely allow to develop.

This house, he assured her, was only local and could not be extended. Besides, he pointed out, even if it were true that there were two religious houses, there would be no problem. The diocese was large enough to accommodate several.

As for the other objects of concern – that, being in the country, the sisters would have no chance of success in their apostolate. He commented that the superiors in France could have no idea of the needs and customs of the Americans, among whom one of the conditions for the success of a boarding school was its isolation. "Your daughters here have already realized this, and make no more difficulties about being located in the country," he told her. He himself did not seem to realize that although the sisters, out of respect for their bishop, had submitted to his arrangements for them without further representations, they were far from easy in their own minds about their location.

Monsignor was truly convinced, as he insisted to Mother Mary, that the city near which he had settled the community offered much greater chance of success, being "richer, more central with respect to the diocese." He added that there were "abundant means of transportation."

The Sisters themselves, across the river from that city, saw their situation quite differently. One who arrived on the scene a year after the first sisters, Mother Mary Cecilia Bailley recorded their impressions and her own:

> The place he had chosen for the new foundation was only a desert place. The dwellings of the few families who lived there in log cabins do not give the impression of a village. It was only a group of settlers just beginning to clear forest land. There was not any convenience necessary and indispensable for a civilized mode of life.

Far from being easily accessible, Mother Mary Cecilia noted, the city of Terre Haute lay across the Wabash River, which at certain seasons of the year overflowed its banks, causing floods far and wide. When the bottom land was inundated, she pointed out, often from fall until spring:

> it is either impossible or extremely difficult to go to town, because it is neither land nor water. It is too overflowed for a team to pass, and to go by boat is impracticable, because the water is beset with trees standing out of it, stumps under it, and any amount of drift and floating debris on its surface. Therefore no place is really less suited for the location of Sisters whose employment of charity consists in educating youth and serving the sick, than this backwoods locality.[20]

On the same day that he wrote to Mother Mary, Monsignor de la Hailandière addressed a letter also to the bishop of Le Mans, again

161

expressing his gratitude to Bishop Bouvier and his satisfaction with the Sisters:

> They have happily arrived here and are working at this moment at getting settled. They are very edifying and seem to me to be very capable, and a good choice. My gratitude is due in great part to you, Monsignor, and very sincerely I offer it. The arrival of these Sisters will be for the diocese the beginning of a new kind of good which was unknown in this country. I place the greatest hopes in this new establishment. Already the good God seems to bless it beyond our expectations; several novices have presented themselves. I have spoken at length with Sister St. Theodore, and it is evident to her that concerning most things it will be necessary to wait and judge before making definite plans.

He repeated to Monsignor Bouvier his reassurances about the location of the Sisters:

> You express to me, Monsignor, the fears they have at Ruillé about the co-existence of two establishments in the diocese, and about the location of the Sisters of Providence in the country. These fears, Monsignor, have no foundation. I think I have made this plain in the enclosed letter, addressed to Madame the Superior-General.[21]

On November 1 the sisters' baggage arrived, in perfect condition, thanks to Mr. Byerley's professional attention. Excitedly they attacked and overcame the sturdy knots and brought to light the articles so necessary and so long awaited. They unwrapped the little statues of Mary and Joseph, the crucifix, the books which would help them set up the novitiate they could now begin in earnest. Somehow, too, they found room for the school supplies which Sister Theodore had secured on the bishop's advice; and for the little surprises which the Sisters of Ruillé had squeezed in: a jar of butter for the winter, some Chalais preserves for feast days. The packing cases helped supply the furniture they needed.[22]

Fortunately, on some days it was still warm enough for them to take recreation outdoors, exploring the woods which met them at their very doorstep. The trees, although now despoiled of the beauty of their foliage, still thrust graceful outlines against the sky. There were still a few fall fruits to gather: wild grapes, persimmons, nuts. Sister Olympiade was not long in finding medicinal plants and herbs. Each day brought its own discovery, and conversation sparkled with hopes and plans.

Sister Theodore considered these plans more deeply in the silence of the chapel, in moments of quiet pacing in the woods, in sleepless hours during the nights. It was only too evident that the new building across the ravine could not possibly be ready before spring. How in the meantime were the Sisters to survive in the cramped space allotted them, ten women, with the prospect of more to come? A novitiate in such circumstances was unthinkable. Further, even when the new convent was completed, would it accommodate both a growing religious community and a boarding school of any size?

Sister Theodore had purposely observed the academies and schools along the way from the East. Not idly had she informed herself of the methods and practices of American religious. Lacking the resources of older European orders, these religious faced first of all the prosaic necessity of earning a living. Teaching orders in the United States met this need by opening academies where the tuition of paying pupils would make it possible for them to minister also to those who could not pay, thus fulfilling their call to serve the poor.

Sister Theodore realized that if the Sisters of Providence were to establish a firm foundation in the United States, they should lose no time in following this example. If the building now under construction could be completed for use as an academy, and the sisters secure ownership of the entire Thralls cabin to serve as motherhouse and novitiate, they could begin the work they had come to do. But there was no time to lose. It was November, already cold, and the long, severe Indiana winter lay before them. She presented her plans, without delay, to the chaplain.

Father Buteux, himself facing the winter with the responsibility of providing suitable lodging for the sisters, and an unfinished house impossible to make ready for them, welcomed her suggestions as a solution to their common problem. His investigations led to the first important community transaction. Mr. Thralls was asking $2,000 for the house and surrounding farm. The house, Father told the sisters, could be purchased for $200. If they could furnish that amount, the bishop might more easily be persuaded to purchase the farm. Accordingly, on November 10 the little community held its first council meeting, where it was formally decided to give the money, almost all they had after the expenses of their journey, to purchase the farmhouse.[23]

When Bishop de la Hailandière arrived a day or two later for his first visit, priest and sisters saw their hopes realized. The purchase of the Thralls farm was one of the events of that important visit. "You are soon going to be rich proprietors," Monsignor wrote on his return to Vincennes. "I have bought the Thralls land. I paid $200 less for having waited. I wanted to leave Fr. Buteux the pleasure of announcing to you the conclusion of the affair. As for me, I enjoyed so much seeing you. I carried away with me so many pious remembrances, consoling, full of hope, that I thought I ought in return to impose on myself this little sacrifice.[24]

Among the pious remembrances which Monsignor carried away, consoling both for him and for the nascent community, was the formal opening of the novitiate on November 12. After intoning the <u>Veni Creator</u>, he conferred on the first postulants their religious names. Mlle Pardeillan was now Sister Marie Joseph; Miss Doyle, Sister Aloysia; Genevieve Dukant, Sister Agnes; Frances Thériaque, Sister Therese.[25]

In a long and detailed letter to Mother Mary following these events,[26] Mother Theodore reported to her superiors in France these and other details of the foundation. This was her first letter from Saint Mary-of-the-Woods. She had written at length along the way, and was at the time of this writing forwarding the last installment of her Journal of Travel.[27] From those she had left, in the meantime, there had been no word at all. She had not found at Vincennes, nor yet at Saint Mary's, the words of affection and understanding for which she had pleaded in her last letter before leaving Havre. She begins therefore on a diffident, even apologetic note:

My very reverend Mother,

I have written to you at such length that I should fear to weary you. Yet I must write. My heart has need of pouring itself forth into yours, and doubtless you will not refuse me this satisfaction......

In her effort to give an accurate assessment of the American establishment, the foundress touches on aspects both consoling and potentially disturbing. Having repeated Monsignor de la Hailandière's own explanations of the location of the Sisters of Providence and the presence of Sisters of Charity in the diocese, she continues:

That is what I have been able to find out about these two questions; as for his intentions in our regard, His Lordship wishes to found a principal establishment, a Motherhouse, to form subjects who will be sent into different parishes of his diocese, which is so poor. In this respect, the house would do incalculable good, and could be self-supporting; for board is expensive here, although food is not. We can buy beef and pork to salt for three cents a pound. Vegetables are hardly more expensive than in France. The consoling and encouraging thing here is that religion is making great progress, and Protestants are beginning to abandon their prejudices.

Especially touching is the manner in which she relates the purchase of the Thralls house. Although she had been named superior-general of the new foundation, and was only fulfilling an administrative duty, after prayerful consideration and consultation with authority, she seems to anticipate adverse criticism. She leads up to the subject carefully:

> To prove his good will, Monsignor has just bought us two tilled fields and a little orchard quite near the house they are building for us; but as the most pressing concern for us was a lodging for the winter, we have bought the house where we are......

She had done what she thought best for the welfare of the Sisters and the success of the undertaking confided to her; but will Mother Mary, unacquainted with the actual circumstances, judge imprudent the employment of their meager funds for the purchase of such a miserable cabin, lost in the forest? Her fear of having incurred further displeasure, and her appeal for understanding lend wings to her pen:

> I still had the thousand francs that Madame de Marescot had sent at Havre. I thought I could not do better than to give them, for otherwise we would have had neither house, nor field, nor orchard. You will blame me, perhaps, Mother, and will say that I have been too hasty. If you had been here and understood our situation, I do not think you would pass the same judgment. It was impossible to spend the winter, which is already very cold, and will become colder, in a cabin open to all the winds, having neither doors nor windows that close. Repairs were necessary, and could not be carried out, for we were mixed in with the farmers and their children in a manner not only annoying, but unsuitable. Now at least, however badly situated, we are by ourselves. We can fulfill our Rule and we shall have the inestimable advantage of having the Blessed Sacrament in our dwelling. It will help us to suffer and to die if we must. With Jesus, what shall we have to fear? We also have Holy mass every day. There is another priest for the mission. We shall have to do their cooking, their laundry, sewing, etc.

Father Buteux himself, in addition to his missionary labors among the settlers and his building endeavors had, as we have seen, been devoting himself conscientiously for some weeks before the sisters' arrival to the direction of the postulants who awaited them. Now that the sisters had come he was finding it difficult to relinquish this charge. The zealous young priest had his own ideas of religious life, different, Mother Theodore soon noted with alarm, from those of the community. She acquaints Mother Mary with a situation, allayed for the time being, but later to develop into a real problem:

> Father Buteux, our Chaplain, seems to be animated by the best dispositions, but he took a little too high a hand in the beginning. He took our young people every week for hours at a time for trifling conversation. Sister Liguori had already followed the example, but I stopped all that after consulting Sister St. Vincent, who would have leaned a little toward the foolishness, but yielded to my reasoning. I asked Monsignor to forbid it, and he did; there will now be no further question of that sort of thing.

Finally, having expressed her joy at the thought of the retreat Father Martin was soon to give the little community, in the closing lines of her letter she makes another attempt to speak her heart to her Superior;

> Adieu, Mother. Pray for me. Heavy crosses are reserved to me here. Happily, I had made my novitiate. I am ready for all that Heaven may please to ordain. I recommend myself and all our poor exiles to the prayers of our Sisters. How happy they are! But no, we can suffer more than they, and consequently have more happiness! I cannot express all the love the good God has put in my heart for the cross. Again Adieu, dear Mother. Accept the very respectful homage of all your American daughters, but especially that of your very obedient child and humble servant,

Sr. St. Theodore

> I must tell you that Monsignor requests that they call me Mère. This name gave me pain; then I found that it cost my Sisters, poor children, very much. What a mother they have! What a difference! Finally I forbade them to call me by that name. Mother would pain them less. I shall say like St. Paul, "I can do all things in Him who strengthens me." The extreme

167

poverty which we suffer, the cold and hunger of these icy countries and all of that nature will not really be my crosses. I foresee others much heavier; but heaven is the price of all, and Calvary is the way.

By November 27 the Thralls family had moved, leaving the sisters in possession of the farmhouse. They set to work immediately to convert the room vacated by the family, which was larger than the one the sisters had been occupying, into a chapel. There, on November 29, Mother Theodore recorded in her account of the foundation: "we had the happiness of having Mass, which was celebrated in our principal room, where we had reserved the Blessed Sacrament on a poor altar, but one still more respectable than the one we had found."[28]

Their first retreat in the New World began that evening. Father Martin arrived from Logansport, bringing them a new postulant, Catherine Doyle. To the relief of the sisters, he preached the retreat in French. At its close with general communion on December 7, the professed sisters renewed their vows, "according to custom," and Father Martin gave them tentative permission for Benediction of the Blessed Sacrament every Thursday.[29] The last day of the retreat brought another postulant, Miss Suzanne Reed.

Renewed by their days of retreat, heartened by the presence of the Blessed Sacrament in their midst, sisters and postulants plunged joyfully into preparations for Christmas. After the chapel, their first concern was for the newly-completed house for the priests, where Monsignor would stay when he arrived to spend the feast with them. With energy and enthusiasm, and with what materials they could assemble, they spent the Advent days cleaning and polishing. Their creative ingenuity even achieved curtains for the little rectory. A reasonably comfortable, cheerful room would await the bishop when he arrived on December 23.[30]

Monsignor had time to admire and approve the arrangements in rectory and converted farmhouse, to ratify Father Martin's permission for weekly Benediction, and to savor the happy pre-holiday bustle.

Then suddenly the dark of Christmas Eve found festive candlelight springing from the windows to gild a path across the snow; and settlers began to arrive from all around to share in the mystery about to be reenacted in this new Indiana woodland Bethlehem.

Chapter 10

The first Christmas in the little sylvan Providence was a simple and joyous spiritual festival. Mother Theodore recorded its highlight in her diary: "Midnight Mass was celebrated in our house for the Congregation."[1] For all who offered together the beautiful Christmas liturgy – bishop, community, parishioners – it was a festival of hope.

Christmas Day found the sisters once again in chapel, for the morning Mass. Then there were hours of holiday recreation, around the table where Sister Olympiade served the feast-day dinner; walking during the afternoon in the wintry woods, and at dusk huddled around the fire sharing memories. The sisters recalled other Midnight Masses, preceded by cherished Noëls and followed by the festive réveillon; the postulants had stories to tell of Christmas in pioneer America.

There had as yet been no word from those whom the sisters had left in France, but they consoled themselves with the thought that among the French the New Year was the time for exchange of greetings. Surely they would be hearing soon! It was a hopeful, happy, although very weary little household that went from chapel to bed at the day's end.

But the joy and hope born of Christmas were destined to brighten only a fleeting interlude between the months of travel and labor just ended and long weeks of anxiety about to begin. During the night Mother Theodore awakened with a violent headache and fever which continued to intensify despite every effort to give her relief. To the Sisters gathered in distress around her it was soon evident that she was the victim of no ordinary illness.[2]

Monsignor, unaware of her condition, had left with Father Buteux for a visitation of the surrounding settlements. Returning on December 29 from Paris, Illinois, and finding the community in distress, he at once shared their concern.

The community physician, Dr. Ezra Read of Terre Haute, was in attendance; Monsignor sent Father Buteux to Vincennes to seek the young French doctor recently established there, Dr. John Isadore Baty. Dr. Baty discerned symptoms of cerebral fever, affecting also the heart and digestive organs. No remedy applied by either physician seemed to avail; each day brought greater suffering to the patient, greater anxiety to those who hovered near her, unable to assist her.

And beneath the anxiety and the forced inactivity of those endless January days there stirred deeper forebodings. The unforeseen crisis awakened doubts and fears which days of absorbing labor had mercifully suppressed. Now the cold winter daylight permeating the sickroom afforded no haven for illusion; with the life of the foundress in danger, the whole undertaking was threatened.

The letters written at the time afford the best insight into the effect of this crisis on the little colony in the Woods and on the bishop himself. Each letter provides a clue to the personality of the writer and the mental and emotional climate of the mission in its beginnings.

There is an almost painfully self-conscious formality about Sister St. Vincent's January 18 letter to Mother Mary. Addressing the superior as "very worthy and good Mother," the reserved and diffident religious painstakingly informs her of the situation in the American mission. She describes the beginning and the progress of the foundress's illness, the distress of the sisters, the solicitude of the bishop, and the patient resignation of the sufferer under the various remedies prescribed for her, noting that "this dear and beloved sister supported this species of torture together with her other sufferings with an admirable courage and submission that only God could inspire."

She records how when the doctor, seeing no improvement, pronounced the invalid in extreme danger, "our good and holy bishop, who did not leave her except to take some nourishment heard her confession, administered Holy Viaticum, Extreme Unction, and even made the recommendation of the departing soul." Mother Theodore was so ill, in fact, that Dr. Baty, having exhausted every effort during eight days, admitted that he could offer no hope. "But the Lord," Sister St. Vincent's account continues:

> finally let himself be moved by the prayers that we addressed to him and the tears we shed in His presence. I would not know, my good Mother, how to tell you to what an extent our good and pious Prelate carried his attentions and his bounty with regard to our good Theodore. It is certain that every spiritual and material help was given her, beyond what we might have expected in so profound a solitude, deprived as we are of even the most common and necessary things. The illness then having yielded less to the efficacy of the remedies than to the voice of the God of all mercy and to the powerful intercession of the most holy Virgin... we are well persuaded that if she is restored it will be to the Mother of God that we owe this benefit. Please, I pray you, my good Mother, engage our Sisters in France to redouble their confidence and love of the Lord and His Mother, and to beg them to continue to be propitious to us.

Her letter reflects Sister St. Vincent's evident desire to inform without alarming her superiors. She writes only when the greatest danger seems to have passed, and she writes not a distressing appeal for advice or help, but a careful and somewhat reassuring account. The glimpse she offers of the destitution of the woodland solitude is incidental – a simple statement of accepted fact.

The sisters had been edified and consoled in their affliction by the solicitude of the prelate who since their coming had often shown them only the forbidding side of his complicated nature. Yet earlier impressions still lingered, and between the lines of Sister St. Vincent's letter discerning superiors might have detected a hidden plea for understanding and encouragement:

> I return to our worthy Prelate who in the beginning seemed to us so cold; experience teaches us never to judge our neighbor by his exterior, for he is good and devoted to us beyond all expression. However, I fear him very much, and I confessed to him that notwithstanding his kindnesses, I experienced a great timidity and embarrassment with him; he told me that perhaps someone had prejudiced me against him, judging him wrongly. I made known to him the thought I had of returning to France if our Mother Theodore should die. He seemed to be pained by this. He urged me strongly not to do it, and especially not to make it known to my Sisters; that if God demanded of us the sacrifice of our Superior, we must resign ourselves, that assuredly her death would cost no one more than it did him.[3]

In a letter dated two days later Sister Basilide conveys her own reactions to events. More impulsive than Sister St. Vincent, more affectionate and outspoken, she directs a pathetic appeal to the distant superiors. For her, Mother Mary is her "dear and very worthy Mother," and she begins with the exclamation, "How long the eight months since I saw you have seemed! They were to me like so many years!"

Her letter is avowedly personal; yet in her forthright urgency she may well be expressing the secret anxieties of most of her sisters. "Would I have believed it would cost me so much!" she exclaims. "I did not know my own heart when I thought I could make so many sacrifices so easily! No, I was incapable of reflection. I was presumptuous, but I did not know what awaited me." It was the present crisis which had occasioned her soul-searching, she confesses:

> I had not made serious reflection until the illness of our Mother, of which I shall not give you details, for I think that Sister St. Vincent has done so... I shall treat you only of myself; if I should lose the only person whom you have given me to take your place and help me acquire what is wanting to me, I should not last long. The profound grief affecting me as I know it would, together with the fatal effect on foreigners of the climate we inhabit, and the thought of the impossibility of your recalling me, would be more than enough. Perhaps you think, my good Mother, that I speak this way because I am discouraged or have lost my usual strength of character...but it is only because it seems to me that unless the good God visibly takes hold of this work, which seems so evidently to be His own, it can hardly subsist...

> Our good Mother offers you and our other Superiors her respects and recommends herself in a particular manner to your prayers. Please accept, my very dear Mother, the assurance of the most profound respect of her who will always be, in the New as well as the Old World, your very submissive and devoted daughter.

Both Sisters had written their accounts to France after Monsignor de la Hailandière's departure on January 13 for Vincennes. The mood of mingled satisfaction and apprehension in which the bishop departed appears in the letter he addressed to Mother Theodore after his arrival in Vincennes – the first of a series of such letters of instruction and spiritual direction:

> Very dear daughter in Jesus Christ,

> That will be henceforth the name I will give you; it pleases you and it comes from the bottom of my heart, of this poor heart which suffered so much when the good God kept you attached to His cross and your soul seemed to wish to soar to His bosom, there to enjoy His embraces. Well, you are still nailed by suffering to your bed, uncertain of your future, as if between life and death. As for me, I believe you are out of danger, and if the best does not come all of a sudden, I see in that a new mark of the goodness of

Providence. If the certitude of your recovery had been given to us all at once, it would have been too much for us. I know some would not have been able to bear it, so keen would have been their joy.....

For my part, nevertheless, I must tell you that I wait with impatience for news in the mail. They have just come from the post office and there was still nothing although it will soon be ten o'clock. I must make up my mind and go to sleep again this time trusting in Providence. Ah! it is so good for all, no doubt, but especially for us! O, let us never forget it! For myself, my heart is full of the remembrance of his last bounties. How many times my eyes fill with sweet tears at the recollection! But what am I doing? You are suffering, and I speak of myself, when I should speak to you only of the good God. O my daughter, do not let yourself grow cold in His love! Be careful not to give anyone a part, however small, of your heart, the heart which belongs to Him alone. Hide yourself so well in Him that only your daughters can find you. O, how I wish you to be holy!

Always pray for the diocese, for our priests, and for their head.... I still intend to return to your house for February 2.

In the meantime he opened his heart in a letter to his friend and vicar-general, Father Auguste Martin. It would be impossible to appreciate fully Monsignor's state of mind at this time without reflecting on the confidences contained in his letter, written just after he had received word from his brother in France of the death of his mother:

I received your last letter so full of sentiments of devotion for the mission of Vincennes and for its poor head. It did more than please me; it was like a great, an immense consolation that the good God sent me as a remedy for the torrent of bitterness which was about to be poured into my heart. My mother is no more of this world, my good, my tender mother! The good God has taken her.....

My reverend Mother Theodore has just been ill unto death; I believe her to be almost out of danger now, but what uneasiness her condition caused us! For my part, I consider it a miracle that she is still breathing. I spent many nights at her bedside. Poor daughter, how much she suffered, and with what patience! I now have her confidence, and I can say that she has given it to me without reserve.[4]

Another letter to Father Martin, written some three weeks later, voices the same blending of anxiety over Mother Theodore's condition and its effect on the young Community and gratification at the thought of the confidence she has shown in her bishop:

> She has shown on the whole a confidence in me so much the more surprising since some people had attempted to turn her against me. This confidence is really without limits, and I think it must be so in order for me to be able to accomplish anything there. Poor woman! She continues to be ill, and we do not know what to expect for her future condition. The first time I spent nearly three weeks at her bedside, believing each instant would be her last. I was recalled there a few days ago, and it was (they thought who sent for me) to bury her and to try to organize a house that one could only compare, if the situation occurred, to a woman without a head! Truly, the fear of losing this excellent religious has caused me more suffering that I can say. I saw in her death the death of our whole house. Pray that the good God preserves her to us![5]

Responding promptly to the urgent summons, Monsignor arrived at Saint Mary's on January 28. He was accompanied by Father Simon Petit Lalumière, the indefatigable missionary who was later to prove one of the Community's staunchest supporters in time of trial. Father Lalumière brought not only his own new friendship, but messages also from the friends the Sisters had made in New York, where in a recent visit he also had met Madame Parmentier and her family and Mr. Byerley.

The letter Father Lalumière delivered brought news of both. Madame Parmentier had charged him, she wrote, to assure the Sisters of the continued attachment of all their friends, and of their interest in the Indiana mission. Father Varela, in point of fact, was offering proof of his respect and veneration by sending with Father Lalumière a very promising aspirant, a young Irish widow desirous of entering religion, whom he was directing to the Sisters of Providence.

Mrs. Anne O'Neill Moore was very highly respected, Madame Parmentier wrote, and would assist the sisters in their work for the glory of God. The young woman did indeed arrive with Father Lalumière, and three months later was admitted to the community with the name of Sister Gabriella. She was to work for the glory of God as a Sister of Providence for over 30 years.

There is no evidence that Monsignor shared his personal sorrow with the sisters. Fortunately he found Mother Theodore somewhat better and an atmosphere of tremulous expectancy in the crowded little house as the community prepared for its first formal religious ceremony. On February 2 in the first religious Reception and Profession of the Sisters of Providence of Saint Mary-of-the-Woods Monsignor conferred the habit on Sisters Marie Joseph Pardeillan and Aloysia Doyle, and received the first vows of Sister Olympiade Boyer.

The religious Congregation which Monsignor had envisioned for his diocese and which the sisters had come so far to found was at last taking form. Yet the experiences of the past months permitted none of those involved to entertain rash hopes for the future. Monsignor judged the moment opportune to present the prospects and the needs of the foundation to the French Motherhouse which had so generously responded to his first appeal.

Accordingly, before leaving Saint Mary's he addressed another earnest plea to Mother Mary at Ruillé. There was much in the sisters' situation to console their superiors, he informed her; "wherever they have passed they have gained the esteem and the veneration of all with whom they came in contact." The blessing of God had also been more prompt and more abundant than they could have hoped for, seven postulants having already offered themselves, and several others being about to do so. Parents were eagerly awaiting the opening of the boarding school. And yet:

> We lack, even for the opening of the boarding school, more than one indispensable Mistress. We have no one who can teach music and drawing. Fortunately we shall find in Sister St. Francis-Xavier, whom you have the kindness to prepare for us for the springtime, a Sister who will render us great service in one of these branches!
>
> .....However great our hopes, I must confess to you that they would vanish like smoke if Sister Theodore were taken from us. In fact, she leaves nothing to be desired, either in qualities of heart and mind, or in the virtues that one desires to see in a superior and foundress. Her submission to the bishop and her confidence in him are especially remarkable; so, I have reason to believe, the greatest understanding will always reign between us.......
>
> In these circumstances permit me, Mother, to beg you, for the charity of Jesus Christ Himself, to send us a Sister who can replace her, and if the good God preserves her to us, help her in the accomplishment of the task you have confided to her and in which the future of this diocese is so deeply involved.[6]

In the same mail he attempted to enlist once more the aid of the bishop whose influence had first obtained the sisters. He wrote to Monsignor Bouvier of LeMans:

> Asking you to read the enclosed letter, I will pray you also to recommend its request to Madame the Superior General. I like to believe that she will understand that to refuse the request I make would be to expose to probability and proximate ruin this nascent establishment, the object of so much solicitude on my part and so many hopes for the poor diocese of Vincennes, 800,000 to 900,000 inhabitants without any means of religious instruction except what they can receive from our priests. Has anyone an idea of so great a distress?[7]

Touched by his brother bishop's plight, Monsignor Bouvier added his plea to that of the Bishop of Vincennes, noting on the reverse of

Monsignor de la Hailandière's letter, "These letters have touched me very much. It would seem to me impossible to recoil before the necessity of going to the assistance of this poor bishop. I pray then the Reverend Mother Superior General and her Council to take the request under serious consideration."

Weeks would pass, of course, before Mother Mary could receive this appeal. On February 4 Monsignor and Father Lalumière returned to Vincennes. The same day there was rejoicing in the community on the arrival of "the first letter from Our Mother."[8] The elation of the French sisters can best be imagined. The Americans, who must have witnessed the demonstrations of joy at first with astonishment, even awe, entered into them after their own fashion as the long-awaited, loving message was translated for them.

"An immense distance seems to separate us, my dear daughters, in body only, for there is no distance between souls." Mother Mary knew well how to begin her letter to her daughters of Ruillé. "Your sacrifice has been great," she continues, "but grace has been in proportion. Providence has been your Mother and your Guide."

She could not know, of course, how great their sacrifice had really been; how truly they had learned to depend on Providence, how closely their beginnings resembled those of the first sisters. At that moment, indeed, the Providence of Indiana rivaled the "Little Providence" of the earliest days – one small house, containing two rooms, for a community crowded to begin with and increasing steadily in numbers. As we have seen, one of the rooms had been arranged as a chapel. One remained as the scene of all other community exercises. The "sickroom" – occupied ever since their arrival, and now by the foundress herself – was in fact only a corner of this one small room. Even judging from her own experience in the first "Little Providence" Mother Mary could scarcely have imagined the situation of the daughters to whom she directed her maternal reassurances and exhortations.

Mother Mary had written her letter on December 7, before Mother Theodore's letter of November 14 could have reached her. She acknowledges the letters written along the way and at the arrival of the sisters at Vincennes, "where the Savior of souls has called you to be victims of His will and His love," but begs for further news:

> Write to us, my dear daughters, about each one of you in particular and about all of you in general, speak of your Americans, of your novices, of your pastors, of your children. Speak to us also of your privations of all kinds, for we do not doubt that you must experience them…..We had wished that you would have been located in Vincennes itself, because of the spiritual advantages which could more easily be procured; as for temporal help, the whole earth is the object of the care of divine Providence.
>
> Finally, it is difficult for us to judge from here what would be for the best there, but we are confident that you will be able to get along when you have sufficient knowledge of the country in which you are living.…..Edify that new world by the practice of all the virtues of which our divine master has given the example. Above all, may they say of you what the pagans said of the first Christians, "See how they love one another."[9]

A little news of their sisters and friends in France transported the missionaries for a time at least into the midst of those whom they had left.

This long-awaited letter from Ruillé would seem to have opened a path to the isolated little house in the Woods. Ensuing weeks were to bring letters from their faithful friends in New York and from the sisters and benefactors in far-off Soulaines. But first there came a hasty note from Vincennes. The bishop, finding the five days since he had left Saint Mary's too long to wait for news of the Foundress's condition, wrote "to force someone to reply."

The invalid herself was able to respond to his request with the news

181

that on February 10 she had felt strong enough to make her first visit to the chapel. The result of this announcement was an enthusiastic letter in which Monsignor expressed his relief and consolation, and once again his great desire to direct her in the way to sanctity:

> ...may the good God give you so much openness towards me, such complete confidence in my guidance, that it seems that I may conduct you to sanctity straightway and without detour; in fact, I feel in myself the desire for this even more strongly perhaps than I have ever felt it for anyone else.....be convinced that I will do all that I can for you. The good God will do more, and our good Mother will not forget you. On your side, always place complete confidence in me. O, how much your simplicity pleased me when you lay there, stretched out, about to die..... always preserve this simplicity, without pride and also without false humility.
>
> The main thing now is to keep your heart raised on high, on the cross, if it pleases God, but still on the cross with love. Love God, love only Him with your whole heart; that is the important thing...and believe firmly that no one is more sincerely devoted to you than I.[10]

Mother Theodore could find in Monsignor's letter much to encourage and inspire, much which echoed her own aspirations. Wholehearted in her quest for God and convinced of her own incapacity, she had always been quick to acknowledge her failures and to seek and follow the direction of those who were competent to give it.

She did not, nor did he expect her to respond to each of the letters which followed one another so regularly during the weeks of her convalescence. "Do not tire yourself by writing to me," he advised... "impose a fast on your pen in place of the one of Lent which you would like to keep and cannot."[11]

Yet the very openness for which her director commended her demanded that she inform him of her preoccupations. The invalid slowly struggling back to health was also the anxious superior faced with the necessity of taking hold of her responsibilities and eager to begin in earnest the work for which she had come to America. Monsignor must be consulted about plans, provisions, furnishings, and expectations for the future. On February 15 she was in chapel with the sisters for Mass and Communion. This sign of improvement occasioned a report to Monsignor; indeed, as he acknowledged, "a good long letter."

She could scarcely have been reassured by his evasive response. He mentioned, for instance, that since Father Buteux had objected that provisions could be obtained more cheaply from New Orleans, he was not sending anything from Vincennes. As for beds – he was awaiting a reply about the cost. His matter-of-fact dismissal of her concerns may well have served to lessen the impact of the spiritual counsels he hastened to include:

But you, my dear daughter, are you not improving also? What! To have been in your chapel, you whom a short time ago we expected to be conducting to the tomb! It is almost a resurrection from the dead. Nevertheless you will still suffer much; that does not surprise me, my daughter; it can scarcely be otherwise. And then, the good God, who loves you so much, wishes to purify you more and more. It may even be that you will have in the future only the half of a shattered health. I would see in that still another proof of the love of the good God for you.... Is it not also true that most of the saints, those especially who being the most familiar to us can best serve us as models, have had only a miserable health? And then, the will of God, that will so admirable and so good, even when it seems harsh, ought we not to love it always?

You pain me, my daughter, when you tell me that you do not believe in the future. Do not have these thoughts.....abandon yourself always to the good God, then sleep, but tranquilly, in peace in the bosom of Providence...Humility, which you desire, demands that we remain calm, although repentant....Let us not look at ourselves; there is nothing of good in us; but let us look much more at God, and especially on Him through whom God is known, Jesus Christ…..Let us keep close to this good Master, better still, let us keep Him within us, this amiable and august guest and friend, the daily Bread! Ah, for us, all is found there![12]

Mother Theodore pondered this letter, accepting both the unmistakable invitation to heroic abnegation and the implied reproach. That reproach was undeserved. She was already well versed in the abandonment and trust which Monsignor proposed. It was not lack of confidence in God's Providence, but awareness of the human cooperation due to that Providence, which had dictated her admission of fear for the future.

Perhaps it was not in the bishop's nature to understand her anguish; perhaps, taught by his own experience and circumstances, he understood all too well, but could see no solution to the situation which challenged them both. She tried to take heart from his assurance, in closing, that he planned to visit Saint Mary's before the end of Lent. Circumstances might speak to him for themselves.

Everything around them cried out for purposeful activity. Beyond the clearing that surrounded their little house the dense forest was suddenly coming alive. Their woodland for long weeks in the grip of a silence broken only by the occasional crackle of a frozen branch, the fall of an icicle during a temporary thaw, the muted crunch of wheels on rutted paths as bishop or chaplain, doctor or tradesman, arrived or departed, now stirred with the flutter of wings and the footfalls of living things newly aroused. From a distance the intermittent clamor of the river steamers announced the reopening of the Wabash to navigation. The harsh Indiana winter was at last giving way before the awakening of spring – such a spring as clothed with enchantment the primeval American forest.

The forest to which Mother Theodore and her sisters awakened in the spring of 1841 still retained its air of ancient mystery and grandeur.

It still flaunted its inexhaustible store of surprises. Each step out of doors was a revelation for the sisters. Each new day was a call to physical and spiritual renewal. And each day Mother Theodore, a little stronger, reached out more eagerly toward the work awaiting her.

As a true pioneer, she must look first of all to the clearing and cultivation of the land around their dwelling. With her customary foresight, she had hired on shipboard a French workman bound for America with his family, Thomas Brassier. Arrived at Saint Mary's soon after the sisters, Mr. Brassier with his son had undertaken the heavy preliminary work. Sisters and postulants were soon busy helping as they could. Mother Theodore noted progress: on February 25, "we sow our first peas." On March 18, "we draw up a plan for a kitchen garden near our little house." On March 20 the first potatoes were planted, followed during March and April by vegetable seeds "of every kind."[13]

A visit to Vincennes gave her opportunity to consult with the bishop and with Dr. Baty, and to make some essential purchases. She returned in time to prepare for the opening of the month of May with all due solemnity, in fulfillment of the promise made during her illness. Although others might entertain doubts of her readiness, her own zeal for her mission forbade her to spare herself.

Her first biographer, Mother Mary Cecilia Bailly, has left this record of those early days:

> At the return of spring she was well enough to begin to take business in hand; from this date her active and useful life in Indiana;.......Her attention was divided between the spiritual instruction of the Sisters and the exterior occupation of temporal affairs. Improvements were commenced; that is, land was cleared, fenced in, and put under cultivation, roads were made, and buildings erected; all this was done under her immediate direction. She wrote much, her correspondence being extensive, and the business writing of the Community, though in its beginning, was of itself considerable. She was out a good deal

directing the labor, and she had to receive all those who came on business of any kind, for she made all the purchases that supplied the daily wants. Yet with this multiplicity of duties she seldom missed giving her every day instruction at its regular hour.[14]

Chapter 11

On her return by steamboat from Vincennes toward the end of April, Mother Theodore glimpsed for the first time the fairyland of leaf and blossom through which flowed the Wabash River in the springtime. It was a sight which each recurring spring time was to captivate her anew. "How truly," she would write, "is this part of the globe named the New World!"[1]

The scene seemed to grow more beautiful the nearer she approached Saint Mary's, where during the three weeks of her absence spring had been working its magic. Wildflowers carpeted the ground surrounding their carefully-laid garden plots; magnolia and dogwood and catalpa with their white flowers shed what she would later describe as "the perfumed snow of the spring time."[2]

The sisters, to whom her absence had seemed very long, hurried out to greet her. Anxious eyes searched eagerly for signs of restored health as they plied her with questions about her stay in Vincennes, basked in her approval of the occupations, indoors and out, which filled their days, and gathered around her once again at the hour of her daily conference.

Before the end of the month there were two new members in the attentive little circle; from Sainte-Marie, Illinois, came Catherine

Guthneck, the first of three sisters to become Sisters of Providence; and from Logansport, Father Martin's second postulant, Mary Ann Graham. The community now numbered 16. A simple novitiate reception ceremony signaled the opening of their first "Month of Mary."

"Could we choose a more beautiful day," wrote Mother Theodore to Father Martin on May 1, "to increase the number of the children of our poor little Institute, who are likewise by so many titles children of Mary?"[3] The postulant he had brought to Saint Mary's in November, Catherine Doyle, was one of those received; with her were Sister Stanislas Reed, her companion since December, and Sister Gabriella Moore, whom Father Lalumière had escorted from New York in early February.

The foundress recorded in her diary the external events of the busy month which had begun so auspiciously. On May 3 the bishop arrived with his architect, Jean-Marie Marcile,[4] to arrange for the completion of the academy building. Monsignor remained until May 12, taking careful notice of every phase of life on the little mission. "This good father made us the gift of his own carriage," she noted.

Monsignor also saw each of the sisters in private and heard confessions. Before he left the sisters had the pleasure of seeing once again the priest who had been their guide on their way. Father Chartier came to confer with the bishop and to visit the missionaries he had served on their journey.

Monsignor left with Father Chartier on May 12, having offered the use of his horse to the men laboring the fields. "They are beginning to prepare the fields for corn and potatoes," the foundress recorded gratefully, "making use of a horse which Monsignor bought us." Her involvement in every aspect of the formidable task set before her casts a glow of excitement and eager anticipation over the most prosaic entries in her journal: "We are sowing potatoes at the end of our garden," again, "Brassier goes to look for wheat," or "we have bought and killed a beef;" and "the wood is brought up for our bridge." Each little measure of progress was somehow momentous.

An event of special note occurred in mid-May, when, the foundress bravely noted, "Two of us go to Terre Haute in the religious habit for the first time." Thus the businessmen and settlers in this Protestant Hoosier town met their new neighbors from across the river, and an era of cordial relations began. The projected school could be counted on to bring a certain amount of welcome trade to the merchants of the rising little city. Both town and institution would benefit by courteous cooperation.

On May 31, the community observed a day of retreat with sung Vespers and a general Communion, "to conclude the month of Mary and to commend our establishment to her."[5]

The demands of the month just ended and those which followed were sufficient to tax the energies of even the strongest members of the little community. For Mother Theodore, not yet fully restored to health, the burden had deeper, personal dimensions.

Beneath the anxieties inseparable from her situation there still pulsed the heartache which had shadowed the outset of her mission – the fear of having somehow forfeited the confidence and love of superiors she herself loved and revered. The reassurance her sensitive and affectionate nature craved seemed long in coming, even as reports from Indiana were slow in reaching France.

Mother Mary, writing on January 22, had just received the letter of November 14 which recounted the circumstances of the arrival at Saint Mary's. The letters telling of the foundress's grave illness were then only on the way; it would be months before any words of comfort and concern could be received. Mother Mary's letter reflects her own austerely supernatural sentiments and takes for granted the same dispositions in its recipient:

If you remember, I did not show you America in speculation,

weeping at the sight of Jesus crucified, yet joining the fleeing Apostles. I spoke to you of that enterprise with the language of truth...Do not be discouraged, expect all, even the impossible, from divine Providence whose glory is to work with nothing; that is why, if you wish Him to use you as an instrument, you must remain in your nothingness by your humility.

"It is unfortunate," you say, "that we have not sufficient education." When God wishes to do something, He has need of nothing, and to be convinced of this, besides the light of faith, one can take us as the most convincing proof that history can furnish. Have confidence and be at peace.[6]

Mother Mary did not overestimate the capacity of her distant daughter to understand and cherish her advice. "You know my heart," the foundress had written in return.[7] "You know whether or not it has been happy to find yours again; whether its gratitude is lacking, whether the counsels you give me are precious." She went on to remind her superior that it was only in the full consciousness of her unworthiness that "with all the ardor of my heart," she had embraced the mission offered her and that if it were to be done again she would accept "with even greater courage and resolution."

Yet she acknowledged a growing conviction of her own inadequacy to meet the needs of her mission:

You have learned from the letters of Sisters St. Vincent and Basilide that I have been very ill. Monsignor wrote you, I think, that the danger was over. With what consolation I would tell you today, if I could, that it has entirely disappeared. It was this which caused me to defer writing to you. But no, such is far from the truth.....I have escaped death only by the special protection of God.

Only after weighing everything carefully before God and having according to your desires examined all on the spot I feel that I must tell you that everything is perfectly disposed here for the success of our work, which will certainly prosper if you will send us a few suitable subjects, even if it is necessary to deprive our house in France. Otherwise, without this sacrifice, our mission will fail.

Her loyalty both to Monsignor and to her superiors prompted an additional earnest plea, unfortunately destined to be misunderstood. Word received in certain letters from France had forecast a signal of disappointment for the bishop and the American mission, and a potential reflection on the superiors in France; as Monsignor expressed it, "They have <u>stolen</u> (that is Father Cardonnet's word) the dear Irma; she has been sent to Brest."[8]

With her wonted verve and candor, on receiving this news Mother Theodore had committed her first reactions to paper; prudent reflection calmed her impetuosity somewhat, but there was still no mistaking the insistence with which she tried to plead Monsignor's cause and save her beloved Ruillé from adverse criticism. After reminding Mother Mary of the zeal and solicitude of the bishop, his sacrifices for the community, his devotion during her illness, and his hopes for their establishment, she continued:

Permit me, my good Mother, to beg you to consider that this young person is not an ordinary postulant. She was confided to your care as a trust, not that you should examine anew her vocation, her judgment, or even her health, but that you should form her to the religious virtues, especially those of a missionary religious. Such were the intentions of her family, her own, and especially those of Monsignor de la Hailandière, who founds the greatest hopes upon this child and who wishes her, as I said in my last letters, <u>just as she is.</u>

The knowledge that I have of the American spirit causes me to participate fully in Monsignor's hopes for Irma. I am convinced that instead of being a hindrance here she will be very useful to the mission, since God has given her everything necessary to succeed. Besides, that is not the point. She belongs to Vincennes.[9]

Always frank and straightforward, in her zeal for the needs of her mission and for the reputation of her community in France, she wrote freely, believing that she was only making use of a permission Mother Mary had often given her to write with all the candor of her nature.[10] Later, to her surprise, she would be called to task for the tone of this letter and sadly realize that once again her single-minded dedication had betrayed her.

Her preoccupation with the awesome demands of the mission and her sense of her own inability to meet them are repeated in her letter to Canon Lottin late in May:

> How much good there is to do here! How great and sublime is the mission which has been confided to us! How holy one should be to fulfill it! I confess to you, Father, that each day I discover better how far removed I am from the perfection of my state and from the qualities necessary for the important work confided to me....To lead souls to God one must be a saint in any country in the world, but here where assuredly more than ordinary sanctity is required, there would be needed also a superior of extraordinary holiness; that makes me tremble. I have written to our venerated Mother to beg her to send us someone who has indeed the spirit of God and especially profound humility with great piety and a great spirit of sacrifice. With that, one could work wonders here....I beg you, Father, in the name of Jesus, in the name of the thousands of souls whom we could gain for him here, to engage that good Mother to send the two persons I ask with so much insistence, one who could replace me or help me, and a musician for our boarding school, with Irma to teach drawing. With that I dare assure you that we will succeed, and without that we will not succeed.[11]

The consciousness of unworthiness and incapacity expressed in these letters was not the effect of enfeebled health or fear of an uncertain future, nor was it evidence of that timidity which recoils before difficulties real or imagined.

The early Indiana missionaries had learned this lesson well, but the circumstances in which they labored did not make its application easy. To accommodate 19th century French mentality to 19th century American conditions presented particular difficulties. A biographer of Simon Gabriel Bruté, the first bishop of Vincennes, having remarked about the phenomenal development of America during this period, was moved to comment:

> The already very rapid material progress (more so than in Europe) in the old states of the East soon proceeded beyond the mountains at a pace hitherto unheard of. One can say without exaggeration that in less than a quarter of a century (1834-1856) Indiana and Illinois evolved materially as much as Europe did in two thousand years.
>
> From an ecclesiastical point of view this was like catapulting from the pre-medieval to contemporary times. Perhaps nowhere else until that time was the movement of history so keenly felt.[12]

Making due allowance for hyperbole, consideration of the historical fact is essential for an understanding of Mother Theodore's life and work in her new environment and the relationships involved. The years 1834-1856 coincide with the period between the establishment of the diocese in which she was called to work and her death in 1856. Thus both the diocese of Vincennes and the Congregation of the Sisters of Providence of Saint Mary-of-the-Woods had their beginnings during the years of "unheard of" progress. It was indeed a new world into which the missionaries ventured, a restless world which demanded of them adjustment to a lifestyle entirely different from that in which their personalities had been formed. The problems it created for them were augmented by difficulties arising from individual temperaments and background.

The first bishop of Vincennes, Simon Bruté, had been living in America since 1810, when as a young priest he offered his services to Bishop Flaget, newly appointed to the diocese of Bardstown. Bishop Bruté's successor, Célestine de la Hailandière, came to the United States in 1836 at the age of 38, after ten years of ministry in a prosperous parish in his native city, Rennes, following a brief but promising career in law.[13] Neither his experience nor his formation had prepared him for the life of a missionary bishop. The French priests who had preceded him to Vincennes or whom he himself had recruited had also to face a similar painful adjustment. On their arrival in 1840 the sisters had noted with surprise and distress the effects of pioneer missionary life on their compatriots.

"They noticed in their countrymen some change in disposition," noted Mother Theodore's first biographer, Mother Mary Cecilia Bailly. She tried to describe the surprise and dismay of the French sisters on meeting an environment not at all usual to them. Their compatriots had lost the effusive manners of the French:

> There was not that gay vivacity, that manner so demonstrative of pleasure which is strikingly characteristic of the French...That warm politeness which is natural manners with the French seemed in those they met to have been chilled by the new atmosphere they had breathed... and their own warmth of feeling to meet them made a contrast which showed the power that foreign climates and people have to change and assimilate strangers into their own characteristics.[14]

There were exceptions, of course. We have seen the reunion of Bretons in Vincennes, the sisters just arrived and awaiting the bishop, and the Eudists at St. Gabriel's College. We have witnessed Mother Theodore's delight in the lively conversation of Father Badin, that "veteran among the missionaries" who after 50 years on the Kentucky mission still retained "all his French gaiety and joviality."

Yet she would confess to Mother Mary that they had found their bishop cold, uncommunicative and indecisive. She was quick to sense a partial cause in his overwhelming burden and his poverty: "He seems to me to be animated by the best intentions but so busy, so poor, that he does not know which way to turn."[15] However she never seemed to tire of praising in her letters to France the solicitude of the bishop and his interest in the foundation. Although to Monsignor's great satisfaction she had shown herself open to his suggestions and advice. It remained a source of wonder to her that his genial and benevolent qualities were hidden under "so cold an exterior."[16]

What was true of the bishop was true in a lesser degree of the few overworked priests under him. They were preoccupied with the effort to survive in their utter destitution, exhausted traveling over primitive roads to bring the Gospel to a poor and often indifferent people, lonely and discouraged. All these might well serve to stifle any natural exuberance in men however dedicated, however animated by the "best intentions." The clear-sighted foundress understood and accepted the demands of the mission to which Providence had appointed her, and the only means of meeting those demands. "To do any good in America," she reflected, "one must be entirely dependent on the spirit of God."[17]

Her greatest fear, as her letters show, was that she might somehow be an obstacle to the workings of this spirit. The atmosphere in which she had to work served to intensify this fear. For the good of the mission and in the interest of her community she had to enter fully into the designs of the bishop; at the same time, she was charged with the observance and the preservation of her Rule. As we have seen, there had been no clarification of mutual responsibilities at the beginning of the mission. A woman of foresight and energy, accustomed to make plans and carry them forward conscientiously, she had now to deal with a prelate whose zeal, enthusiasm and understanding of his office left no room for the enterprise of others.

One of the potential difficulties in the way of success on the missions was such failure on the part of a zealous and overworked bishop to realize that the courageous women who had braved the wilderness to render their services were intelligent, experienced and capable of directing the enterprise for which they were responsible without detriment to the respect and deference due to the bishop. The bishop of Vincennes was convinced of the importance of the foundation at Saint Mary-of-the-Woods. Indeed he went so far as to identify its success with that of the diocese itself.[18] Perhaps for this reason, given his understanding of his episcopal responsibilities, he felt the need of personal involvement in every detail.

He was meticulous in his surveillance, as a list of directives he drew up early in May indicates. Very little was left to the discretion of the superior, even though she was an experienced educator whose work in France had won recognition. Even though on the journey from New York to Indiana she had taken advantage of the occasion to observe practices in American Catholic schools.

"Everything considered, dear Mother," Monsignor began his memorandum,[19] "this is what I have decided about the boarding school. His list of personnel included the novice Sister Aloysia as assistant; as teachers, Sisters Basilide, Marie Joseph, and "one of our Americans;" as housekeepers, Sister Olympiade or Catherine and an assistant, Sister Liguori to give writing lessons. Detailed instructions followed:

1. You would have the tact necessary to abandon the direction of the instruction to the Sister Assistant, who would even in a short time replace you when the parents presented themselves. You could, and perhaps should, remain in the novitiate.

2. In directing the instruction, Sister Aloysia would do it in the manner of this country, without excluding the improvements your French methods might add.

3. The French sisters would learn the American method under her direction and could later be sent to found some other establishments where they could complete their mastery of English and their acquaintance with American customs....

Further directives followed from Vincennes early in June:

I believe that if it has not already been done you should announce in the Terre Haute newspapers the opening of the boarding school.....

Without knowing what is going to become of Mrs. Williams.....I thought that we might secure her for music lessons....I am sending you a list of the books purchased, so that Sister Aloysia can order from Cincinnati through Mr. Buteux those which are lacking.

I rejoice to see your sisters prepare themselves soon for the conducting of the boarding school, or rather for their charges as mistresses. They should not forget that they can scarcely teach anything before having studied the books that they are putting into the hands of the children, not <u>even arithmetic.</u>

Responding to the need for complete submission of her own judgment and will, Mother Theodore acceded gracefully, even gratefully, it would seem, to Monsignor's directions. In the same letter in which she begged Canon Lottin to use his influence in favor of the American mission, she who had directed schools with distinction apparently adopted Monsignor's judgment on the novice Aloysia, She describes her as "a converted Protestant who after having spent some years with the Sisters of Charity in the East generously gave herself to the poor mission of Vincennes and entered our novitiate." Despite her personal convictions about Aloysia changing her community, she was able to characterize this instance as "assuredly a mark of Providence, for without her who would teach us English? Who would have been our interpreter with our postulants? Who would now be prepared to begin a boarding school?"[20]

The month of May had ended with a day of retreat and a fervent commendation of the new school to Mary. June opened with the promise of Our Lady's acceptance of her charge. "We have been approached for the first time about boarders," Mother Theodore confided to the diary on June 2. The following day she was called to consult with Mrs. Williams, Father Buteux's protégé in Terre Haute, who wished to register her daughter. That same day brought an application from a third prospective boarder. The beginnings were slow, it is true, but encouraging, and the woodland blossomed with hopeful activity.

While the field hands worked energetically at preparing the ground and sowing corn and beans, the sisters applied themselves to household preparations. Mother Theodore found time also to prepare a detailed and surprisingly comprehensive prospectus for the little school. Modeled on that of the boarding school in Ruillé, it aimed at appealing at the same time to the educational aspirations of Americans.

On June 25 Mother Theodore recorded, "We went to Terre Haute for provisions for the boarding school." The following day, armed with cleaning implements, they braved a heavy downpour to make their way from the convent to the new building to prepare it for the benches and tables the workmen were assembling for refectory and classroom. In the midst of the storm without and the rush of activity within Monsignor arrived, accompanied by a seminarian, to observe progress at first hand. He departed on July 1, again in the midst of torrential rain, which continued the next day, but did not keep the community from work until "the first furnishings were placed in our big house."[21]

They were still busy making final painstaking touches when on Saturday, July 4 1841 the first boarder arrived. Our Lady's special interest seemed evident, and the grateful foundress, after noting in the diary the day and the child's name, Mary Lenoble, added "Glory to Mary! Glory to our Mother!"

On Sunday, Susan LaLumière and Susan Williams arrived and that evening after Father Buteux, assisted by Father Parret, had blessed the premises, the boarders, with the sisters assigned: Sisters Aloysia, Basilide, Marie Joseph, and Thérése, spent their first night in the new school.

Monday brought four more pupils. On Tuesday, July 7, the work so long awaited, so anxiously prepared for, was officially inaugurated with all the solemnity their primitive circumstances permitted. Teachers and pupils assisted at a Mass of the Holy Spirit and the chanting of the <u>Veni Creator</u>. After Mass an excited little group followed their teachers from the crowded little chapel and across the ravine to the waiting Academy. Six additional pupils soon brought to 13 the total enrollment of the first session of the little "pensionnat" in the Indiana Woods.[22]

First Academy at Saint Mary-of-the-Woods
Opened July 4, 1841

Chapter 12

Mother Theodore's dream of establishing a school for the education of young women was officially underway. Being an experienced school woman, she recognized the importance of increasing the enrollment at the new academy. Mother Theodore made use of the press, of the positive experiences of the students and the excellence of the education offered to draw new students to the academy.

She placed the following advertisement in the Terre Haute *Wabash Courier* for seven consecutive issues.

Providence at St. Mary-of-the-Woods situated in Sugar Creek Tsp., Vigo Co., 4 miles northwest of Terre Haute.

St. Mary's Academy for young ladies will open the second of July. Branches taught are as follows: Reading, Writing, Arithmetic, Geography, and History, both Ancient and Modern, English Composition, Natural Philosophy, Chemistry, Botany, Mythology, Biography, Astronomy, Rhetoric, Plain and Fancy Needlework, Bead Work, Tapestry, and Lace Work.

Terms – Boarding, including the above branches, per annum $100.00

Extra Charges: French Language, per annum $10.00

Music, Instrumental and Vocal $30.00

Drawing and Painting in Water Colors, Imitation of Oil Painting on Linen $20.00

Oil Painting on Velvet, Oriental Painting, Embroidery and Artificial Flower Work $10.00

Washing and Mending per annum $12.00

Stationery $5.00

Medicine at the apothecaries' rate.....

Those who wish to learn the Latin, German and Italian languages can do so. Terms the same as for the French for further particulars, application must be made to the Mother Superior. All letters addressed to the Institution must be post paid. A prospectus will be published in a few weeks.

Mother St. Theodore[1]

This advertisement was also published in the Chicago *Democrat*, the Springfield, Illinois *Journal* and the *Indiana Journal*.

Support for the new academy came from many sources. Editor Dowling of the *Wabash Courier* "...had ferried across the river and driven along the planks of the neglected National Road, turning off to see the new school[2] and reserve a place for his daughter. In an editorial he praised the academy situation as "...healthful and the building is extremely neat and well adapted to the purpose, being a three story brick of the most tasteful construction."[3]

As the people in Terre Haute found out that the Sisters from France intended to start a school at Saint Mary-of-the-Woods, the word spread quickly. There were few opportunities for girls to be educated in those pioneer days and parents were eager to give their daughters an education. Students came from Terre Haute, Vincennes, and cities in Illinois.

Despite the hardships of those beginning days, the students grew to love their school and took the many inconveniences in stride. Mother Theodore was deeply grateful for their patience. Fortunately, the first school term was a short one, ending in August and resuming in September.

The students left Saint Mary-of-the- Woods for their end of term vacation with great excitement. Going home to family and friends after completing their first term at St. Mary-of-the-Woods Academy brought much joy. Leaving their new friends at school, however, was hard to do.[4]

Semester break was a time for Mother Theodore and her faculty to regroup. Mother Theodore being an experienced and capable school administrator recognized the need to re-evaluate schedules, re-examine faculty assignments and assess program needs.

They had hardly completed these important tasks when Mother Theodore received word from Bishop de la Hailandière that she and Sister Aloysia were to come to Vincennes for the consecration of the Cathedral. Inviting Mother Theodore for this occasion was totally appropriate, but inviting a novice showed favoritism that the other sisters had noticed on his many visits. Sister Aloysia welcomed the bishop's attentions and used them to take over circumstances that were Mother Theodore's responsibilities. This was not lost on Mother Theodore.

Being an insightful administrator and superior she saw Sister Aloysia as a very troubled young woman who sought control within the academy and the community. Since Sister Aloysia was the protégé of the bishop and an ardent follower of the chaplain, Father Buteux, she was successful in influencing their decisions.

Father Buteux, the first chaplain at St. Mary-of-the-Woods... "possessed an exaggerated idea of his authority over the community. He interfered daily in the interior government of the community. He believed the Congregation should have an American government and favored Sister Aloysia, an American."[5]

Sister Aloysia was quickly taken in by the views of Father Buteux.

The two of them began planning in secret to found a new community for American postulants. It was expected that Sister Aloysia would be the superior. She went so far as to approach "four of the American postulants to persuade them to join the intended American community that spring."[6]

When this became known to Mother Theodore her own words described her action.

> I took our little buggy and set out for Vincennes on January 19th, in spite of the cold and the snow thickly falling, wrapped up in an old buffalo skin robe and sheltered by an umbrella, I arrived at the Bishop's house at nine o'clock that night. The next day by way of resting and thawing out, I was most ungraciously received, but His Lordship ended by promising to come and send away this unworthy subject, Sister Aloysia, who had already given us so much trouble. The circumstances were delicate in the extreme. The Bishop had considered Sister Aloysia essential to the success of St. Mary-of-the-Woods. This action caused Monseigneur very much pain. He had conducted her, directed her, sent her here to this place before we came and had given her, from the beginning, marks of preference and esteem which wounded the others. Yet, he was the first to say that she could not remain any longer.[7]

Bishop de la Hailandière gave Sister Aloysia the news himself. Mother Theodore, as superior, presided at Sister Aloysia's divestiture. Sister received the order to leave without trying to defend herself, without tears, without emotion of any kind. Her silence at her dismissal was of short duration.

Mother Theodore and her sisters suffered deeply from the scathing criticisms made by the former Sister Aloysia to the people of Terre Haute. Mrs. Williams, one of the first Catholics in the area took Sister Aloysia, now known as Mary Doyle into her home and strongly supported her. The ex-sister continued to make her complaints against the sisters public. "Protestants warmly espoused her cause, so that she became, for awhile, very popular in town; and what is strange even some Catholics took her part."[8]

Mother Theodore and her sisters had worked hard to win the respect of the townspeople only to have it nearly destroyed by the ill-will of the dismissed Mary Doyle. Because of her condemning statements the enrollment at the academy began to fall.

A letter from Mother Theodore to Mother Mary in Ruillé reads:

"I have just discovered that there is a conspiracy in Terre Haute to destroy our institution. The persons responsible for this had begun prejudicing against us the families that were here last year. Only one pupil returned this fall. And she, it seems, had no other home. I was greatly distressed, for burdened as we are with debts and having no funds with which to pay them. I looked upon the failure of our boarding school as a great misfortune, all the greater because it would render impossible fulfilling the end of our vocation, the education of youth."[9]

The enrollment problems at the academy were a direct result of the new school that Mary Doyle had opened in Terre Haute in competition with the academy at Saint Mary-of-the-Woods. Hard feelings toward the sisters continued and prejudice against them was rampant.

In a letter to Bishop Bouvier of Le Mans, France, Mother Theodore poured out her soul. "My Lord, truly we have much to suffer in our deep forest surrounded by enemies, having no other support, no other consoler than God alone."[10]

A major suffering for Mother Theodore at this time was the serious lack of support from Father Buteux, their Chaplain. He complained to Bishop de la Hailandière that Mother Theodore was not suitable to be the superior and did not have the qualities necessary for that position. When the bishop's response to him was that Mother Theodore was sent there by her superiors and was where God wanted her to be, Father Buteux took another approach. He faced Mother Theodore directly and tried to convince her that she would do harm to the mission because her character was so different from the American character. This was very upsetting to her, since she had not experienced difficulty in relating to the American people. Quite to the contrary, those who knew her felt drawn to her recognizing her goodness and closeness to God.

When Father Nicholas Petit arrived for the sisters retreat, Mother Theodore confided Father Buteux's criticisms to him. Father Petit assured Mother Theodore that God had indeed blessed the work she was doing. He told her that Father Buteux was "…half crazy" and he needed to leave because of "disturbing the peace of their house."

Bishop de la Hailandière wrote to Mother Theodore telling her…

> Fr. Buteux is your Chaplain, nothing more. As such, he hears the confessions and there in the sacred tribunal he gives whatever advice he judges fit. He may not speak in private to any Sister, Novice, or Postulant. It is not in any way his duty, as he seems to think, to form them otherwise than by the administration of the sacraments. This would be going contrary to your rule. One additional duty it seems to me is incumbent upon him, that of giving an instruction every week to the Community. At least that is what I recall to my mind. I wish his relations to go no further than this."[11]

The bishop soon became aware of Father Buteux's subterfuge and removed him as chaplain from Saint Mary-of-the-Woods.

In a letter to Mother Mary, Mother Theodore admitted "I had difficulty in consenting to this, for I know the purity of his intentions, but not withstanding my prayers, even my tears, the Bishop removed him."[12]

Father Buteux's removal was a great loss to the other sisters because they were very attached to him. They had spent hours with him in spiritual direction and he managed to very subtly weaken their confidence in Mother Theodore. This was quite painful to her. It was difficult enough to experience the disloyalty of the chaplain, but to have her own sisters turn from her at the urging of the Chaplain was extremely hard to bear.

Father Buteux's efforts "to destroy the struggling convent at St. Mary-of-the-Woods were not however in any degree checked, but only driven underground. He continued his clandestine relations with the sisters and ex-Sister Aloysia."[13]

An anguished Mother Theodore again wrote to Mother Mary concerning the removal of the chaplain, Father Buteux.

"We all wept for he was a holy priest, but much too amiable and affectionate, despite his grace and modest appearance to be in frequent contact with young girls whose hearts, like glue, attach themselves to everything. I congratulate myself on his removal, although I liked him very much."[14]

The slanderous words and actions of the former Sister Aloysia and Father Buteux were a heavy cross to carry. Mother Theodore opened her heart to Mother Mary and pleaded with her for love and understanding.

Unknown to Mother Theodore someone wrote an anonymous letter to Mother Mary telling her the sisters at Saint Mary-of-the-Woods were suffering greatly and experiencing grave difficulties. Mother Mary's anxious letter of reproof to Mother Theodore stated:

If what we are told is true, should we not reproach you for having written us nothing but romances since you have been in America? For in none of your letters is there mention of suffering or of extraordinary difficulties, the heat and cold of the climate excepted. …if you were alone, my dear Theodore, I could more readily forgive the dissimulation which you have practiced toward us. I would have admired your courage in suffering in silence, for the love of God, all that is most crucifying in the trials and privations of that life. But if you have the right to be silent concerning your own trials, is it lawful for you, under the circumstances, to hide from us those which weigh upon your Sisters? I do not think so. On this account I order you, without consulting anyone whatever, by the obedience which you owe us, to inform us of all that concerns you in general and in particular. I wish to know everything, my dear Theodore. Consequently, I oblige you to tell me the whole truth, no matter from what quarter your sufferings and your difficulties may proceed."[15]

This letter from Mother Mary written in December reached Mother

Theodore on February 26, 1842. Her heart was heavy as she read the words accusing her of withholding the truth from her superiors. She knew the anonymous letter, supposedly written out of concern for the sisters, was intended to wound her reputation and have her recalled from her forest home.

> "Mother Theodore and her Sisters were too peace-loving and too submissive to the will of God to attempt to discover who had been the cause of this trial. Bishop de la Hailandière was, however, of different mettle. He took the whole occurrence deeply to heart and demanded and received the original letter from Mother Mary though absolute proof was lacking, he was convinced that it had been sent by Father Buteux."[16]

Mother Theodore immediately began to answer Mother Mary's letter. It was with sorrow that she wrote, "You have taken the resolution of leaving me in the depth's of the forests of America, without the hope of receiving any consolation from you who are always my most dear Mother. That, Mother, is the heaviest cross that your daughter could ever carry."[17]

Mother Theodore continued to assure Mother Mary that she had never deliberately hidden any of their sufferings from her. She reminded Mother Mary that she, herself, told "her Theodore" that life would be very different in America. The customs, language, manners, religious views and character of the people were so unlike the French. Mother Theodore told Mother Mary that even the priests in whom one should find consolation have been rendered insecure.

It was difficult for her to have to tell Mother Mary that Bishop de la Hailandière experienced the effects of the Indiana wilderness in his manner of relating to his priests and religious women.

> "He is sad, gloomy, even colder than the Americans, never satisfied with anything. Still he shows the liveliest interest in our work, the truest affection. He talks of nothing but his Sisters. He almost seems to work only for them, even to the point of displeasing his priests, who blame him."[18]

Since Mother Theodore had been put under obedience by Mother Mary to tell her all that was happening, would she finally accept Mother Theodore's account of the trials and tribulations the sisters were enduring in America, as well as the consolations that were theirs? Time, alone, would bring the answer to that question.

One by one, students began returning to the academy. As Mother Theodore had hoped, the reputation of the academic excellence offered at the academy prevailed and ever increasing numbers of students arrived at Saint Mary-of-the-Woods for their education.

Soon the school flourished. Mother Theodore's exceptional administrative skills provided a peaceful environment in the academy so long besieged by criticism from the supporters of Mary Doyle.

The school opened by Mary Doyle in competition with the academy did not last long, but the damage she had done by vilifying Mother Theodore and the sisters continued in peoples' minds and actions for a long time to come.

Chapter 13

Mother Theodore drew her strength from God who had brought her to this Indiana wilderness. Despite the continuing hard feelings and prejudice against the Sisters of Providence congregation, Mother Theodore never gave in to despair.

The Terre Haute merchants long-standing refusal to provide her credit continued to cause her serious concern. There was little or no money to purchase food for the sisters. In her own words Mother Theodore wrote to Mother Mary

> Friday morning a boy whom I had sent to Terre Haute brought me a note from a dealer in whom I had confidence and who furnished us what we needed. We had paid this man about four hundred and fifty francs on our account. On Friday, however, he wrote that he would give us nothing more except for cash, all the others to whom we owed anything seemed to have given word to one another to come, almost all together, to ask for their money. We were reduced to the necessity of giving them linen, dresses, pieces of muslin and calico, and so forth, or the coffee and sugar the Bishop had procured for us in Louisville in exchange for butter, soap and other things of absolute necessity.[1]

Mother Theodore's heart was heavy as she realized her helplessness.

She turned to God and begged him to help them in this time of great need. She reminded her sisters that "many things are wanting to us, yet we dare not complain. Shall we not be, and are we not already in our own little nook? Besides, did we not come here to suffer – we who were so well provided for in France?"[2]

With the increased enrollment at the Academy, Mother Theodore had expected that money for tuition, room and board would provide additional revenue for the necessities of life. What was unforeseen was that the families of the students were experiencing their own financial difficulties and could not pay their debts to the sisters.

As Mother Theodore wrote to Bishop Bouvier in France

> I, in particular, have trials which are personal, were it only that of having charge, almost alone, of a congregation already numerous, to whom I have not always bread to give, and often I do not know where to procure what is absolutely necessary for the morrow.[3]

Mother Theodore saw her sisters' pain. She saw their hunger. Her heart ached and she did what she always did in time of need. "I turned to my God and felt my confidence reanimated. If He takes away our last support, is it not because He wishes to be the sole support of His daughters of the Woods? There never was such pressing need of His help as now."[4]

God seeing their immediate need heard their prayer. People who worked for them were aware of their hardships and brought them flour and oats sharing the bounty of their own tables with the sisters. They also brought them seed to plant that would provide crops at the time of harvest.

Mother Theodore's heart was full as she recognized God's Providential care. Those who had kept such distance from them formerly were reaching out to help them in their need. Relationships were changing. Mother Theodore and the sisters were quick to show their gratitude and nurture their new friends and neighbors.

As spring arrived the land was cultivated, the seed sown, and all of nature came to life. Mother Theodore watched the young plants appear through the softening earth and felt great hope. The spring rains fell gently on the soil and the newly planted seedlings took on a life of their own.

Mother Theodore walked the farmlands watching diligently as inches turned into feet with the growth of the crops. She and her sisters enjoyed the spring and summer harvest of fruits and vegetables that filled their table.

Looking to the fall, Mother Theodore longed for the harvest of hay, wheat and corn that filled their fields. All of it would provide much needed sustenance for them through the fall and harsh winter.

As Providence would have it, at summer's end, the crops were bountiful and provided fruits, vegetables, and grains that would give nourishment to their bodies and their spirits. There was much rejoicing among the sisters as they helped with the harvesting. By the time they finished gathering in the harvest the new barn was filled to overflowing. Their gratitude to God for his Providential care was great.

In a letter to Mother Mary, Mother Theodore wrote

A hundred and fifty bushels of wheat, nearly the same amount of oats, also hay and corn sufficient for the winter forage for the animals, were safely stored in the large barn with the other provisions for the winter; bacon, lard and shucks for the ticks.[5]

When Mother Theodore looked upon the harvest she felt a deep thanksgiving that their table would not be empty again.

October 2nd dawned bright and sunny. It was a beautiful, crisp autumn Sunday. About noon cries of "fire" shattered the peaceful quiet, as billowing smoke and flames rose from the log house provided for the male employees. The fire quickly spread to the large new barn and the flames leaped onto the stored harvest.

The sisters, neighbors and employees looked on in horror as the flames began to consume the fruits of their labor. Neighbors and employees worked side by side with the sisters to quench the flames, but the winds whipped them higher and higher out of control.

There was little water power to extinguish the blaze. The small stream that ran down the ravine could not provide the amount of water that was needed. In Mother Theodore's own words to Mother Mary she wrote

> In less than three minutes the two buildings containing our wagons, plows, and all the farm implements constituted an immense oven from which a bright and circling flame rose to a prodigious height and threw to a great distance a shower of sparks.[6]

Mother Theodore looked upon the destruction from the frenzied fire and knew in the depths of her soul that she needed to go to the chapel and beg God to save his dwelling place. Her feelings as she prayed ran the gamut of disbelief that all the food of the harvest was burning before her very eyes, to whatever would they do now, to "our hope is in the Providence of God, which has protected us until the present and which will provide somehow, for our future needs."[7]

Mother Theodore experienced an immediate strengthening and returned to assist those who were battling the blaze. Every hand was needed in an effort to extinguish the inferno. Mother Theodore joined the others in an effort to beat back the flames but to no avail. As she later told Mother Mary,

> The fire was burning with inconceivable fury. Everything was on fire. Nothing could be seen, but fire, and sparks fell on us, particularly from the trees. The men were there working at top speed. We had them cut down those trees which, though the most dangerous because of their height. They took their axes and hewed away with all their might. Some half-consumed pieces of wood fell around them and immediately fire broke out in the clothes of one, in the hair of another and in the hat of a third. Almost all of us have burns, but by a special Providence, no one has been seriously hurt. My hand is burned, but that is a small matter.[8]

The prayers and supplications of Mother Theodore and her sisters were heard. The winds ceased and though the loss was tragic, the sister's convent was spared.

With their storage of wheat and corn destroyed, the sisters salvaged the last of the season's corn that was at the grist mill and sold it for wheat flour. At least there would be bread for a few months. It was also necessary to slaughter some of their animals and exchange others for corn and oats.

The psychological damage of their loss caused great stress for Mother Theodore. How often that winter she woke from a deep sleep imagining that she heard crackling flames and smelled the billowing smoke. Only those who had experienced that terrible fire would understand her fear. She had heard that convents all around the country had been set on fire by those who felt prejudice against sisters. Mother Theodore and her sisters had experienced widespread prejudice in Terre Haute and wondered if the ill-will of their enemies was the cause of their fire. They were never to know.

In writing to Bishop Bouvier in France, Mother Theodore confided that at times she felt depressed and disheartened. At other times her calm, peaceful heart and joyfulness rose to the surface and she was able to thank God for the grace of suffering for him.[9] It was because of this that she could say to her sisters, "Let us take courage, my very dear sisters; the cross, it is true, awaits us at every turn, but it is the way to heaven."[10]

The next two years were years of great poverty. In the Life of Mother Theodore written by Mother Mary Cecilia Bailly, she recalls

"The food consisted chiefly of corn bread and pork and not always enough of that; the table could hardly be poorer than it was. The same with regard to wear – shoes were scarce. Any kind that could be gotten were worn. Clothes were mended and patched without end."[11]

With no credit extended by the local merchants to Mother Theodore and her sisters, they found themselves in dire straits. Bishop de la Hailandière

215

sent three barrels of flour to help tide them over. Mr. Sanford seeing their massive loss, let them have what they needed from his mill and allowed them to pay when they could.

Had it not been for the kindness of Bishop Bouvier of France and the superiors at Ruillé in sending one thousand francs to the sisters at that particular time of need, they may indeed have starved. Once again, Mother Theodore recognized the Providence of God watching over them and wrote to Bishop Bouvier

"We had but one dollar remaining of what Mr. Byerly had lent us and we did not know where to get a cent for the wants of the house. Still, how could I mistrust divine Providence? Now, I get flour on credit in the firm hope of soon being able to pay. So, my good Father, we have bread, shoes, etc.

Thanks to your liberality. May we not in truth call you our Father?[12]

The French superiors at Ruille did not realize the extent of the new mission's poverty. Mother Theodore had tried to inform them, but letters took months to cross the ocean. By the time the letters arrived the news was old and circumstances had often changed.

Mother Mary at Ruillé was anxious for Mother Theodore to open new establishments in Indiana. Her letters to Mother Theodore urged her to begin new foundations that would offer an education to young girls. Mother Theodore did not want to go too quickly in forming another establishment for fear the sisters that staffed it would not be sufficiently developed in the spirit of the Congregation. Having experienced the dire poverty of Saint Mary-of-the Woods on her arrival, Mother Theodore was not willing to send her sisters into a similar situation.

In September of 1841, Bishop de la Hailandière wrote to Mother Theodore about the new pastor of the Church of St. Joseph in Jasper, Indiana. His name was Father Joseph Kundek and he was described as a "human dynamo of energy and zeal."[13]

The bishop informed Mother Theodore that Father Kundek had built a fine house for the sisters. He had also provided "a garden, an orchard, a meadow and ground for cultivation. What more could be desired?"[14]

Because Father Kundek had the foresight to build a school and a convent to house the sisters, he was in a good position to approach Mother Theodore to ask for sisters to staff his school. She informed Father Kundek of conditions that had been adopted by the Congregation for new establishments in America. She concluded by saying:

> We should be extremely grieved if you would not be able to comply with our wishes, for again, we love this mission of Jasper very much. Yet, we believe we ought not to give the sisters to it, if we cannot fulfill our other duties. So then, the future of this house is in your hands. See before God what you can do."[15]

Upon receiving this word, the parish priest responded by making certain the conditions Mother Theodore required were met. On October 15, 1841, Mother Theodore and her council made the decision to accept the Jasper mission. It was their first establishment away from Saint Mary-of-the-Woods.

Mother Theodore wrote to Mother Mary about her decision to take the Jasper Mission:

> My dear Mother, on the 19th of next month, Feast of our Glorious Father St. Joseph, the Saturday of Passion Week, the day devoted to honoring the passion of the divine Savior, and consecrated for centuries to the cult of the Blessed Virgin, this day, I say, is chosen for the installation of our good Sisters at Jasper, a little town forty miles on the other side of Vincennes. The people are German and almost entirely Catholic. We are sending there Sister Marie Joseph who is German. She is a person of solid piety and very good judgment. We are giving as companion an Irish Sister who knows English well and who has made astounding progress during the 13 months she has been here. These dear Sisters have no idea whatever of the way to conduct a religious house or a school."[16]

Because of this, Mother Theodore arranged for Sister St. Vincent Ferrer to assist them for a few months in their new ministry. This would give them time and experience in beginning a new school.

In her motherly way, Mother Theodore decided to accompany these sisters to the Jasper mission and help them get settled in their new home. It was her intention to do this as each new mission opened.

Having Mother Theodore with them provided a sense of security for the Jasper sisters. All they had known was Saint Mary-of-the-Woods where they spoke French much of the time and diligently attempted to learn English. Now, with Sister Mary Joseph who spoke German, Sister Gabriella who spoke English, and Sister St. Vincent, who, though temporary, had excellent organizational skills, they had what they needed to make a strong beginning in their Jasper school.

In France, it was the custom of the Sisters of Providence to open a free school for poor children whenever they opened a school for children whose parents could afford to pay tuition. In a letter to Mother Mary, Mother Theodore wrote:

> "In a month we will open a school for little girls of our woods and just now, while I am writing to you, a Catholic mother is begging me to take the boys. I do not know what the sisters and his Lordship will think of this proposal. I count on putting Sister Liguori at the head of this little school. She is getting to speak English quite well now."[17]

As the reputation of the Sisters of Providence as educators grew, many Catholics, desiring a good education for their children moved into the area. The number of children justified the building of a free school for the village which opened in the Spring of 1842.[18] A spacious brick school was built in the village in 1923 where both girls and boys received an excellent education.

It pleased Mother Theodore very much to know that she was able to continue the tradition of providing instruction for the poor, as well as for the children whose families paid for their education.

Mother Theodore continued to receive many requests to open schools in various parts of the State of Indiana. Before accepting any offers, she made sure that the conditions she and her council had agreed on for the new establishments had been met.

St. Francisville, Illinois, though poor and isolated was such a place. There were 30 Catholics of French descent and 19 non-Catholic families. Father Ducoudray, pastor of the parish, wrote to Mother Theodore:

> "The whole country, hereabouts, is counting upon a school kept by your sisters. Two of your good religious will accomplish much good in this district. Be certain that on my side I will neglect nothing to make it pleasant for them, and with the aid of God, I hope to succeed."[19]

Mother Theodore decided to send Sister Ligouri, a French sister and Sister Augustine, an American sister, to establish the school. As was her custom, Mother Theodore accompanied the two sisters to St. Francisville on October 20, 1842. The people welcomed the sisters with open arms, knowing that their children would have a good education.

It was not long, however, before all the responsibilities that fell to the sisters: the school, the convent, the care of the church, the pastor's meals, laundry and mending[20] became more than they could manage. Both sisters became ill. Sister St. Ligouri and Sister Augustine's little mission lasted only one year. The two Sisters were dearly loved by their students. A single entry in the diary by Sister Saint Francis Xavier during Mother Theodore's absence in France records the end: " Our Sisters leave St. Francisville." In a later letter Bishop de la Hailandière stated that he withdrew them because "they were without a priest or means of subsistence."[22]

Sister Ligouri and Sister Augustine had touched the souls of many parents and children in that tiny hamlet. The goodness that they brought would not be forgotten. In the words of Mother Theodore:

God, alone, can console you, strengthen you. He, alone can give you the courage to overcome nature and to make him all the sacrifices He has required of you this year. What a year it has been for poor nature, and above all, what a year of grace. Only in heaven will you understand the treasure with which your soul has been enriched these months.[23]

Having established the academy at Saint Mary-of-the-Woods, the school at Jasper, Ind., the village school for girls and eventually boys and the school at St. Francisville, Mother Theodore felt the time was right to make a journey back to France. An uneasiness was growing in her and her womanly intuition told her that "all was not well" between the superiors at Ruillé and the American mission at Saint Mary-of-the-Woods.

Chapter 14

Trusting that providence will not fail made Mother Theodore realize that she needed to secure the future stability of her congregation and could not risk again the near ruin they had experienced after the fire.

She consulted with Bishop de la Hailandière, her council, and the sisters, knowing in her heart that she had to make a trip to France for three major reasons:

1. To seek financial aid for the American mission.
2. To talk with Mother Mary and her council about the hardships and misfortunes of the Indiana mission, particularly the interference of the bishop in community decision-making.
3. To raise questions concerning the relationship between the Indiana mission and the Ruillé community.[1]

Mother Theodore had made these needs clear to Mother Mary in the numerous letters she had written to her since arriving in Indiana. Because Mother Mary did not respond to Mother Theodore's queries in those three areas, Mother Theodore was at a loss for the guidance she sorely needed. A personal visit to Ruillé was essential.

In the meanwhile, unknown to Mother Theodore, Mother Mary had plans to severe all ties between the Ruillé Community and the American foundation. Writing to Bishop Bouvier Mother Mary stated:

Reasons Against the Union of the Two Communities

1. The supervision necessary and obligatory for the Superior is impossible. One cannot respond to what one does not know, and the true and just knowledge can be transmitted to them, just as it can be hidden from them, denied or distorted.

2. The changes which would become necessary would be disastrous for the temporal welfare, because of the enormous expense of travel.

3. The uncertainty of the success of this congregation, whose failure would entail receiving members whose spirit, manners, and habits would be different from the Sisters of Ruillé-Sur-Loir: which could not have good results.

4. The union wishes the Community of temporal goods; that of Ruillé can provide for only its own needs for several years to come.

5. If one gives as example the Sisters of the Sacred Heart, reply that this religious group, when they found a house, whatever part of the world it may be, send out from the Motherhouse all the persons needed for the foundation."[2]

These words were written on June 21, 1843, and are clearly an indication of Mother Mary's strong desire to crush obstacles that might lessen her control over her community. She also sought to win the sympathy and support of the Bishop of Le Mans. Her plan was to use these arguments with Mother Theodore when she came to Ruillé for her meeting with Mother Mary, her council and Bishop Bouvier.

In the intervening time, Mother Theodore's strong intuition was causing her fear that the promises Mother Mary made to her and her five companions before they left France would not be kept. Having been told that they would never be cut off from the congregation at Ruillé was central to their agreement to come to America. The one query "Will we be separated from Ruillé?" was answered in the negative.[3] Why, then was Mother Theodore's spirit in distress? Why was her sense of foreboding serving as a prediction of what was to come?

Mother Theodore's pressing need for permanency with the Ruillé community and her continued spiritual guidance from Bishop Bouvier of Le Mans were driving forces for making the journey to France.

Realizing it would be necessary to have the permission of Bishop de la Hailandière to go, she conferred with him several times about the trip. At one moment he would tell her he had no money to give her for travel. The next day he would tell her to go to France and bring back money for the American mission. Some days later he would tell her she would have to travel alone for he had no money for a companion. Finally, he agreed to pay the way for Sister Mary Cecilia Bailly to accompany Mother Theodore and care for her if she became ill.

Writing to Mother Mary on April 8, 1843, Mother Theodore said:

> I would consider it a very tender mark of God's Providence if it were given to me to see you again, for, dear Mother, your opinion would be not only useful now, but is very necessary. This foundation belongs to you, to you, I say, who have watched over it amid the countless troubles it has caused you, to undertake this work of God. I feel, dear Mother, that you have the grace and experience for laying the foundation stone of the edifice we would like to rear in this country, and I could not but consider it a great favor from heaven to be able to have your direction, or at least your counsels in the matter. It is almost impossible to tell you everything by letter at so great a distance. Before acting, one would have to understand well these people whose customs are so different. With what confidence and gratitude I would gather up your words. Oh, my good Mother, I believe one learns to appreciate her Mother more and more when one is so far away from her..[4]

Mother Theodore chose Sister St. Francis Xavier to be the superior and care for the spiritual welfare of the sisters during her absence. She chose Sister Basilide to take charge of the temporal needs of the community.[5]

Having put all things in order, Mother Theodore felt the time had come for the journey to France. On April 26, 1843, she and Sister Mary Cecilia Bailly left their beloved Saint Mary-of-the-Woods for France.

The letters of recommendation given to Mother Theodore by Bishop de la Hailandière provided the confidence she needed in her appeals for money. The bishop's letter stated:

> I have weighed before God your reasons for undertaking a voyage to France. I approve of this voyage. I hope that God grants you success and that He will bring you safely back to your daughters rich in alms, which will have been bestowed upon you. Go, my dear Sister, to that France so charitable, so zealous for our poor missions, and whose resources seem to increase in proportion as she gives.[6]

Landing in New York the travelers were once more welcomed by the Parmentier family who had offered them hospitality when they originally arrived in New York from France in 1840. It was a joyous reunion, for the Parmentiers had kept in contact with Mother Theodore during the ensuing years. There were many stories shared about the West and Indiana mission. Through laughter and tears their story was told.

By the middle of May the two sisters set sail aboard the ship, the *Sylvia,* bound for Havre, France, scheduled to arrive by the middle of June.[7]

Once aboard ship, Mother Theodore experienced much peace. This passage was quite different from their voyage to America in 1840, when the sea was violent and they felt sure they would die. Her words to her sisters on that voyage "Come, if we have to die, let us die, but say nothing"[8] are often quoted by the congregation

There was time on this ship to pray, to journal and to reflect. Many questions surfaced in her mind concerning the relationship between the

Congregation of Saint Mary-of-the-Woods and the Congregation of Ruillé. It was important for her to know:

- What help the American foundation could expect from Ruillé.

- If the six sisters sent by Ruillé have a right to return to France if they wished.

- Do the superiors at Ruillé have a right to give orders to the six sisters and recall them?

- Have the sisters been given to the Bishop of Vincennes to found a Congregation on the model of that of Ruillé in all that is possible or to found a Congregation according to the views of this prelate?

- May the bishop accept establishments and decide upon the conditions without consulting the council?

- May the bishop admit to vesture or profession a postulant or novice who has not been presented by the council?

- May the bishop place and displace the sisters in the different employments of the Congregation?

- What should be done if the bishop does not approve that the superior or her delegate visit the establishments, but he does not forbid it?[9]

These questions were pondered in Mother Theodore's heart all the way to France. She knew the answers she wanted and feared the answers she might get. She begged God to protect her and her sisters and their relationship with the Ruillé Congregation. She agonized over the bishop's efforts to gain control over the Saint Mary-of-the-Woods Congregation. Talking to Mother Mary and getting her advice concerning the bishop's actions was of utmost importance to her.

Little did Mother Theodore know that Mother Mary had already decided to separate the Ruillé Congregation from the fledgling Congregation of Saint Mary-of-the-Woods. This decision, made without conferring with Mother Theodore and her council would severely grieve the heart of Mother Theodore when she learned of it.

The rest of the voyage was smooth sailing and on June 6th, the ship docked in the harbor of Le Havre, France. To be once again in her beloved France brought great joy to Mother Theodore. How she had missed her native land. And yet, America, her new home had become her dwelling place. In her own words: "This land was no longer for me the land of exile; it was the portion of my inheritance, and in it I hope to dwell all the days of my life."[10]

Mother Theodore and Sister Mary Cecilia traveled to Le Mans to pay their respects to Bishop Bouvier, bishop of Le Mans. He was Mother Theodore's spiritual father and was there for her through all her trials and tribulations. His words of wisdom gave her the strength and fortitude she needed when she felt she was carrying on her shoulders the weight of America's highest mountains and in her heart all the thorns of its wilderness.[11]

At their initial meeting on June 9th, she shared with him her reasons for making this journey to France. She presented him with her credentials from Bishop de la Hailandière and after reading them Bishop Bouvier wrote on the back of the document an authentication that read:

"We certify that the letter written on the other part of this sheet is really from the Bishop of Vincennes; that this Bishop is personally known to us and has both our esteem and our affection. We compassionate in their great need the Sisters whom we have given to Him and whom He recommends to the liberality of charitable souls.

J.B., Bishop of Le Mans

Le Mans, June 9, 1843"[12]

This dignitary, despite his great responsibilities toward his own diocese, was always willing to give Mother Theodore his sound judgment and advice. She had complete confidence in his decision-making and knew he cared deeply about the Sisters of Providence in America.

At the conclusion of their visit with Bishop Bouvier, the two Indiana missionaries began their travels to Ruillé, the place Mother Theodore dearly loved. There was such longing to see the sisters there and all the old familiar places, particularly the chapel where she spent endless hours in prayer; where she had taken her Vows; where she had poured out her heart to God to help her through the many crosses she had to bear.

On her arrival at Ruillé, the sisters ran to meet her. There was much joy and celebration on her return. It was obvious to the sisters how frail she appeared despite her gaiety. It was remarked:

> Only to see Sister Theodore one would judge her incapable of accomplishing any great or lasting work, so marked was the contrast between her fine and lofty mind, her heart overflowing with devotedness and generosity and her incomparable grace of eloquence and speech. All these excellent gifts of mind and heart united to a physique so delicate and fragile that the least fatigue would seem able to destroy.[13]

Mother Theodore delighted in introducing Sister Mary Cecilia Bailly, the "demi-Indienne" to the French sisters. What they had heard and read about American Indians was a far cry from the elegant gracious young sister who spoke fluent French with them.[14]

Mother Theodore guided Sister Mary Cecilia through the motherhouse buildings, filling her with the history of each special place. It was her great desire that Sister Mary Cecilia would breathe in the very sacredness of this dwelling that was their roots.

The one person Mother Theodore longed to see was Mother Mary. While desiring to be greeted by her, she felt fear of rejection and displeasure, since she had not asked Mother Mary's permission to come to France. There were many questions that she needed answered by Mother Mary.

In mid-September, the annual retreat was to be held at Ruillé. Mother

Mary and Bishop Bouvier would also be present for it. Taking advantage of this opportunity, Mother Theodore asked to meet with them and present her questions and concerns. During the meeting it was clear to Mother Theodore that Mother Mary was determined to separate the two Congregations and that her decision was firm and irrevocable. Even so, Mother Theodore implored her to reconsider. She reminded Mother Mary of her promise that the six sisters going to America would not be separated from Ruillé, but Mother Mary would not listen. Instead, she brought up the five reasons against the union of the two Congregations that she had written to the Bishop Bouvier. Mother Theodore listened with a grieving heart and begged Mother Mary not to separate them. Her plea fell on deaf ears, but God's grace gave her the strength to regain her courage. She asked the questions she had wrestled with on shipboard:

1. What would the relations of the Congregation of Saint Mary-of-the-Woods be with that of Ruillé?

   She was told that the Woods was a foundation formed from that of Ruillé. It would be self-governing under the authority of the Bishop of Vincennes, its Superior.

2. What help has the Indiana Congregation a right to expect from Ruillé?

She was told NONE, except benevolence and charity.

3. Will the six Sisters sent to America by the Ruillé Congregation have the right to return to France if they wish?

She was told YES and they will always keep that right, since they went only on that condition.

4. Do the superiors of the Ruillé Congregation have a right to give orders to the six sisters they have in America and to recall them?

She was told no, not without the consent of the Bishop of Vincennes.

5.   Will the Congregation of Ruillé pay the traveling expenses of any of its sisters who no longer wish to remain in America?

She was told the sisters should write to the superiors and await their response.

6.   Have the sisters been given to the Bishop of Vincennes to found a Congregation according to the views of this prelate?

She was told the Sisters have been given to his Lordship according to his request to form a Congregation on the model of that of Ruillé in all that is possible; and the desire of the Bishop of Le Mans, of the superiors of Ruillé and especially of the sisters of Saint Mary-of-the-Woods is that the Constitutions and Rules be the same for the two Congregations in all that is not absolutely impossible.

7.   Should the changes which may be deemed necessary be made by the Bishop of Vincennes without the participation of the council of Saint Mary-of-the-Woods?

She was told no, but if the bishop gives an order the sisters should obey and discuss the point when they find the opportunity.

8.   May the bishop accept establishments and decide upon the conditions without consulting the Council?

She was told no, these things should be done together.

9.   May the bishop admit to vesture or profession a postulant or novice who has not been presented to the council?

She was told no, the council must always regulate these things, but His Lordship has the right to refuse his approbation of a subject whom he judges undesirable, even though she might have the votes of the Council.

10.   May the bishop place and displace the sisters in the different employments of the Congregation?

She was told that this was impossible.

11.   If the bishop does not approve that the superior or her

delegates visit the establishments, but if he does not forbid it, what should be done?

She was told she should visit her establishments. That is indispensable.[15]

Each question posed by Mother Theodore was met with responses that were explicit and precise, cold and calculated. Mother Theodore felt as though a knife had pierced her heart. Trying to maintain control over her feelings at that moment was one of the hardest things she had ever experienced. She loved Mother Mary deeply, yet she and her sisters had just been torn away from their motherhouse in France, the place that had nurtured them, taught them and formed them in religious life. No more would the chapel where they had pronounced their Vows, made their retreat and prayed together, be theirs. No more would the Sisters they had known and loved at Ruillé be of the same religious Congregation as they were. How would she tell the sisters at Saint Mary-of-the-Woods? With all the problems occurring with Bishop de la Hailandière would the sisters even want to stay with the American Congregation?

In her desolation, Mother Theodore realized that it was the will of God that for the future she must lean upon him, alone.[16] Trusting in his Providence, she said, "I turned to my God and felt my confidence reanimated. If He takes away our last support is it not because he wishes to be the sole support of His Daughters of the Woods? There never was such pressing need of his help as now."[17]

Mother Theodore left Ruillé after the meeting with Mother Mary and Bishop Bouvier filled with apprehension. She set out to procure funds for her American mission planning to appeal to the generosity of their friends in Paris and all those in France who would be disposed to support their temporal needs.

The time of their arrival in Paris was unfortunate, as the city was quite deserted. Those persons belonging to the higher classes had left the city for their country estates and would not be returning until December.

In addition, there was so much need in France that contributions to charity had taken a serious toll on the peoples' finances.

Because of this, Mother Theodore and Sister Mary Cecilia traveled to Brittany to visit the families of the sisters in America. She knew these families would be anxious to have news of their daughters and relatives. She also knew her sisters at the Woods would rejoice in first-hand news of their loved ones in Brittany. What was lacking in money their families and friends made up for in hospitality. The two sisters were welcomed with open arms and enjoyed the warmth of French conversation and cuisine. Many questions about loved ones filled their time together. How good it felt to be among friends who were hungry to hear about America.

Since it seemed useless to continue their financial quest, they decided to return to Ruillé and prepare for their departure to America with the little money they had collected.[18] Bishop Bouvier encouraged Mother Theodore to leave before winter came upon them. She realized the wisdom of his words.

Mother Theodore's faith in the Providence of God was rewarded. She desired to attend Mass once more in Paris, at the old baroque church named Our Lady of Victories to beg the Queen of Heaven to protect them. Mother Theodore's grief and sadness spilled out to her heavenly mother. She narrates "It was on this precious day that we became in a particular manner Children of Mary, that the Blessed Virgin deigned to take the poor children of the Woods of Indiana under her maternal protection. It was not long before we experienced the effects of this protection."[19]

The next day a letter arrived for Mother Theodore informing her that His Excellency, the Keeper of the Seals for the King would give them an audience in an effort to assist them in their quest for alms. They were received graciously and highly advised to write a letter asking Queen Amelia for an audience with her. M. Martin, Keeper of the Seals, promised to deliver the request to the Queen personally

The Queen's answer did not arrive for some days and Mother Theodore's hopes had dimmed. On Saturday evening a letter from the Queen was placed in Mother Theodore's hands. What joy there was when it informed them that the Queen would meet with them the next day. Mother Theodore writes:

> We were ushered into the Queen's apartment. She entered a moment later, gave us seats herself and had us sit beside her, giving us the most gracious reception. She inquired about our situation like a tender mother, and listened to the details with the greatest interest.[20]

The queen expressed a true understanding of their situation and asked how she could help them. There was no hesitation in Mother Theodore's reply as she asked if the queen could pay their passage home. Queen Amelia agreed immediately to pay the passage for Mother Theodore, Sister Mary Cecilia and two new postulants who would be joining the American community. But that was not enough for the queen. She wanted to assist them at Saint Mary-of-the-Woods and assured Mother Theodore that her family and friends would provide additional funds at her solicitation. However, they must ask the bishops of France to also contribute.[21]

Mother Theodore wrote in her journal:

> After that she continued to speak with touching kindness of all who might contribute to the welfare of our work. In a moment of holy exaltation she said, "Ah, Yes, Sisters, let us save souls!" There was in her manner, her eyes, and above all in her voice so intimate a conviction of the price of a soul that my heart was touched by it, and is so even yet in recalling that incident to my mind.[22]

Mother Theodore knew from whence help had come. She went right back to the church of Our Lady of Victory to thank their protector and mother. Kneeling before her beloved Mother Mary, she poured out her heart in thanksgiving for the Blessed Mother's intercession. Her prayers had been answered and once more, the Mother of God had come to the protection of Her loving Daughters of Indiana.

Because of the kindness and generosity of the queen, Mother Theodore would not have to return to America empty handed. In fact, the queen continued to send money to Saint Mary-of-the-Woods long after Mother Theodore's visit with her in France. A special bond was born between these two women who would touch the lives of countless others by their sharing, one from her plenty, the other from her need.

It was time, now, for Mother Theodore to put all her strength into dealing with the situation at Saint Mary-of-the-Woods. Mother Mary had received a letter from Sister Basilide at the Woods, telling her that Bishop de la Hailandière was interfering in the administration of the community in Mother Theodore's absence. That all was not well at Saint Mary-of-the-Woods became apparent when Mother Mary opened mail at Ruille addressed to Mother Theodore from her sisters at Saint Mary-of-the-Woods. Having read the sisters fears, Mother Mary wrote to Mother Theodore:

> I continue to think that your presence is of absolute necessity at St. Mary's and that all the gold in France could not repay you for the injury which your absence may cause to the spiritual good of your rising Community. Provide yourself with a good measure of protection at the feet of the Immaculate Virgin in order to go forth to endure a combat with no other arms than humility, meekness and constancy of heart.... make haste, my dear Theodore, fly to Vincennes to repair the damage.. though your return to France has been useful, your presence at home is still more necessary.[23]

Mother Theodore did not receive Mother Mary's October 16, 1843 letter until November 1843 a month later. She had no idea that Mother Mary had communicated to Sister Basilide in Indiana, that the separation of the two congregations had taken place and the sisters at Saint Mary-of-the-Woods were no longer members of the Ruillé Congregation.

Mother Mary Lecor

Chapter 15

Additional letters began to arrive for Mother Theodore from her sisters at Saint Mary-of-the-Woods. The anguish of the sisters over the separation from the Ruillé community filled each page. They needed her to be with them. As she read each letter she felt once again that hers, and hers alone was the right to share the news of separation. That she had been pre-empted by Mother Mary was the cause of great pain, not only for her, but also for them.

The letters also cited the irregularities of the bishop's actions and his determination to take control of the Congregation in her absence.

In an abstract in the Annals of the Community, Sister St. Francis writes:

> The Bishop's first question was about the retreat; we replied that we wished to wait till our Mother's return, which we hoped would be in the autumn, fearing he would want to clothe in the habit and admit to profession some of those whose fitness we did not feel satisfied. Hearing the objections, the Bishop began to accuse Mother Theodore of despotism and several other offences. What he called her 'horrible fault' was the constancy she showed for the preserving of our rules and constitutions. Among other things he said that to oppose the Bishop was to revolt against God Himself; that he alone (the Bishop) had any authority over

us, and that the last priest in the diocese had more power over us than our Superior General.[1]

The bishop sent frequent letters to St. Mary-of-the-Woods with his demands, distressing the sisters who were trying so hard to hold on in Mother Theodore's absence. He admitted Sister Agnes and Sister Mary to Vows; founded a new house at St. Peter's, Ind., where he placed the two young Sisters who were withdrawn from the school at St. Francisville, Ill. which he had just closed. He demanded that the habit of the Sisters of Providence be given to two young women, members of the Congregation of the Sisters of Charity of Emmitsburg, Md until their Superiors wished to withdraw them from the school in Vincennes. He put the Sisters of Providence in charge of the Vincennes school and changed Sister St. Vincent from Jasper to direct it. Finally, he went so far as to depose Mother Theodore as Superior and called for an election in her absence without consulting the sisters or the Rule.[2] These were the same issues that prompted Mother Theodore's questions to Mother Mary at their meeting in Ruillé. Her intuition had been accurate.

On August 15, the Bishop assembled the six professed sisters: Sisters Basilide, St. Francis Xavier, Ligouri, and Olympiade, Agnes and Marie. Monsignor declared that the meeting was called in order to proceed to the election of a superior general. He had deposed Mother Theodore whose term of office he said had expired.[3] By doing this he violated the community Constitutions which said:

> Chapter 3 – Election of the Superior General, "the Superior General must be chosen from among the members of the congregation who are at least ten years professed. On the day fixed for the election, Monsignor the Bishop or his delegate with two assistants, deposes the Superior in the presence of the community; He receives from her hands the keys, the seal of the congregation and her pectoral cross, gives her the cross of a simple Sister, relieves her to take her place among the Sisters. He celebrates the Mass of the Holy Spirit, assembles the members

of the Council in the common room, gives them an exhortation and the election then takes place.[4]

Each sister present was told to cast a vote. When the votes were drawn from the bishop's hat they were all for Mother Theodore. Chagrined at the failure of his scheme, the bishop asked that the meeting be kept secret and the sisters agreed. Several years passed before the other sisters found out what their bishop had done.

On receiving word, about the attempted election Mother Theodore and Bishop Bouvier of Le Mans were stunned that Bishop de la Hailandiére had acted so irresponsibly. He was informed that in France, the election was judged as ridiculous.

This caused Bishop de la Hailandiére great embarrassment and he became hardened toward the sisters at the Woods, particularly Sister St. Francis who had been left in charge during Mother Theodore's absence. The bishop, once Sister St. Francis' friend and advocate, turned his rage on her because of her loyalty to Mother Theodore.

Sister St. Francis did everything she could to hold firm to the Rules and Constitutions. The bishop took away her assigned position and gave the authority over the Congregation to Sister Basilide. He knew he could influence her and bend her will to his own. Sister Basilide was flattered by his attention and sought to please him in numerous ways. She seemed to accept his ideas more readily and basked in his friendship and esteem. But it would not be long before her disillusionment would be felt in very painful circumstances. Lacking in ability to stand up to the bishop as he continued to violate the Rule of the Congregation, she found herself torn between two authorities. It was clear to her that the bishop wanted total control of the community. Yet, Mother Theodore was the rightful authority over the community.

Sister Basilide's weak nature could not bear the constant stress that afflicted her. She wrote long, detailed letters to Mother Theodore when any opportunity presented itself.

It was clear to Mother Theodore that she must leave for America immediately. She and Sister Mary Cecilia returned to Ruillé, packed their bags, met with the postulants that would be joining them, the gardener that they had hired for the Woods, said their tearful goodbyes and left Ruillé for the final time.

How Mother Theodore's heart ached knowing that she would never see her beloved France again. Her deeply loved family, her sisters at Ruillé, her friends and benefactors would be cherished all the days of her life. Her courage in the face of all these sacrifices rose to the surface and she offered all of them to God. Not looking back she placed her trust totally in the Providence of God.

On Nov. 28, 1843, Mother Theodore and her companions arrived in Havre, France. Approaching the wharf, to their great shock they saw their ship, the *Nashville,* leaving the harbor. Mother Theodore writes:

> The Commissaire de Marine was informed of our difficulty and sent the order to let us pass, the ship was already some distance out, but we overtook it in a rowboat and shortly after, the steam tug towed us out to sea.[5]

The ship was kept in the channel for five days, tossed and turned by opposing winds. All on board recognized the mighty power of the ocean. Mother Theodore described their initial experience:

> There is nothing, perhaps, more diverting than the first gust of wind which changes the decks of a ship into a hospital ward: children crying, women moaning, men holding their heads in one hand and a basin in the other.[6]

The days and nights to follow were catastrophic. Constant storms pitched the *Nashville* like it was a toy, while passengers and crew cried out in fear. Mother Theodore encouraged all of them to pray and ask God's help. It was hard for those who did not ordinarily pray to believe that God would listen to their pleas. Mother Theodore reassured them that God would help them if they trusted him.

Suddenly the force of the winds and water caused the ship to capsize and water rushed in all the openings of the vessel leaving the passengers to feel they were doomed. But as Providence would have it, a counter gust of wind righted the ship and prevented it from being submerged. Mother Theodore's trust in God and the prayers of those on board ship had saved their lives. It was Mother Theodore's words and confidence in God's protection that strengthened their courage and enabled them to pray.

The days that followed brought storm after storm in the sea. Mother Theodore cared for the sick, using the knowledge she had from her pharmacy training. She reached out to the hungry, sharing the meager food that she and her companions had with those who had none. She brought solace and comfort to those in despair and prayed for those who had no hope.

Mother Theodore, Sister Mary Cecilia and the postulants prayed the Rosary and their other exercises of piety promising to give honor to St. Ann, patron of sailors, who had brought them to safety over the seas.

This materialized in what is known as St. Ann's Shell Chapel. The original chapel, built in 1844, was of logs. Eventually falling into decay, it was replaced in 1876 by a stone structure on the same spot, of the same dimensions and lined with the same shells.[7]

After two months of a horrifying voyage they reached the mouth of the Mississippi River on Jan. 24, 1843. Mother Theodore wrote to Mother Mary at Ruillé: "The dangers of the sea are over and those dangers have been great.... We pray you all, our good Mother and dear sisters to obtain the grace for us from our Lord that these lives which He has spared may be employed in serving Him with fidelity and love."[8]

The customary course of travel for ships headed for New Orleans was to sail north of Cuba. The Captain knowing the beating the *Nashville* had taken on the ocean waters and the rough currents ahead, wisely chose another route.

Entering the Mississippi River from the ocean waters brought great joy to the travelers. Mother Theodore wrote in her journal:

> "At length we cast anchor and the perils of the sea were over. I cannot express the feelings which at that time moved our grateful hearts. The fog had disappeared and we were lost in admiration of one of the fairest scenes of the world. The vast sea which we were on the point of quitting; the sea of another kind which we were about to enter; that forest of ships from all parts of the world, either preparing to cope with distant storms, or coming, like ourselves, to repose after their voyage – it was a magnificent spectacle."[9]

A steamer came to tow the *Nashville* to port, much to the delight of the passengers. "On January 27, they left this vessel on which they had suffered so much."[10] Mother Theodore gave thanks to God for bringing them to safety on American shores. It was not "her Indiana", however. How her heart ached and longed for her Indiana home. Her arrival at New Orleans brought refuge from the undulating movement of the sea. She could, at last, place her feet on solid ground and steady her whole being.

The Ursuline Sisters were there to welcome the weary travelers into their spacious house. As Mother Theodore had done when she first arrived at Saint Mary-of-the-Woods, she and her companions hastened to the chapel to thank God for his protection on their journey from France.

The next morning at Mass, Mother Theodore was afflicted by a burning fever and was confined to bed for seven weeks. The Ursuline Sisters took loving care of her as if she were one of their own family of Ursulines.

Even in her illness, Mother Theodore realized she needed to send her traveling comrades on to Saint Mary-of-the-Woods. How she wished she could join them, but her illness would not permit such a risk. She placed Sister Mary Cecilia in charge of the small group, but wisely kept one of the Postulants to stay with her. She entrusted Sister Mary Cecilia to tell all her sisters of the Woods about what had transpired in France and on the journey back home. She sent her love and care to each one of them and promised she would be home with them again.

As Mother Theodore began to regain her strength, she took a horse drawn carriage ride through New Orleans. It was not what she expected to see. There were "slave markets" on many streets. Negro men and women were paraded in front of raucous buyers. Some were displayed in ostentatious clothing while others were without any clothing on at all. The pain and degradation on their faces cut Mother Theodore to the core. In her words, "I would have wished to buy them all that I might say to them Go! Bless Providence. You are free"![11] At this period of history the buying and selling of Negros was a business and those who engaged in it felt no pity for the human beings that were trafficked like cattle. The grave injustice of this outrageous exploitation caused Mother Theodore deep pain and she begged God to help these slaves who had no way to help themselves.

Stopping at the cathedral she found to her dismay the same ruins that she encountered at the cathedral in Vincennes - falling walls, crumbling bricks, faded paintings, dust and dirt. To the eyes of a visitor it had all the appearances of being abandoned, but to Mother Theodore, God was present and she knelt in adoration. The great cathedrals of France in all their splendor could not compare with this humble dwelling where, in simplicity, the God of heaven and earth did dwell.

March 17th, the day scheduled for departure from New Orleans finally arrived. Mother Theodore felt such gratitude to the Ursuline Sisters for their love and excellent medical care. Had it not been for them she might not have lived to begin this journey home. Boarding the steamer they began their five day journey. She and the postulant marveled at the ease with which this vessel transversed the turbulent waters. When she sighted the Indiana shores Mother Theodore said with deep emotion: "I would have loved to kiss its soil. This land was no longer for me the land of exile; it was the portion of my inheritance, and in it I hope to dwell all the days of my life."[12]

The steamboat docked in Evansville, Indiana late that night and Mother Theodore and the postulant were met by the father of Sister Mary Magdalen Linck, a novice at Saint Mary-of-the-Woods. How comforting it was to be greeted by someone who had a connection with her Indiana home. The Linck family provided over-night hospitality to the weary travelers and took them to Mass the next morning, the feast of the Annunciation. This feast was very important to Mother Theodore since she had promised Mary, the mother of God, that she would make her known and loved always.[13]

The next day Mother Theodore and the postulant, Julienne set out by stage coach for the 55 mile journey to Vincennes. The corduroy roads jerked and jolted them so severely that their pain was acute. Not only did Mother Theodore have those hours of physical suffering to bear, but the anxiety of meeting with Bishop de la Hailandière was the source of much tension. Numerous letters from Saint Mary-of-the-Woods had warned her of the Bishop's decree to never permit her to return to Saint Mary-of-the-Woods again.

> To be ill for so long at such a time when she was so urgently needed by her Community in the woods of Indiana, seemed a heavy cross indeed, yet she bore within her frail frame the heritage from generations of hardy Breton mariners, a heart of steely courage against misfortune, tempered and exalted by supernatural faith and love. Her tender feelings, however, rendered her crosses a doubly heavy burden and often when

morally she was able to bow beneath some new trial, accepting it lovingly from the hand of God, she was nevertheless physically overwhelmed by the shock.[14]

Sisters Basilide and St. Francis Xavier implored Mother Theodore to be very careful when she met with Bishop de la Hailandière. His determination to expel her from the congregation and the diocese was known far and wide. Other warning letters urged her to act with great deference and caution toward His Lordship on the occasion of their first meeting.[15]

It was also known that unless Mother Theodore signed the articles of agreement that the bishop had drawn up, she would not be permitted to return to Saint Mary's. Sister St. Francis Xavier knew that Mother Theodore would not sign anything that was against her conscience or the Rule.

Mother Theodore was a born leader in every sense of the word. Her Sisters read it in the calm and steady gaze of her dark eyes, in the quiet courage with which she met the ordinary and extraordinary difficulties with which her position in America was beset from the very inception of the Indiana mission. She was facing now, she knew, one of the crises in her career, but she looked straight into the threatening future with a trust born of her unalterable confidence in divine Providence.[16]

Arriving in Vincennes, Mother Theodore went immediately to the convent where four of her sisters lived. The door was opened to her with cries of joy and tears.

Their mother was with them once again. Weary though she was, her gentleness and cheerfulness touched them deeply. When they sat down to eat their evening meal, Mother Theodore noticed how impoverished they were. In her Letters and Journals she wrote "They had neither a glass nor a table napkin for me, and the sum of the delicacies they could set before me was a little corned beef. But what of that? We did not even notice it."[17]

After supper the three younger sisters left Mother Theodore and Sister St. Vincent, the superior, to talk. Knowing that the Bishop had every intention of preventing her from going to Saint Mary-of-the-Woods and being with her sisters again, praying for strength, the next morning, accompanied by Sister St. Vincent, she went to see the bishop.

> Trembling with physical weakness and oppressed with apprehension and sorrow, Mother Theodore stood before Monseigneur de la Halandiere in his study. The momentous interview upon which turned the fate of the Sisters of Providence in Indiana, perhaps even in America, lasted for two hours.[18]

At first, the bishop refused to acknowledge her presence. Finally, he began to heap on her serious and harsh accusations concerning things she had never said or done.

> His Lordship then changed the conversation to speak about the money I had "stolen" from him in Paris. He said I would have to refund it to him and immediately. I tried to explain how it was that I happened to get it. He answered there was not a word of truth in what I was saying. How angry this good Bishop was![19]

Mother Theodore was exhausted and so fearful that in this tirade he would absolutely forbid her return to Saint Mary-of-the-Woods. Her daughters were anxiously awaiting her arrival. It was not to be that day. The Bishop directed her to return the next day for further conversation concerning these matters.

It was a sleepless night for Mother Theodore. Would the bishop expel her from the Diocese? Would he prevent her from returning to Saint Mary-of-the-Woods and her beloved daughters? Would the mission to America end in failure?

Arriving at the Bishop's office the next morning, Mother Theodore silently begged God to give her the strength she needed to accept whatever suffering she might have to bear. In her words:

> We returned and found Monseigneur a little less ill-disposed through one of the providential and loving dispositions of our God. Now he treated me better, and I began to think I would be able to return to St. Mary's. Believing the moment favorable, I asked permission to write a few words to announce my arrival. It was granted, and upon the Bishop's desk, itself, I wrote a note saying I would leave for St. Mary's by the first steamboat. I added that I was writing under the eyes of his Lordship, who sent his blessing to all the community.
>
> Among the countless accusations heaped upon me, one was that I was not sick at all at New Orleans, but had remained there to plot something against my Superior. The state of weakness, however, to which I was reduced was my justification. I availed myself of it to ask that nothing further be said to me about these matters and that permission be given to me to leave. It was granted.[20]

Mother Theodore boarded the steamboat that very day. She could wait no longer to go home to her beloved sisters. Arriving in Terre Haute she engaged a carriage for the remainder of the journey to Saint Mary-of-the-Woods.

Her heart beat rapidly as the carriage approached the deep ravine where they had originally arrived in 1840. Mother Theodore stepped out of the carriage, descended the slope of the steep ravine and climbed up the opposite bank with new energy. She was home.

Her sisters welcomed her with open arms. They had waited for their Mother with anxious hearts not knowing if she would ever be permitted to return. As she had done on her first arrival at the Woods, she and her sisters went to the chapel and knelt before their loving God in thanksgiving for bringing her home. Mother Theodore reflected on her journey from France, how God had been her refuge on the stormy seas, her support in that painful meeting with Mother Mary at Ruille, her strength in her quest for money in France, her survival in enduring her critical illness in New Orleans and finally God changed the heart of Bishop de la Hailandière so that she could come home to the land she loved so well.

Chapter 16

After a night of much needed rest Mother Theodore met with her beloved sisters to tell them of her experiences in France. She told them that she and Sister Mary Cecilia were warmly welcomed at Ruillé. The French sisters wanted to know all about their sisters in America. Their questions were many and specific.

- What did Saint Mary-of-the-Woods look like?
- Did they have schools yet?
- What foods did they eat there?
- Did they follow the same rule?
- How many sisters did they have now?

Mother Theodore and Sister Mary Cecilia answered all their questions with detailed descriptions. Both were so pleased that their French sisters cared deeply about the Indiana community.

Difficult as it was, Mother Theodore knew she had to tell them about the very painful meeting she had with Mother Mary. It was at this meeting that she heard for the first time that Mother Mary had decided to separate the Ruillé community from the Indiana Community. Mother Theodore told her sisters that she pleaded with Mother Mary to reconsider, but she was told the decision was final. Hearing these words was like a sword had pierced her heart. The sisters who had come from France had been told they would never be separated from the Ruillé community. That had been promised to them before they left France.

Mother Theodore told her sisters that she knew the suffering they would experience when this word reached them. This was why she had wanted to inform them in person at Saint Mary-of-the-Woods. How sad she was to learn that Mother Mary notified them of the Congregation's separation from Ruillé instead of allowing Mother Theodore that courtesy.

To lighten the conversation, Mother Theodore told the sisters who had originally come from France about the visits she had made to each one of their family homes. Their delight was audible as she gave detail after detail of each visit.

The Sisters were well aware that a major objective of her trip to France was to seek alms for their community. Having a letter from Bishop de la Hailandière authorizing her solicitation of alms, Mother Theodore presented it to Bishop Bouvier of Le Mans, France. He supported her endeavor and added an endorsement of his own. She began her appeal in Paris. Unfortunately, she could find no one there for whom she had letters of introduction. These residents had all left for their vacation homes in the country which was a great disappointment for her. Mother Theodore told the sisters of Sister Mary Cecilia's continual encouragement to go to the Chancery in Paris for financial help. Mother Theodore had resisted that step, but at Sister Mary Cecilia's final prodding she agreed to go.

When they arrived at the Chancery they were told that officials would inform the Keeper of the Seals, Monsieur Martin du Nord,[1] of her need. He sent a courier early the next morning granting them an audience. At their meeting he promised he would help them in whatever way he could. His first suggestion was that Mother Theodore write a letter requesting an audience with Queen Amelia. She did so and a week later received word from the Queen that she would meet with them the next day. The Queen welcomed them in a most gracious manner.

Describing the meeting Mother Theodore wrote:

> She inquired about our situation like a tender mother, and listened to the details with the greatest interest. Finally, after having manifested the most tender sympathy for our work, she asked us what we wished of her.[2]

One of our greatest needs at that time was our passage home. When she asked how many of us would be traveling, I told her four. She immediately offered to pay for all of us.

Having heard about our ministry in Indiana, the Queen offered to assist us financially and solicit others to contribute to the welfare of our missions. In a moment of elation the Queen said "Ah, sisters, let us save souls!"[3] It was evident that she was touched by our mission. Mother Theodore continued telling her Sisters that because of the Queen's generosity and that of many others, their table would no longer be empty. They would have food to nourish their bodies and their spirits. They would be able to pay their debts and the wages of their faithful employees. The Providence of God had once again come to their rescue.

Mother Theodore had saved the hardest topic for last – Bishop de la Hailandière. She told the sisters that their letters describing the actions of the bishop in her absence had reached her in France. How was she to respond to them without speaking ill of the Bishop? It was evident that the Bishop had resolved to direct the affairs of the community, totally disregarding the authority of the superior. He had freely changed sisters from one establishment to another; received sisters of another Congregation into the Sisters of Providence after persuading them to leave their own Congregation; appointed postulants to assist in the opening of a school. The list of interferences seemed endless. The bishop had said more than once that he had never wished to prevent the sisters from following their Rule, yet he continually violated them in his action. She added, "We have crosses here of every kind. It is in the midst of these crosses that our Congregation grows strong."[4]

Now that she was "home", she would protect their Rule with great vigilance. She praised Sister St. Francis and the members of the council for holding firm to the Holy Rule when the bishop attempted to transgress it, knowing how difficult that must have been for them. She also knew that she would be responsible to confront the bishop when he tried to circumvent her authority and violate the Rule. She went on to say:

> If ever this poor little Community becomes settled, it will be established on the cross; and that is what gives me confidence and makes me hope, sometimes even against hope.....[5]

> Calling on their trust Mother Theodore continued: You may have to wait longer than you would like, you may have to bear privations; but bear and forebear. Have confidence in the Providence that so far has never failed us. The way is not yet clear. Grope along slowly, do not press matters; be patient, be trustful.[6]

Bringing her conversation with them to a close, she told them that she would like to spend the rest of that day walking among the trees and farmland, drinking in the beauty of their woodland home. In a day or two, she would begin meeting with each of them to listen to their fears, their hopes and dreams. Now that she was home, it was time to put her energies into strengthening the life and spirituality of the community.

After their noon meal, Mother Theodore began her walk around the Saint Mary-of-the-Woods property. Signs of spring were everywhere. The beautiful trees that graced the land bore buds that soon would burst into color. the fruit-bearing cherry trees; the heart-shaped linden tree that regenerates itself; the elegant, fragrant magnolia with its glorious flowers; the sturdy oak with its valued hard wood; the pine, mimosa, ginkgo and maple. All these marked the land of Saint Mary-of-the-Woods and contributed greatly to its beauty.[7]

The more Mother Theodore walked, the more she saw: hills and dales, ravines like the one she climbed when she arrived in 1840; wide, open fields for planting; birds of many colors and song; animals both wild and tame. Nature had indeed built a playground for all to enjoy and all this beauty surrounded their home. How blessed she felt. This spring they must also plant flowers to add splashes of color to delight the eye. How good it felt to be home.

The next day Mother Theodore began meeting with each professed Sister, each novice and postulant individually. It had been so long since she had had that opportunity. Each one of them shared her anxieties brought on by the bishop's actions. They needed her to strengthen their confidence and trust and she made every effort to do so. Without passing judgment on the bishop, but letting them know she understood their pain, Mother Theodore said:

"Continue, my dear and truly chere fille, to walk in the presence of God, to do your actions solely to please Him and to bear courageously all the trials which He may permit you to have. Let the evil one make all the noise he wishes around you. Do not mind him, but put yourself entirely beyond the reach of his malice by keeping close to our Lord."[8]

Mother Theodore had a precious gift for a superior – a tender and compassionate heart.[9] She could listen to the things that worried her sisters and by her motherly way, calm their troubled spirits. How relieved and happy they were to have her home with them again.

After meeting with each of the sisters at the Motherhouse, she began to make plans to visit the establishments and her sisters on the missions. It was with eagerness that she visited the Academy at Saint Mary-of-the-Woods. The French school in the Vigo County woods had become, to a certain extent, the "model" and the best families from all over Indiana began to send their young daughters to receive solid training in their mother tongue. Booth Tarkington, esteemed writer, chose to immortalize his mother's old school in these words:

> I think that my mother's days at "old St. Mary's" were among the happiest of her life. Certainly she always spoke of them with happiness and the recollection of them was bright and vivid sixty years afterward. Two of the sisterhood whom she must have held dearest of all, for their names were so often upon my mother's lips, remain in my own memory to this day, Sister Cecilia and Sister Basilide. They must have been women of exquisite manner as well as distinguished education. They must have possessed unusual charm as well, to be so adored throughout the life of their pupil. Something rare and fine was brought from France to Saint Mary- of-the-Woods, and none of those who were students there remained unaffected by it. For lack of a better word, I must call it "distinctive". The visible effect was a manner of simplicity and gentle dignity. The students were well taught. They were really educated, and they were also given what we once spoke of as "accomplishments," for they "learned the harp, the piano, and guitar" and acquired a fine accent in the French language. What most distinguished the girls of Saint Mary-of-the-Woods, was that lovely manner they were taught there. They were taught it so well that it was not a superficial veneer. Indeed, it was rather absorbed than learned, and it was something that came from within outward. Although my mother spoke rarely of this, more often dwelling upon her affection for the Sisters and the beauty of the place itself, the manner of Saint Mary-of-the-Woods is what remains most deeply impressed upon me. It always springs to my mind whenever I delve for the true meaning of "lady".[10]

Mother Theodore would have felt so proud to read these words of Booth Tarkington. In the beginning there were many years of hardship for the school, but God had blessed this first of their establishments and his Mother Mary watched over her namesake with loving care.

On Oct. 20, 1844, Mother Theodore received word from Bishop de la Hailandière for the second time that he was opposed to her visiting her establishments without written permission from him. Since the Holy Rule required her as superior general to visit the establishments, she began this visitation at the Academy. If this angered the Bishop she would tell him once again that the Holy Rule superseded his demands.

The Academy that she visited was no longer a struggling little forest school. Its curriculum was on a par with the best and the school was drawing students from all over Indiana and other far and wide locations. Because of this:

> "The courageous spirit of the early sisters quickly built up a tradition of solidarity and amiability which was at once admired and loved by their pupils."[11]

Observing these strengths in the Academy, Mother Theodore felt that this "first-born" of their establishments was doing exactly what it was created to do, provide an excellent education for young girls.

Wanting to educate those who could not afford to attend the Academy, Mother Theodore attached to it a free school for the poor. This was a practice in France and she wanted to keep that tradition in America. As the number of Catholics in the neighborhood increased, it was evident that a school in the Village was needed. Sister St. Francis dearly loved teaching those children whose parents could not pay tuition. She especially cherished preparing them for their First Communion. Their ages ranged from 6 to 19 years, boys and girls. Some of those she prepared had never heard the word "God". Others did not know the word soul. Yet, Jesus had said, "Suffer the little ones to come unto Me." The Village school was built and many children received an outstanding education.

Looking beyond Saint Mary-of-the-Woods, Mother Theodore decided to visit the school and mission of Jasper for which she had a warm spot in her heart. After all, it was the Congregation's first establishment away from Saint Mary-of-the-Woods. She loved to call it our "eldest mission daughter." She left a vivid description of rural Jasper in spring:

> The beauty of the forests of Indiana in the Spring in the rich and lovely month of May surpasses all description. The rivers, swollen by the rains, flow through long lanes of verdure. Caressing the islands they seem to carry with them in their course and which look like floating nosegays. The trees raise their straight trunks to the height of more than one hundred and twenty feet and are crowned with tops of admirable beauty. ... how truly is this part of the globe named the <u>New World</u>.[12]

The Jasper school had suffered great poverty for several years. The early colonists of Jasper had no material wealth. Only brawn and spirit were theirs, courage to conquer the hardships of the wilderness and their grand old German faith, their best heritage from their rugged fatherland.[13]

Mother Theodore sent money to alleviate the Jasper sisters financial stress. Usually, when the sisters left the motherhouse for the missions, they were under the authority of the parish priest who was responsible for their spiritual and earthly needs. However, the priests themselves were experiencing great poverty and had little money to meet the needs of the sisters. This cycle repeated itself in the early missions of Indiana. The sisters in Jasper gave their best efforts to the school at great physical cost-overwork, fatigue and hunger. Yet, in the midst of these many sufferings, the school flourished. The parents were well pleased with the education their children were receiving and word spread quickly. As Mother Theodore visited each classroom, she was moved by what she observed. The sisters had taught these children so well that their knowledge was very evident. An excellent teacher herself, Mother Theodore felt very proud of these sisters and the success they had in the most unlikely circumstances.

Visiting with her sisters in their home once school was over, she praised them for the great difference they had made in the lives of these children. Mother Theodore had witnessed their educational keenness, but she had also seen evidence of a deep reverence and love of God. It showed in their prayers, in their religion class and in their preparation for the sacraments. How she thanked God for making all this possible.

After visiting the Jasper mission, Mother Theodore set off for the mission of Saint Peter's, opened by the bishop while she was in France. What she found was very unsettling.

> Poverty, poor diets and exposure to the sweltering humidity in summer and the frigid cold in winter left the Sisters exhausted and susceptible to illness. Tuberculosis was prevalent. These factors, combined with the physical and spiritual hardships inherent in life on the frontier, frequently led to death.[14]

In a letter to Mother Theodore, one of the two sisters serving at that mission told her how hard the winter had been. They had little wood and could barely stay warm. The snow even came into their log cabin home and covered their table. When Mother Theodore saw the way the sisters lived she wept. She wrote:

> Their log house is open to every wind, and inside there is nothing, nothing …not a key to lock out, not only the thieves, but even the wild animals that would enter their cabin. Every night we were obliged to draw up a school desk against the door to keep it closed.[15]

Seeing the conditions that existed at Saint Peter's, Mother Theodore resolved "to formulate strict guidelines to be followed when establishments were opened in the future."[16]

Observing the severe poverty of the sisters she told the bishop that the sisters must also receive wages for their teaching. She also stipulated that:

> They would give an accounting of it only to their Superior; that, in keeping with the Sister of Providence Rule, provisions would be made for a free school; and that a furnished house

would be provided for the Sisters. The Bishop looked at the guidelines and said "Do as you wish. Do whatever seems best. I approve in advance of all that you will do."[17]

Mother Theodore was stunned that the bishop so readily supported her stipulations. This agreement would ensure that her sisters would never again have to suffer living conditions such as those she had just witnessed. Being a loving superior, she recommended to the sisters that they leave their log hut and go back to Saint Mary-of-the-Woods with her. Living in dire poverty as they were, they still begged Mother Theodore to permit them to stay at Saint Peter's and continue to teach the children in their school. How could she stand in the way of such apostolic zeal? She told them she would reassess the situation at the time of the retreat and praised them for their willingness to endure such hardship for the good of others.

The last of the visitations to be made at this time was to Vincennes. This school also had been established by Bishop de la Hailandière in Mother Theodore's absence. The superior of this school was quite ill and therefore could not give the proper supervision to her teachers. As a result the classes in the school were in great disorder. Mother Theodore wrote:

> We spent three days at Vincennes to give the Postulants some idea of the art of teaching. We taught the class in front of them. We gave them a method and advice we thought necessary to give a little emulation to these little hearts already so cold.[18]

The postulants were exceedingly grateful for Mother Theodore's help. Her expertise as a teacher was very visible to them and they hung on every word she spoke. "Example is the best teacher" they had frequently heard and the proof of that was right in front of them.

After visiting all these establishments, how happy Mother Theodore was to see all the good her sisters were doing in educating the children of Saint Mary-of-the-Woods, at the Academy, the Village School, Jasper,

Saint Peter's, and Vincennes schools. Indeed, the reason for the sisters coming to America was being fulfilled. Providence was guiding their footsteps one step at a time.

Returning to Saint Mary-of-the-Woods after all her visitations brought joy to her heart. Being home with her sisters lifted her spirit and energized her whole being. How blessed she felt to be with such committed and spiritual women religious.

While she had been in Vincennes she had been approached by a young priest, Father Delaune, who had been appointed pastor at St. Michael's Church at Madison, Indiana. He asked Mother Theodore if she would send Sisters of Providence to staff the school at Madison. She told him that she would be glad to mail to him stipulations that had been set for new establishments. On her return to the Woods she wrote and sent the detailed stipulations. He responded quickly stating that he would provide a suitable dwelling for the sisters, plus two hundred dollars a year. He went on to say that, in time he would pay the rent and furnish their home. Mother Theodore was pleased with the efforts of this young priest to provide adequate housing for the sisters and accepted the new mission in Madison. She chose Sister St. Ligouri to be Superior and Sisters Mary Celestia and Catherine to teach the children. As she did with each new establishment, Mother Theodore accompanied these three sisters to their new mission. She did all she could do to help them settle in and spent a few days with them, helping them organize their school.

Unaware of the storm their arrival had awakened, they looked upon Madison as a promising field for their zeal. It was not long before they began to experience "hardships of a different character, but greater than they had yet experienced anywhere...."[19]

Madison was a stronghold of Protestantism: Prejudice against the school and the Sisters was present from the beginning.

The Sisters were ridiculed; stones were thrown at them in the streets; they were insulted....ruffians followed the Sisters on the 2 mile daily walk to Mass and back, throwing stones and eggs and snowballs, even spitting upon their religious habit. The Protestants were enraged that the Sisters were in Madison.[20]

It took some years for this prejudice to change. The excellent education that the sisters provided for the children ended the intolerance that had prevailed for so long. The Sisters of Providence gave 60 years of devoted service to the people of Madison, Indiana.

On July 21, 1846, Mother Theodore wrote in a letter to Bishop Bouvier, "We are opening a new house after retreat in Fort Wayne, in the northern part of the state. They propose to give us a brick house with a garden and a little meadow."[21] Because of this, Mother Theodore approved the opening of a parish school in Fort Wayne. Mother Theodore, Sister Basilide and the three sisters that would be missioned there: Sister Mary Magdalen, Sister Catherine and Sister Caroline set out to make the foundation. This would be Mother Theodore's first new establishment in northern Indiana. It is recorded on the first page of the house register in the handwriting of Mother Theodore:

"The establishment of the Sisters of Providence was founded in September, 1846 by the Reverend Mr. Julien Benoit, Pastor of Saint Augustine's Church."

Father Benoit, on meeting Mother Theodore recognized that he was in the presence of a saint. "Her crystal clear glance revealed to him the depths of that candid, upright and courageous soul on fire with the love of God."[22]

St. Augustine's School opened in September, 1846 and there were 60 students enrolled immediately. This foundation became very important as it was the first catholic school in Fort Wayne.

During the final months of 1846, Mother Theodore felt pressured, once again, to ask the bishop for the deed to the land at Saint Mary-of-the-Woods, which he had refused to give her so many times. She felt that the deed was being withheld from her because of his anger toward the community. All she ever wanted from him was the deed to their land and his approval of their Holy Rule. Finally, after entreating the bishop one more time, he gave her the title to the land. Now the sisters could build a much needed addition to the Academy at Saint Mary-of-the-Woods. Sad to say, the document that he gave her carried a clause that rendered it null and void. Because of this, Mother Theodore could not enlarge the boarding school on land that was not theirs. The bishop had once again given them reason to distrust him. No matter what they did, they were always under the shadow of the bishop's discontent.

Word that the bishop had submitted his resignation to Rome began to reach Mother Theodore. Many hoped it would be accepted and he would soon leave the governing of the diocese. "Mother Theodore did not think there was any one in the world so universally despised as the Bishop of Vincennes. Yet, she said, he had many good qualities. He was pious, zealous, serious, possessed of excellent morals, etc. How much harm she thought, is done by the least faults in persons placed over others."

"If, Monsignor remains, I will have to go," she said.[23]

In a letter to Bishop Bouvier, Mother Theodore wrote:

> When I arrived in Vincennes on May 18, 1847....I went with my traveling companion to present myself to the bishop. His Lordship refused to receive us. We presented ourselves a second time; we were no more fortunate than the first[24].

Mother Theodore decided since the bishop would not see them, that they would leave by stage coach for Saint Mary-of-the-Woods. It happened that Sister St. Vincent, the superior of the Vincennes school had to see the Bishop the next morning. Mother Theodore said to her "If you can succeed in inducing Monsignor to see me for only a few moments, that would be a good way to stop the scandal".[25]

Mother Theodore was referring to the refusal of the bishop to see her. This was known throughout the town and the people were talking. When Sister St. Vincent asked the bishop if he would see Mother Theodore for just a minute he agreed. That good news was received with great joy. Mother Theodore left for the Bishop's office asking God to be with her. When she arrived the Bishop was very angry with her and heaped upon her a tempest of reproaches bitterly condemning her for things which she had never even thought.

> "He said I was ambitious, that I was usurping the superiority to the prejudice of my sisters. I replied quietly that I was not opposed to an election, that I still would not oppose it, but that I feared that the community would not consent to one."[26]

At these words the bishop became still more angry and said to her severely:

> "Very well, I forbid you to return to Saint Mary's. I withdraw from you all your rights as superior. I release you from your vows for Indiana and I forbid you to have any relations, even by letter with the Sisters of Providence of Saint Mary's and to remain in this Diocese."[27]

Mother Theodore endured these castigations for over a quarter of an hour. When she begged him to allow her to go to Saint Mary's to take care of the things that needed to be finished, he refused. "After a moment of reflection" wrote Mother Theodore, "I knelt down, and begging Monsignor to pardon me the faults of my administration, I asked his blessing and said goodbye, assuring him of my submission."[28] The bishop locked her in that room and left for his dinner.

When the bishop left she realized that this was the final blow. She had just been deposed, dismissed from the Congregation, forbidden to return to Saint Mary-of-the-Woods or to communicate with her sisters. Tradition has it that she was also excommunicated since the Bishop had always threatened to do so.

Her heart was broken when she realized that all this took place because of her constancy and fidelity to the Rule she had vowed to observe.

Jesus' words "Blessed are you when they shall persecute you, and revile you and speak all that is evil against you untruly for My sake: rejoice and be glad, for your reward is very great in Heaven."[29]

These words gave her the strength and hope she so needed. The sisters fearing the worst went looking for her in the bishop's house. He finally unlocked the door and Mother Theodore fell on her knees begging his blessing. He blessed her and silently motioned her out. Sister St. Vincent and Sister Marie Xavier took her back to their home. Mother Theodore told them all that had transpired and asked them to send word to the sisters at Saint Mary-of-the-Woods since she could not return there due to the order of the bishop.

The next morning she made arrangements for her departure from the diocese. She gave Sister St. Vincent and Sister Marie Xavier her keys, the money and papers she had with her, keeping only a small amount of money for travel, as she left the diocese. That night, the stress of all that had happened to her, broke down her frail health and an attack of pleurisy brought her near death. She asked for a confessor but the vicar general refused to come. A young priest consented to hear her confession. "I was happy to die," she wrote later, "for it seemed to me that only thus could the Congregation be saved from total ruin."[30] Her anguish of mind increased the fever and the doctor forbade her to leave Vincennes. For three weeks she remained under his care sometimes at the point of death.

Sister Mary Xavier, who had observed Bishop de la Hailandière's dismissal of Mother Theodore returned to Saint Mary-of-the-Woods the next day to inform the sisters of what had taken place. As soon as the sisters received word of Mother Theodore's expulsion, they immediately determined that they would all go with her. They sent this word to the bishop, but he returned their letter unopened. Father John Corbe, their chaplain, sent his resignation to the bishop who retaliated with the questions, "What do you want to leave the diocese for? Those who make the trouble ought to be the ones to stay and settle it?"[31]

Immediately the bishop sent a letter to all the professed sisters, (including the lay sisters) at Saint Mary-of-the-Woods giving them the right to elect a new superior general. That proposal was not accepted and all the sisters, novices and postulants unanimously agreed not to stay in Indiana, but to join Mother Theodore wherever she would go.

They began packing trunks with all the important papers of the community and all of the money they could gather from their savings. They were arranging to sell their cows for four strong horses to pull the heavy wagons that they would use for their departure. They were very aware that the Bishop had declared that any one of them that followed Mother Theodore would be excommunicated.

Every sister wrote a letter to Mother Theodore encouraging her and promising their loyalty to her. The community sent Sister Olympiade to give Mother Theodore her experienced nursing help. Her physician, Dr. Baty, gave orders that Mother Theodore must have rest because of her extreme weakness. Sister Olympiade would be the perfect one to keep others from interrupting Mother Theodore's quiet.

The Eudist President of Saint Gabriel's College, Father Bellier came begging to see Mother Theodore to share important news from France with her. He showed her a passage in a letter that had a quote from Pope Pius IX stating "I have accepted the resignation of the Bishop of Vincennes and have named his successor."[32] This was very good news and it brought much hope to Mother Theodore. A week later Bishop de la Hailandière received a letter from his brother in France telling him the Holy Father had named his successor. The bishop said the word from Rome was not official and he had no intention of leaving the diocese. His plan was to stay and assist the new bishop, Very Reverend John Stephen

Bazin, Vicar General of the Diocese of Mobile. Bishop de la Hailandière was not correct in citing church law concerning his present position. In fact, his jurisdiction over the Vincennes diocese ended the moment he received word that Rome had accepted his resignation. As a result, Father Corbe decided to wait for the new bishop to arrive before making any life changes and returned to Saint Mary-of-the-Woods where he was warmly welcomed.

Mother Theodore, still in the grip of fever, was unable to assess her present situation. Was she still bound by all the penalties imposed on her by the bishop? Was she still deposed, dismissed from the Congregation, forbidden to return to Saint Mary's, cast out of the diocese and even possibly excommunicated? How would she even find out? Because the Holy Father, Pope Pius IX, had accepted his resignation as bishop, Bishop de la Hailandière sent a letter to the sisters renouncing all his rights over them. It was clear to the sisters that his legal authority over them was finished. This letter was a release for Mother Theodore and the interdictions that had held her captive. Writing to Bishop Bouvier she said, "It seemed to me that Providence had intervened and I could now return to Saint Mary's."[33]

Because of her weakness she was carried aboard the steamboat. In a matter of thirty hours she was at Saint Mary-of-the-Woods. She arrived home on June 10, 1847, to a loving welcome from all her sisters who met her in procession. The people of Terre Haute fired a canon in her honor and the workmen at Saint Mary's fired a volley of gunshots to welcome her. Their neighbors and the students of the Academy joined in this wonderful day of rejoicing.

Being home, Mother Theodore had time to convalesce. Her forest was verdant and the songs of the birds brought her much joy. She would walk this land she loved so much. Gradually her body began to heal and her spirit grew stronger, "all will be well," she said, "all will be well."

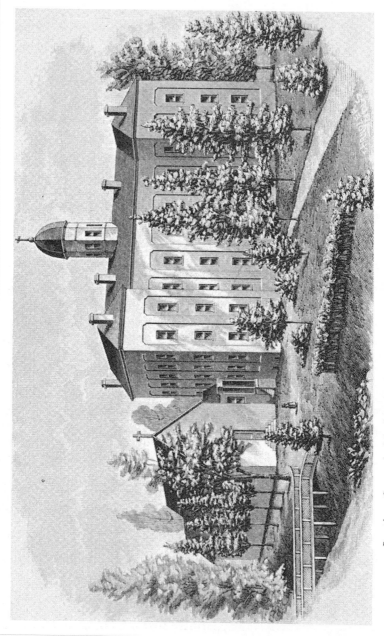

Providence Convent built by Saint Mother Theodore Guerin in 1855 was destroyed by fire in 1889.

Chapter 17

After Mother Theodore's recuperation from her illness she was anxious to return to the many responsibilities that awaited her attention.

Unexpectedly, Bishop Basin contacted her and expressed a strong desire to open a pharmacy in Vincennes for the sick poor. Knowing her former training in pharmacy work, he invited her to expand the ministries she had begun in the diocese and take on this new venture to care for the sick.

An article in the Constitutions stated: "They will have a pharmacy in each establishment, will give remedies gratuitously to the poor, sell them at a modest price to the rich and with the profit they draw from this, support the pharmacy."[1]

Mother Theodore was delighted to have the Bishop invite her to begin this ministry in Indiana. She and Sister Olympiade gathered all the herbs that would be needed from their own woods. Mother Theodore chose Sister Joachim to direct the little pharmacy that was housed in the school of the Sisters of Providence in Vincennes on March 22, 1848. Many sick people, both rich and poor, frequented the pharmacy and found relief from their pain and discomfort. To be able to fulfill the Constitutions with the establishment of this pharmacy brought Mother Theodore much joy.

Soon after having his dream fulfilled by Mother Theodore, Bishop Bazin suddenly became very ill with pneumonia. Father Corbe received word that the pneumonia had advanced and the bishop was dying. He sent for Father de Saint Palais to be with the bishop during his final hours. Mother Theodore was also contacted and was present in the room quietly praying for him. Bishop Bazin said to her, "Tell your sisters that if I had lived, I would have tried to do much for them." He took his last breath on Easter Sunday, April 23, 1848, six months since his consecration as Bishop.

Vincennes grew quickly with the presence of a pharmacy in its city. Not so Terre Haute. It was a typical frontier town with streets of mud, horses tethered to posts outside the few stores and wagons hardly able to navigate the flooded areas.

Father Simon Petit Lalumiere arrived in Terre Haute in December 1842. Catholics were very few in numbers, but Father Petit Lalumiere had a strong longing to build a school to provide an education for their children. He bought land for the school on June 28 1848. After committing himself to provide the building for the school, he asked Mother Theodore to take charge of the building and supervision of the establishment. She readily gave her "yes". However, the inclement weather, lack of money and illness prevented the school from opening until Jan. 2 1849. As was her custom, Mother Theodore accompanied the sisters who would teach in the school that would be dedicated to Saint Vincent. On opening day there were only a small number of students, but day by day that number increased as parents heard the children's excitement about what they were learning. In November 1849 enrollment had reached 90 students and continued to grow.

Mother Theodore visited the classes at Saint Vincent's school frequently and held public examinations so the students would have the opportunity to demonstrate their achievements. One mother was quoted as saying:

> I do not know how they do it, but they teach the girls all they wish, and after classes teach them all sorts of crafts. The children love them so much that they call them their mothers. Indeed, I would not object if they made a Catholic of my daughter. That religion must be good which can produce such kind beings.[2]

The protestants of Terre Haute "all agree in saying that the Catholic religious are the best educators of youth."[3] With the enrollment reaching 140 in 1855, it was recognized that "the sisters were breaking down the barriers of hostility and misunderstanding among the Protestants."[4]

At that time in history, the ravages of epidemics were taking a terrible toll particularly on the lives of the poor. Parents frequently fell victim to these epidemics and left their children orphaned. Mother Theodore's heart was deeply touched by the plight of these children. Being a woman of action she opened an orphanage for girls in the convent and in the school at Vincennes on Aug. 29 1849. This event took place at the beginning of the new Bishop de Saint Palais' administration, although all the arrangements had been made by the recently deceased Bishop Bazin.[5]

Mother Theodore was not comfortable taking charge of the orphaned boys at that time. She felt the boys needed a male influence to give them guidance. Because of this, Bishop de Saint Palais entrusted the care of the boys to some pious lay people. Unfortunately, this arrangement was unsuccessful.

Father Sorin at Notre Dame, Indiana, was approached to see if some of his Holy Cross Brothers could assume this ministry. However, Father Sorin was unable to take charge of the orphaned boys because cholera had caused a great loss to his community. He had lost 30 of his brothers to the disease.

In her own inimitable way, Mother Theodore's tender heart enabled her to include the abandoned boys in her care. Their new home was the orphanage at Highland, near Vincennes. The boys moved in on April 1 1851. Mother Theodore wrote to Bishop Bouvier in France, "There are at present 47 girls and 32 boys."[6] She remembered the words of Jesus who said, "Because you have done it to the least of these, my little ones, you have done it to me,"[7] and so it was done.

Mother Theodore recognized that the Thralls house that had been a home for the Sisters of Providence for so many years could no longer house the increasing number of sisters at Saint Mary-of-the-Woods. Young women seeking to give their lives to God continued to enter the community. By 1851 there were close to 70 members in the Congregation. While the bishop was at Saint Mary-of-the-Woods for retreat he determined that the sisters must have a new and larger home. Placing his decision before the council and promising to supplement the cost with a gift of $500.00 to be given at once and again when he came back from France. Mother Theodore rose to the challenge. That summer of 1851 was spent amassing the building materials for the new motherhouse. Her trust in Divine Providence never failed her. In July 1851 she could write to France:

> We are now well ahead in paying off our debts; in fact, we might say that we have no more debts. We still owe fifteen hundred dollars to one person in Madison, but it is for property which we purchased and which is worth more than that amount. The other debts are of little consequence.[8]

As Mother Theodore contemplated the new motherhouse, she recalled the wretched cabin which served as a chapel when she and her sisters arrived at Saint Mary-of-the-Woods. She was determined that never again would the Eucharist be housed in such miserable surroundings.

Work on the motherhouse building was slowed because of the severe winter weather, yet the men kept hauling stones over the frozen roads. Just keeping up with money for the weekly payroll caused Mother Theodore a great deal of anxiety. She wrote to Mother Mary: "We are beginning to build a house which will cost more than fifty thousand francs, a terrible undertaking for little persons like us. I feel my courage is slipping away at the thought."[9] But as time went on, the missions that Mother Theodore had established began to contribute solid amounts of money to help defray the payroll and supplies needed for the motherhouse building. Mother Theodore writing to Mother St. Charles in France said:

> Providence has succored us in a remarkable manner in the past year. Never did a workman come for his wage without my being able to pay it. I have paid out including this year, twelve thousand dollars, sixty- three thousand francs….we have paid fifty thousand francs for our motherhouse. Our debts, yet standing are from twenty to twenty-five thousand francs.[10]

In July, Mother Theodore wrote her circular letter inviting the sisters home for their annual retreat. Her heart was filled with love and gratitude to God for this last great benefit – their new home. She recalled to them the poor frame house where they had been received in charity twelve years earlier.[11]

Tears flowed when the mission sisters and the motherhouse sisters beheld their new motherhouse for the first time – particularly their new chapel. Remembering their crowded quarters in the Thralls farmhouse, they rejoiced in the spaciousness of this new motherhouse. On Sunday, Aug. 7 1853, Mother Theodore prayed, "O my God, grant that all who dwell in this house may love thee much, may love one another, and may never forget why they came here."[12]

As others began to observe the teaching skills of the Sisters of Providence, many requests were made to Mother Theodore to open schools staffed by her sisters throughout Indiana. Father Deydier, pastor in Evansville, IN begged Mother Theodore to provide a school there to educate the children of the immigrants who were arriving in droves. The population of the city increased in three years from 3,225 to nearly 8,000. The need for a good school was evident, but money was scarce because of the funds required for the motherhouse building. Bishop de Saint Palais came to their rescue by buying the house near the church that would serve as the school. It was in need of many repairs, but the sisters were zealous in their desire to get the house ready to become their school.

Mother Theodore and the four sisters that were named for the Evansville mission left Saint Mary-of-the-Woods on Aug. 19 1853. Arriving in Evansville they found that no preparations had been made for them. There was not a piece of furniture in the house and everything was dirty. They spent the next day cleaning the house and the next week sleeping on straw on the floor.[13]

Mother Theodore smiled as she remembered sleeping on the straw in the Thralls' house when they first arrived from France. How long ago that seemed. She used the little money she had to buy the most necessary furniture for the house where these sisters would live and teach the children.

Amazingly, on September 5, they started classes. Sixty students who came from very poor families arrived. There were no desks, no benches and no books. But the Sisters of Providence knew how to teach and those who had originally jeered at them finally realized that the children were learning a great deal. In less than a month the school named Saint Joseph had almost 100 students.

Soon after the Evansville school was established, the pastor of St. Michael's church in Madison, Ind., Father DuPontavice, contacted Mother Theodore hoping that she would send sisters to staff the school he had built in North Madison. Since Mother Theodore was fully occupied in setting up the school in Evansville, she sent word to Father DuPontavice that she would send two sisters to teach at his school. She asked Sister Mary Cecilia to accompany the two sisters to North Madison. The house that was promised to them was not secured and no dwelling was available when they arrived. The pastor proceeded to rent two rooms for the sisters in the home of a family in the parish. Father DuPontavice had built a brick church under which was a large schoolroom where in December of 1853 there were 80 children taught by the two Sisters of Providence. Mother Theodore had planned to go to North Madison as soon as she was assured that the school in Evansville was running smoothly.

As she left Evansville she was attacked by the dreaded malaria. Her 10 days of suffering caused her much anxiety because of her worry about her sisters in North Madison. As soon as she was physically able, Sister Olympiade was sent to accompany her to North Madison. When Mother Theodore arrived there she was distressed to see the two rooms that had been provided for the two sisters in a parishioner's home. After some prodding from Mother Theodore, Father DuPontavice built a stone house for the sisters.

Having Mother Theodore there with them gave them renewed energy. Their school had opened in September and they had to teach in the two rooms they had rented for their living quarters. Living and working in such tight quarters of course took a toll on their relationship with each other. Mother Theodore, being the observant person that she was, tried to encourage them. She told them "Bear with the defects of one another. Endeavor not to cause others to suffer, and you, yourself, try to endure the little annoyances which are unavoidable in the necessary relations with others. We often cause pain to one another on account of the differences of our dispositions and natural inclinations."[14]

Mother Theodore warmly praised these two sisters for providing an excellent education for the children. How skillful she was in drawing forth the best in everyone.

The small village of Lanesville in southern Indiana near the mighty Ohio River was one of the important stage coach stops in Indiana. Mother Theodore was quite familiar with it when she traveled south. Because by 1843 many Catholics had moved there. Father Charles Opperman built a church for the parishioners with an adjoining rectory. In March of 1854 the newly appointed pastor, Father Alphonce Munchina, began immediately to build a school for the children of the 120 families who lived in the parish. He turned over the rectory for the living quarters for the Sisters he hoped would come to teach the children.[15]

Accompanying the three sisters who were chosen for the Lanesville mission, Mother Theodore looked forward to helping them provide an education for all the children there. The pastor had already visited the 120 families in his parish to see if they would support the new school. Their response was an overwhelming, "yes." When Mother Theodore and her sisters arrived, the parishioners gave them a joyful welcome and took them in procession to their convent home. The appreciation of these parents touched the hearts of the sisters and gave them the confidence they needed for this new mission. Mother Theodore stayed to help them prepare for the opening of school. To Sister Basilide who was assigned to teach in the new school she said, "Well, my daughter, ours is a preparation for the generation that will succeed us, and eminent good will be done this way by us. You may not live to see it, but you will have sown the seed, and your sisters will come to reap what will have been sown."[16]

The time had come for Sister Basilide and Mother Theodore to leave Lanesville. They boarded a steamboat to reach Madison and asked to be called when it was time to leave the boat that night. However no one remembered to notify them and the boat pulled away from the wharf and traveled some distance up the river before the mistake was discovered. The decision was made to get off at the first stop and wait for the next boat that would take them back to Madison.

After several hours of waiting, a boat heading down river arrived and they quickly boarded it, only to find out after they left the shore that it, too, did not stop at Madison. The captain promised to let them off in a skiff which came along side in the middle of the river. But rough water made their disembarking very dangerous. In her own words she described the accident:

> In descending to a canoe Sister Basilide and I both fell into the river, the boat being pushed off too soon by a man leaping into it. Sister was rescued immediately, but I was hanging on for some time in the water sustained by my left hand only, which caught onto the edge of the skiff. My strength was fast failing, but the angels came to my assistance. May God be blessed![17]

Mother Theodore was quickly taken to the sisters' home in Madison where every precaution was taken to offset the consequences of the accident. This prompt treatment delayed the full effect on her body. It was months before that was realized.

When Mother Theodore returned to Saint Mary-of-the-Woods she did not tell anyone what had happened. The experience was so terrible for her that she could not even give voice to its remembrance. The sisters noticed that she seemed weaker than usual and she would tire more quickly.

A little girl who was brought to the boarding school from the town where Mother Theodore landed told a little about the accident. The sisters at Saint Mary-of-the-Woods were in shock when they heard the details about what had happened. When they came home for the annual retreat, Sister Basilide informed all the sisters who had come from the missions. No wonder Mother Theodore had not wanted to speak of it. From this time forward her health seriously declined and she was unable to carry out her responsibilities until spring came.

In July of 1855, Reverend Edward Martinovic came to Saint Mary-of-the-Woods to ask Mother Theodore for sisters to teach at his school in Columbus, Ind. Columbus was a town where she had frequently stopped on her way to Madison. She was well acquainted with Father Martinovic and she gladly said "yes" to his request for sisters. Her one disappointment was that she could not accompany the sisters to their new mission because of her illness. She asked Sister Mary Cecilia to be her representative, knowing that she would help the sisters prepare for the opening day of school on Sept. 8, 1855. There were only 40 students, but the education there was of great value for years to come. The school lasted until the beginning of the Civil War.

This school in Columbus was to be the final establishment of Mother Theodore's life. She, who was recognized by the French government for her excellence in teaching, had opened many schools, two orphanages and a pharmacy in the few years she had been in Indiana.

In the fall, Mother Theodore's health grew stronger and she was able to visit the missions for the last time. She brought to these schools many years of experience in the classroom, demonstrating the best methods available. Speaking to her sisters she said:

> Have you sometimes thought, my dear daughters, that you are called to do on earth what our Lord Himself did? He instructed and you instruct. He was surrounded by little children and you spend your lives among them. You must possess the indispensible virtues. They are justice and kindness. Justice, in order to reward and punish each one of our pupils according to her merits. But if it is necessary to be just, it is necessary above all to be kind....I recommend to you never to use rough words or ridicule to punish your children; speak to them with respect and they will respect you and respect themselves.[18]

After visiting all the mission schools Mother Theodore's health deteriorated once again and she had to return to Saint Mary-of-the-Woods. She realized that she had made her last visit to the establishments. She carried each place in her heart, remembering details of each school. Not to be able to visit the children and their teachers again was a great sorrow for her.

Mother Theodore's dear friend, Sister St. Francis, was quite ill when Mother Theodore returned home. Always delicate, her body could not resist the violent attack of "tetanus", an infection of the nerves for which there was no cure. The ravages of this illness left her with a raging fever and slight delirium. It was difficult for the sisters to see Sister St. Francis in such pain. She had been with them for "14 years, having witnessed the sublime life of divine love. She was now to show them in a short illness of eight days how the saints die."[19] Mother Theodore sat at her side talking to her friend, praying for her, preparing her for her journey to God who loved her so much. Sister St. Francis turned to Mother Theodore and told her she would be joining her in heaven soon.

On Wednesday, January 30, after many days of actually seeing Jesus and the utter beauty of heaven, Sister St. Francis sat up in bed, looked lovingly at her crucifix with eyes full of love and died.[20]

This was a great blow to the heart of Mother Theodore. It was a personal loss in many ways. In a firm voice she said to her grieving sisters, "my dear sisters since we have a sacrifice to make let us make it generously...."[21] Her own heart was breaking, yet she wiped her tears, called upon the strength and courage that only God can give to make preparations for the funeral of Sister St. Francis. Mother Theodore, herself, was not physically strong enough to attend the funeral beyond the Chapel for the Requiem Mass. How she yearned to be able to be with her dear friend when she was buried. After the sisters returned from the grave-site, Mother Theodore spoke to them about the loss they were all experiencing because of Sister St. Francis' death. She spoke of her virtue and the example she had given to all of them. No one could possibly know the deep hurt of her own heart in the loss of this sister whom she dearly loved.

In writing to the Superiors at Ruillé, Mother Theodore said:

I am bringing Sister Mary Cecilia to the Motherhouse. A new era is about to begin for this congregation.....I hope it will be an era for its progress and well-being....the death of Sister St. Francis has plunged our little congregation into the greatest consternation. She was loved by all her sisters and she loved them all.[22]

Soon, after the death of Sister St. Francis, Mother Theodore's health began to deteriorate rapidly and she became weaker by the day. She remained in her room except for daily Mass and the instructions she had always given them. Only now her instructions focused on the things she wanted them to remember after her death.

Love her as they did, it was difficult for them to even imagine being without her. Who would lead them? Who would give them advice? Who would exhort them to be better than they were? Who would love them as their "old Mother Theodore" did?

So many fears welled up in them all.

Mother Theodore could read their worries. After all, they were truly her daughters and she knew them so well. She told them she would welcome them to come and talk with her and they did so. One by one they came and her words brought peace to their troubled spirits.

Remembering the words of Sister St. Francis as she was dying, that "Mother Theodore would join her in heaven very soon", Mother Theodore realized how true those words were.

Her sisters prayed without ceasing. They could not believe that she would die and implored God to spare her life. As Mother Theodore watched her life ebbing away she said, "Do not let me die without the sacraments." Father Corbe, their beloved Chaplain, administered the last rites. It was May 12, 1856, two days before her death. After receiving the sacraments a great quiet and peace came over her. All the memories of Etables, Ruillé, Rennes, Soulaines, the journey to America, Saint Mary-of-the-Woods, Indiana, the many crosses they experienced, and most of all her beloved daughters, passed one by one through her consciousness. Yet, there was no pain in the memory of them. Where there had been suffering there was now peace. Where there had been joy, there was now the abundance of delight in its memory. How blessed she was.

Her sisters were gathered at her bedside silently weeping as she quietly prepared herself for her final moments. On her last night, the sisters took turns sitting with her, so she would not be alone. It was May 14, 1856.

While her body was in the pangs of death, her soul was very much at peace. She knew her life from birth to death had been lived full of love for God. And now she was about to enter into God's presence and the eternal happiness of heaven. What greater joy could there possibly be! She took her final breath and went home to the God she loved so much.

Beatification

All those who knew Mother Theodore recognized her holiness. Pope John Paul II beatified her on October 15, 1998 in Saint Peter's Square, Rome. Thousands of pilgrims from around the world were present to honor Mother Theodore. Pope John Paul II agreed with the investigative findings that a "miracle healing" had taken place with Mother Theodore's intervention. Pope John Paul II described her spirit and character as "a perfect blend of humanness and holiness." He went on to say "Mother Theodore lived a life of extraordinary love. Her love of God totally filled her being. From that love came her deep caring for people in their sufferings and their joys. Her love embraced even those who caused her pain and anguish. She transformed the hardest hearts by her inspired words", he said.

A few months after that special day of Beatification in Rome, the bishops of Indiana gathered to celebrate Eucharistic Liturgy in the Church of the Immaculate Conception at Saint Mary-of-the-Woods. The church was filled to overflowing with pilgrims from each of the dioceses in Indiana and beyond. Archbishop Buechlein of the Archdiocese of Indianapolis invited all present to keep close to Mother Theodore and follow the virtues that were so evident in her life.

There is a plaque on her casket that reads; "What have we to do in order to be saints? Nothing extraordinary; nothing more than what we do every day. Only do it for his love."

Canonization Of Blessed Mother Theodore Guerin

On February 21,2006, Blessed Mother Theodore Guerin, foundress of the Sisters of Providence of Saint Mary-of-the-Woods was approved for sainthood by Pope Benedict XVI. This wonderful news was received by the General Superior who immediately relayed it to all Sisters of Providence in our Congregation, to the Archbishop and other bishops of Indiana. Our donors, families, and the public all received the news within the span of a few short hours. The whirlwind of activities began at once. There were committees to form, travel plans to be made, prayers to be written, hundreds of questions to be answered. In France, M. Leon wrote, "God sustained her, fortified her heart, lifted up her soul in proportion as her duties became more numerous. No one knew her without loving her."

Pope Benedict announced in July that Mother Theodore's canonization would be Oct. 15, 2006 at Saint Peter's Square, Vatican City. A journey to Rome that eventually included more than 1,000 pilgrims was planned. The Congregation announced that a book of names would be taken to Rome listing those who wished to join the canonization in spirit. Several hundred asked to be included.

For the Sisters of Providence of Saint Mary-of-the-Woods, Indiana and the Sisters of Providence of Ruille, France this day was a wonderful spiritual experience. We had known all along that our Mother Theodore was a saint, but to have the world know it and to share her with the world was the greatest gift.

End Notes

Chapter I – Notes

[1] "Etats de Service de Laurent Guérin," ASMW.

[2] Birth Certificate, Anne-Thérèse Guérin, Etables, October 3, 1798. Registre des Actes de Naissance, An VII, acte 2. Mairie, Etables-sur-Mer. Copy, ASMW.

[3] Jean-Baptiste Moisan, Conférences ecclésiastiques de 1892, in Le Diocese de Saint-Brieuc pendant la période révolutionnaire, Notes et documents, Saint-Brieuc, 1894, p. 250. Laurent Tréguy (1758-1804) was born in Etables. At the outbreak of the Revolution he was stationed at the Catherdral of Saint-Brieuc. He returned to his native canton, where he remained all during the years of turmoil. "He did not cease to do good, night and day. He retired here and there, even in the village, in the midst of the insurgents, so to speak....Under various disguises, he visited and consoled, insofar as he could, the poor sick. Trustworthy persons in every part of the parish kept him informed. Then they announced to the others that on such a day or night, at such an hour, M. Tréguy would hear confessions, baptize, and celebrate Holy Mass."

[4] Letter of the Abbé Le Mené, Curé-Doyen of Etables-sur-mer, to Mother Mary Cleophas Foley, February 28, 1912. ASMW.

[5] Sister Mary Theodore Le Touzé, Notes, Notes 13, 14. ASMW.

[6] Letter of Mother Theodore to Mother Mary, Saint Mary-of-the-Woods, October 3, 1842. ASMW.

[7] Birth certificate, Marie-Jeanne Guérin, <u>Registre communal de l 'an XI, 20 de pluviose, acte no. 4,</u> Mairie, Etables-sur-mer.

[8] Information furnished by Sister Ange de Jésus, Archivist, Sisters of the Holy Spirit, Saint-Brieuc: The Daughters of the Holy Spirit arrived in Etables in 1761. On March 25, 1761 they took possession of the "House of the Little Charitable Schools" situated <u>sous le bourg</u> near the Gouret Spring. They succeeded Mademoiselle de Villeroy....In 1793 there were two Sisters, Anne Guguen, Superior, and Marie-Helene Briand, who were expelled from the house. Marie-Helene Briand (Sr. Mie Therese) withdrew to her mother's house at Etables; returned to Etables at the latest in 1803. In 1808 Anne-Marie Burel is named as Superior, with Scholastique Maillot. The instruction in the "Little Charitable Schools" was very elementary: reading, writing....There was question rather of a Christian education, of the formation of good housewives among the children of the people, according to the <u>Rule of the Daughters of the Holy Spirit</u>, of 1778.

[9] Sister Mary Theodosia Mug, <u>Life and Lifework of Mother Theodore Guérin,</u> New York, 1904, p. 21.

[10] Sister Mary Theodore, <u>Note 10</u>, Sister Mary Theodosia, p. 23.

[11] Marc-Etienne Duval-Villebogard (1751-1823). Born at Saint-Brieuc. Having refused the oath, was banished to Jersey in 1795. After his return, appointed to Etables May 21, 1804; installed as Dean of Uzel February 26, 1898. Retired in April 1818 to Saint-Brieuc, the parish of St. Michael. He died September 23 or 24, 1823. <u>Registre de la paroisse St. Michel de St. Brieuc.</u> Information furnished by the Archivist of the Diocese of Saint-Brieuc, J.R. du Cleuziou.

[12] Sister Mary Theodore, <u>Note 4</u>.

[13] Birth Certificate, Laurent-Marie Guérin, Etables, April 10, 1809. <u>Registre communal de 1809, acte 30.</u>

[14] Death Certificate, Laurent Guérin, November 20, 1813, Etables, <u>Registre communal 1813, acte 72</u>.

[15] Death Certificate, Laurent Guérin, Mairie, Etables-sur-mer, <u>Registre des Décès, no. 44, September 5, 1822</u>. This is a registration furnished from the <u>Registre des décès de l 'Etat civil de la Commune d'Evenos, arrondissement de Toulon, department du Var, June 17, 1814</u>.

[16] Information furnished by Canon Francois Auffray of the Diocese of Saint-Brieuc, Saint Quay-Portrieux, 1984.

[17] Mother Mary Cecilia Bailly, <u>Life of Mother Theodore Guérin</u>, mss. Saint Mary-of-the-Woods, 1873, p. 3.

[18]<u>Ibid</u>., p. 4.

[19]<u>loc</u>. <u>cit</u>.

[20]J.F. Alric, S.J., <u>Histoire de la Congrégation des Soeurs de la Providence de Ruillé-sur-Loir, Paris, 1948, pp. 35, 48.</u>

[21]<u>REgistre des fondations</u>. ASPR.

[22]Note from Mother Theodore to Sister Marcelle, in her letter to Sister St. Eloi, Saint Mary-of-the-Woods, February 27, 1851. ASPR.

[23]Bailly, p. 5.

[24]<u>Registre de la date d'entrée des postulantes</u>, Vol. I, p. 27. ASPR.

Chapter 2– Notes

[1]J.F. Alric, S.J., <u>Histoire de la Congregation des Soeurs de la Providence de Ruillé-sur-Loir (Sarthe)</u>, Paris, 1948, p. 1.

[2]Tony Catta, <u>Le Père Dujarié (1767-1838, Fondateur des Soeurs de la Providence de Ruillé-sur-Loir et des Frères de Saint-Joseph Maintenant Freres de Sainte-Croix</u>, Montréal, Paris, 1960, pp. ix, 164.

[3]Appendix B. For a well-documented life of Father Dujarié, see Philéas Vanier, <u>Le Chanoine Dujarié, fondateur des Soeurs de la Providence de Ruillé-sur-Loir et des Frères de Saint-Joseph, recueil documentaire</u>, Montreal, 1948. On the foundation of the Sisters, pp. 57-72. See also Catta, <u>op</u>. <u>cit</u>., and Etienne and Tony Catta, <u>Le T.R.P. Basile-Antoine Moreau et les origines de la Congrégation de Sainte-Croix</u>, Paris, 1950, Vol. I, pp. 242-247.

[4]Vanier, p. 52. The Sisters of Notre Dame de la Charité d'Evron, founded by Perrine Brunet, served in many small establishments in la Sarthe and Mayenne.

[5]<u>Ibid</u>. p. 47. Report of minutes of the installation of the curé of Ruillé-sur-Loir, ASPR.

[6]Alric, p. 16. Mention should be made of an early collaborator, Marie Lair. For the difficulties encountered by Father Dujarié because of this woman, see Vanier, pp. 185-208; Catta, pp. 56-66.

[7]Vanier, p. 191. (From Report of Father Dujarié to the Prefect of La Sarthe, cited Vanier, pp. 190-196).

[8]In his "Memoire sur la vie et les actions de notre Père," Frère André Mottais gives these details: "He told me that to build this house of <u>Little Providence</u> he took the little children who attended his catechism lessons, he put in his pocket an apple and a piece of bread for his dinner and he

went then with his little troupe into the fields to pick up stones." (Vanier, p. 529) Brother André was born at Larchamp in Mayenne, and entered the new Institute of Brothers of St. Joseph, one of the first, on October 22, 1820; he was professed August 25, 1836, died at Le Mans March 15, 1844. Always loyal and devoted to the Founder, the Annals of the Congregation indicate that without injustice to Father Dujarié, Brother André might be considered co-founder. It was he who was charged with most of the tasks of direction and administration of the new Institute in its beginnings. (Vanier, p. 136.)

[9] Catta, p. 68.

[10] Chaptal's Report on public instruction in 1901, cited by Catta, p. 53.

[11] Sévrin, Histoire de l'enseignement en France sous la Révolution, le Consulat, et l'Empire, cited by Vanier, pp. 57-58.

[12] Alric, pp. 16-19.

[13] Alric, p. 21. Father Dujarié said 1812. In the codicil to his will he states, "…In 1806 I had built the house of Providence situated three quarters of a league from the town, where I provided for two Sisters, for the education of youth and the care of the sick of those regions. In 1812 I built the chapel of the Providence for the convenience of the Sisters and of the inhabitants of the neighborhood." Vanier, p. 527.

[14] Alric, pp. 21-22; Catta, p. 69.

[15] This hospice was given letters of patent in 1786, and continued its good works all during the darkest days of the Terror. "The secluded location where this Institute exerted its zeal, the poverty of the establishment, and the purpose of the work, dear even to the Jacobins, permitted it to come through the Revolution without being disturbed. In 1812, legal existence was granted." Vanier, p. 62, n. 10. The story of the heroic founders is told in Gaetan Bernoville, Une Fondation sous la Terreur, René Berault et Anne de la Girouardière, Paris, 1954.

[16] Bernoville, pp. 169-170. Alric, pp. 19-20. Alric notes, "Unconcerned about the future, he did not even bother to leave us the names of the seven first novices formed at Baugé. Besides Sister Madeleine Beucher (Born at Ruillé-sur-Loir in 1799, professed in 1820, died June 13, 1821) who governed the Little Providence in 1820, tradition preserves only one name, that of Sister Félicité, whom she succeeded." p. 22. A list in the handwriting of Sister Basilide Seneschal mentions, among others, Sister St. Vincent Levellian, first econome of Ruillé. ASMW.

[17] The Sisters of Providence recited the Little Office of the Sacred Heart

of Mary until 1857, when the diocese of Le Mans adopted the Roman liturgy, of which the Little Office of the Blessed Virgin, approved by Pope St. Pius V, was a part. Alric, p. 20, n. 1.

[18]Vanier, p. 62, n. 10. In 1984 the Sisters of Baugé graciously sent a complete copy of this Rule, approved by the Holy See in 1821, and a photograph of the Foundress. (Letter of Soeur Ch. Audureau to Sister Joseph Eleanor, been incorporated into the revised Rules recently approved by Rome. (The same to the same, April 11, 1985, ASMW).

[19]Alric, p. 23.

[20]See Appendix C for a sketch of the life of Mother du Roscoät. See also Alric, pp. 24-48; 60-72; Clementine de la Corbinière, L'Indiana, (Paris, 1886), pp. 129-140.

[21]Letter of Zoé du Roscoät to an unnamed friend, Ruillé, January 9, 1819, cited Alric, pp. 39-40.

[22]Alric, pp. 41-42.

[23]Appendix D. Aimée-Perrine Lecor was born December 29, 1792, on the Ile de Bréhat, at the extreme limits of Brittany; she was associated with Mlle du Roscoät from 1813. Alric, pp. 49-59.

[24]Ibid., pp. 60-64.

[25]Ibid ., pp. 64-72.

[26]Ibid ., pp. 75-76.

[27]Ordonnance du Roi, November 20, 1826, No. 4 099. ADM, Soeurs de la Providence, Ordonnance du roi.

[28]Louis Calendini, La Révérende Mère Francoise Jamin, Le Mans 1825, pp. 72-73. "Not content with giving an asylum to the unfortunate, to children, and to the sick, Mother Jamin strove to assure to whoever might ask the most gracious hospitality. One day, there are 15 Trappistines, another twenty, another still, some religious from the young Congregation of Ruillé-sur-Loir." p. 71.

[29]Father Dujarié to Mère Jamin, Ruillé, November 1, 1822. Vanier, p. 214.

[30]Letter of January 8, 1899. Alric, p. 39.

[31]Registre de la date d'entrée des postulantes, Vol. I, p. 27, ASPR.

Chapter 3— Notes

[1]Mother Marie Armelle to Mother Mary Raphael, Ruillé, January 23, 1937. ASMW.

[2] <u>Registre indiquant les divers changements faits dans le personnel de establissements</u>, Vol. I, p. 34. ASPR.

[3] Rev. Louis Nicholas Petit, S.J., (1789-1855) Born in Haiti, July 8, 1789. His father, a wealthy planter from Lyons, France, lost his life in the native uprising, and the mother brought her children to Baltimore, where Nicholas was educated by the Sulpicians until, in his twelfth year, the family removed to France. He received his seminary training in France, where he entered the reestablished Society of Jesus on January 15, 1816. After many years of missions and retreats, among them the retreat to the Sisters of Providence at Ruillé-sur-Loir in 1823, he went in 1830 as missionary to the diocese of Bardstown, Kentucky, which See included the state of Indiana, where he made missionary journeys. As early as 1832, he offered Mass in Terre Haute, in the home of Mrs. Susan Williams, the only Catholic in the city at that time. He visited St. Mary-of-the-Woods in 1841. At the request of Bishop de la Hailandière he translated the Sisters' prayers into English. He was several times proposed as Coadjutor by American bishops, but his Jesuit Superiors did not give permission, and he was not appointed. For years on the faculty of St. Mary's College in Marion County, Kentucky, he was among the Jesuits who were withdrawn from that college to begin what was to become Fordham University in New York. He died in Troy, New York, on February 1, 1855. (B.J. Webb, <u>The Centenary of Catholicity in Kentucky,</u> Louisville, 1884, pp. 386-389; Charlies LeMarié, <u>Monsigneur Bruté de Rémur,</u> Chapters IV, VIII; <u>Les missionaries bretons de l'Indiana au XIX siècle,</u> Montsurs, 1873, pp. 115-116, 117, 120, 127, 219, 347; Robert Trisco, <u>The Holy See and the Nascent Church in the Middle Western United States (1826-1850)</u>, Rome, Gregorian U. Press, 1962, pp. 118, 135.

[4] Sister St. Charles (Hélène Jolle 1799-1864) Born at Rennes, September 30, 1799, of a Breton officer, Claude Jolle, and Christine-Marie Klemhof, of Holland, a Lutheran. While her father was in service, her mother took the child to live with her sister at Montauban-de-Bretagne, the husband of the latter succeeded in obtaining the conversion of his wife, and then of Madame Jolle. After the death of her mother in 1814, Hélène was raised very strictly and piously by her aunt, and educated in the convent of the Ladies of St. Thomas of Villanova. She entered the Little Providence in 1821 was appointed Mistress of Novices in 1823, Assistant in 1825. In 1831 she replaced Mother Mary as Superior-General; in 1837, became again Assistant, which post she held until her death September 6, 1864. Alric, pp. 79, 96-99, 254-256.

[5] Registre indiquant les divers changements faits dans le personnel des etablissements. ASPR.

[6] Sister Mary Theodore, Note 25; Mother Mary Cecilia Bailly, Life of Mother Theodore Guérin, St. Mary-of-the-Woods, 1873, p. 7; Proc. Ord. Cenom., Copia Publica, f. 68.

[7] Mother Theodore to Sister St. Charles, January 6, 1847. ASMW.

[8] Mother Theodore to Sister Basilide, January 28, 1851. ASMW.

[9] Registre des fondations, ASPR.

[10] Information furnished by Sister Gabriel Marie Gouin, Secretary-General, from archives of the Motherhouse at Ruillé-sur-Loir: "Where was Sister Theodore from September 1825 to September 1826? Having no indication that she passed that year at Ruillé in illness, it is probable that she returned to Preuilly after her first vows. The house in Preuilly was closed in 1830. According to tradition, the illness of Mother Theodore occurred during her novitiate, hence January 6, 1825."

[11] James Roosevelt Bayley, Frontier Bishop, Huntington, 1971, pp. 16-23, 33-36, quoting Memoirs of Bishop Bruté.

[12] Henri Poisson, La paroisse de Saint-Aubin en Notre-Dame de Bonne-Nouvelle, essai de monographie, Redon, 1935.

[13] Ibid., p. 131.

[14] Ibid., p. 146.

[15] Proc. Ord. Cenom., Copia Publica, Test. 1, ff. 30-31.

[16] Bailly, pp. 7-11.

[17] Proc. Ord. Cenom., Publica, Test. 1, ff. 30-31.

[18] Exhortation on the "Instruction of Children" from Chapter Exhortations. ASMW, M. Th. 271.

[19] Mother Theodore to Sister Francis Regis, November 8, 1855. ASMW.

[20] Sister Emmanuel (Marie Paré, 1798-1884) Born at Thuboeuf (Mayenne) May 1, 1798; entered novitiate at Ruillé April 21, 1823; received the Habit July 6, 1824; first vows August 5, 1827. She was sent as novice to Rennes in 1824, remaining there until 1833. ASPR.

[21] Mother Theodore to Sister Basilide, January 28, 1851. ASMW.

[22] Exhortation on attitude towards the sick, from Chapter Exhortations, ASMW, M. Th. 271.

[23] Sister St. Felix (Louise Victoire Dubois, 1810-1885) Born at Blois, January 19, 1810; entered Ruillé May 17, 1828; received Habit July 16, 1829; at Rennes from 1829-1844. ASPR.

[24]Sister St. Felix to Mother Theodore, Rennes, August 20, 1841. ASMW.

[25]Bailly, p. 12.

[26]Letter of Mother Marie Lecor to Msgr. la Myre-Mory, Bishop of Le Mans, giving the names of the Councilors. ADM, dossier: Sisters of Ruillé, Constitutions et Statuts.

[27]Pierre Louis Francois Coëdro (1788-1840) Superior of the "Missionaries of Rennes" founded in 1822. As friend of Msgr. Guy Philippe Carron, bishop of Le Mans 1829-1833, he was in a position to assist Mother Mary Lecor, who relied on his counsel. "homme de règle, un peu rigide et sévère. Peutêtre ses avis contribuèrent à donner à Mère Marie l'orientation dans ses difficultés avec Dujarié" (Lemarié, p. 24). See Catta, pp. 171-173.

[28]Msgr. Guy-Philippe-Marie Carron (1788-1833) Bishop of Le Mans from 1829-1833. (Ritzler-Lefrin, Hierarchia Catholica, VII (Padua 1968) p. 144.

[29]Letter of Mother Mary Lecor to Msgr. Philippe Carron, Bishop of Le Mans, December 3, 1830 (Vanier, pp. 347-348).

[30]Sister St. Charles Jolle to Msgr. Carron, April 12, 1832. Vanier, p. 402.

[31]Registre des Professions de la Congrégation des Soeurs de la Providence, ASPR; Registre de l'entrée des postulantes, V. I, p. 27. ASPR.

[32]Poisson, p. 148.

[33]Contract between M. Lebreton, manufacturer of stockings, and the Directrice of the Ecole de la Providence, Rennes, September 25, 1829. ASAR; Copy ASMW.

[34]Bailly, p. 12.

Chapter 4– Notes

[1]S. Dosithée Hardy. Tableau de la Congrégation des Soeurs de la Providence, Diocèse du Mans. ADM.

[2]Ibid.

[3]Claude-Louis de Lesquen (1170-1855) Bishop of Rennes 1825-1841. Ordained at St. Brieuc in 1806, consecrated at Paris July 13, 1823. Bishop of Beauvais 1823-1825; nominated Bishop of Rennes by Charles X in 1825. He resigned in 1841 and retired to Dinan, where he died July 17, 1855. (Guillotin de Corson, Pouillé historique de l'archevêché de Rennes, Vol. I,

pp. 744-746. "L'Eglise de Rennes...sanctifiée par Msgr. de Lesquen, de si douce mémoire," Vol. VI, p. 551).

[4]Msgr. de Lesquen to Sister Theodore, Rennes, July 29, 1836. ASMW, Lesquen, 6.

[5]Bailly, p. 17.

[6]Proc. Ord. Cenom., Copia Publica, f. 34. Testimony given by Mother Marie Armelle.

[7]Vanier, pp. 81-88.

[8]Alric, p. 81.

[9]The Brothers of St. Joseph were recognized by royal ordinance of June 25, 1823 as a "charitable association." Its members were exempt from military service, were to be granted certification upon presentation of their letters of obedience, and might receive contributions and legacies, but only through the University, which retained control. According to the Ordinance: "Our royal University of France will receive legacies and donations which may be made in favor of said Association, or each of its schools under its jurisdiction to benefit respectively by the said legacies and donations, in accordance with the wishes of the donors and testators." Brother mphrem, C.S.C., The Curé of Ruillé (Notre Dame, 1941), pp. 122-3.

[10]Vanier, pp. 91-94.

[11]Brother André Mottais, "Mémoire sur la vie et les actions de notre Père." Vanier, p. 528.

[12]Notes of Brother Remi, Vanier, pp. 552-553.

[13]Alric, p. 89.

[14]Msgr. Carron to Mother Mary, Le Mans, September 14, 1830. Vanier, p. 344.

[15]The details are recorded in the report entitled "Partage des biens entre les deux Communautés de Ruillé," Vanier, pp. 366-380.

[16]Catta, pp. 204-206.

[17]Vanier, p. 553.

[18]Msgr. Carron to Mother St. Charles, Le Mans, June 24, 1831. Vanier, p. 381.

[19]Mother St. Charles to Msgr. Carron, April 12, 1832. Vanier, p. 402.

[20]Basile-Antoine Moreau to Msgr. Carron, August 28, 1832. Vanier, pp. 408-9.

[21]Bailly, pp. 16-17.

[22]Msgr. de Lesquen to Sister Theodore, Rennes, September 13,1834. ASMW, <u>Lesquen 1</u>.

[23]Msgr. de Lesquen to Sister Theodore, Montauban, November 4, 1834.ASMW, <u>Lesquen 2</u>.

[24]Msgr. de Lesquen to Sister Theodore, Rennes, January 7, 1835, ASMW, <u>Lesquen 3</u>.

[25]Msgr. de Lesquen to Sister Theodore, Rennes, June 6, 1835. ASMW, <u>Lesquen 5</u>.

[26]Jean Botrel (1797-1885) Born in the diocese of St. Brieuc, September 23, 1797, he was ordained priest December 23, 1820, and served as secretary to the Diocese of St. Brieuc. From 1825-1835 he was vicar-general of Msgr. de Lesquen, who in 1834 proposed him as auxiliary Bishop. He was not approved by the Ministry of Justice and Religion. In 1835 he went to Paris, where he assisted Msgr. Forbin-Janson in various works. Active in the promotion and devotion to the Holy Face, he was in correspondence with the Carmelites of Tours. He died in Paris June 16, 1885. (<u>La semaine religieuse de diocese de St. Brieuc</u>. June 25, 1885. pp. 335-337.)

[27]Botrel to Sister Theodore, Rennes, September 21, 1834. ASMW.

[28]Bailly, p. 5.

[29]René Jean-Francois Lottin (1793-1868) Born at Vimarcé, January 12,1793; he was ordained priest August 11, 1816, and immediately appointed curate at Chateau-du-Loir. He was a professor at the Grand Séminaire from 1819-1830, and then was appointed secretary to the diocese; named titular Canon July 21, 1831. He died January 20, 1868. Canon Lottin was for long years adviser to Mother Mary, and was most helpful to the Sisters setting out for America.

[30]Msgr. de Lesquen to Sister Theodore, June 29, 1836. ASMW. <u>Lesquen 6</u>.

[31]Joseph Claude Anselme Récamier (1774-1852) Of an excellent family, his early training led him to choose a profession which would be useful to humanity. Outstanding as physician with the navy, then at the Hotel Dieu of Paris; member of the Academy of Physicians from its inception in 1820; successor to Laennec as professor at the College de France 1827-1830. He was animated by profound Christian charity, and was noted for his care of the poor. Michaud, <u>Biographie Universelle – Ancienne et Moderne</u>, Paris, n.d., V. 35, pp. 292b-296a.

[32]Msgr. de Lesquen to Sister Theodore, Rennes, October 8, 1827. ASMW, <u>Lesquen 7</u>.

[33]Msgr. de Lesquen to Sister Theodore, Rennes, January 2, 1838. ASMW, Lesquen 8.

[34]Bailly, p. 17.

[35]Loc. cit.

[36]Sister Mary Theodore Letouzé, Notes. ASMW.

[37]Sister Thaïs (Félicité Durand) entered at the Little Providence May 16, 1820, received the habit in August, 1820, pronounced her first vows September 8, 1826, and perpetual vows September 5, 1831, in both cases with Sister Theodore. She was dismissed by the General Council September 8, 1841. Registres d'entrée et de changements de personnel. ASPR.

[38]Registres de l'état-civil de Soulaines: "Donation de M. Perrault de la Bertaudière á la Congrégation des Soeurs hospitalières de la Providence de Ruillé-sur-Loir, 2 février 1829."

[39]La Vie Paroissiale, No. 14, May-June 1948, pp. 6-7.

[40]Claude-Marie Perrault de la Bertaudière (1771-1849) Born August 31, 1771, at Angers. Cavalry officer, Mayor of Soulaines 1808-1821. He never married, and dedicated the remnants of his fortune to good works. He died at Soulaines, April 27, 1949.

[41]Honoré Lechacheur (1807-1883) Born at Rabley (Maine and Loire), May 5, 1807. He was physician at Brissac, of which he was mayor from 1848-1851. His services extended to the neighboring town, Soulaines. He died at Angers November 28, 1883.

[42]Proc. Ord. Cenom., Copia Publica, f. 60. Testimony of Sister Xavier-Joseph Lecouble, Directress of the Christian School of Soulaines 1904-1920.

[43]Proc. Ord. Cenom., Copia Publica, ff. 57-58. Testimony of Sister Joseph-Alphonse Jegu, Directress of the Christian School of Soulaines 1920-1935.

[44]M. De La Bertaudière to Sister Theodore, Soulaines, June 30, 1836. ASMW.

[45]Alric, pp. 107-109.

[46]Premier journal de voyage. ASMW. (Journals and Letters, p. 14.)

[47]Ibid., p. 55.

[48]Francois Brillouet (1800-1852) Born at Montigny-sur-Moine, January 10, 1800; ordained a priest June 9, 1827; appointed to Soulaines October 1, 1830. Died September 6, 1852 at Soulaines.

[49]Bailly, pp. 23-24; Parish archives at Soulaines: "Note sur la Congrégation des Soeurs de la Providence de Ruillé-sur-Loir a Soulaines."

[50]<u>Registre des deliberations du Conseil Municipal de Soulaines</u>, August 31, 1845.

[51]Bailly, p. 24.

[52]Father Brillouet to Mother Theodore, January 15, 1841. ASMW.

[53]Louis Marie (1787-1860) Born at Couture May 6, 1786. Retired Captain, Chevalier de la Légion d'Honneur, Mayor of Soulaines for 28 years. Died at his manor, La Possonniere, April 16, 1860.

[54]Letter of Madame Prévost Marie, Noizé, January 15, 1841. ASMW.

[55]Letter of authorization for the reception of boarding pupils, Angers, May 13, 1839. ASMW.

Chapter 5 – Notes

[1]Before its conquest by the English, Indiana, as part of New France, was administered by the Bishop of Quebec.

[2]Rogier, De Berteier de Sauvigny, Hajjar, <u>Nouvelle historie de l'Eglise</u>, Vol. IV, <u>Siècle des lumières, Révolution, Restauration</u>, Paris, 1966, p. 387. John Carroll (1735-1815) was born in Maryland, educated in France; a Jesuit before the suppression of the Order in France; cousin of Charles Carroll, one of the Signers of the Declaration of Independence.

[3]Clementine de la Corbinère, <u>l'Indiana</u>, Paris, 1886, pp. 32-33. It was Msgr. Dubourg, Bishop of Louisiana, who from 1815 sought in France aid for the American missions, a fact which played its part in the definite formation of the "Work of the Propagation of the Faith." Cristiani, <u>Marie-Pauline Jaricot</u>, Lyons, 1961, p. 27.

[4]<u>Catholic Historical Review</u>, XXXIX, No. 2, p. 177, note.

[5]James R. Bayley, <u>Memoirs of Rt. Rev. Simon Gabriel Brutè</u>, New York, 1865, pp. 59-65. In the diocese of Vincennes there were only four Sisters, at Vincennes. Msgr. Bruté had for a long time sought others.

[6]APF, Rome, Scritt. Rifer. A.C. Vol. II, ff. 623-639v; Thomas McAvoy, "The Report of Bishop Bruté to Rome in 1836," <u>Catholic Historical Review</u>, XXXIX, No. 2, p. 177.

[7]<u>Ibid.</u>, p. 198.

[8]Lemarié, <u>Les missionnaires bretons</u>, p. 16.

[9]<u>Ibid.</u>, p. 14.

[10]Alric, p. 24.

[11]Jean-Baptiste Bouvier (1783-1854) Born January 16, 1783; died in

Rome December 29, 1854. "One of the greatest bishops of Le Mans," Louis Calendini, <u>Histoire de l'Eglise du Mans</u>, Le Mans, 1916. President of the major Seminary, Vicar-general, and then Bishop of Le Mans 1834-1854. He favored the development of priestly and religious life in his vast diocese; a man of doctrine, Bishop Bouvier devoted himself to everything that concerned the teaching of religious doctrine: catechism, synodal statutes, instructions and exhortations, constitutions of religious orders.

[12]<u>Registre des délibérations du Conseil particulier de la Congrégation des Soeurs de la Providence</u>, Vol. I, p. 48, ASPR.

[13]Bailly, pp. 14-15, <u>Constitutions et Règles des Soeurs de la Providence de Ruillé-sur-Loir</u>, Preliminary chapter, No. 9, p. 2: "The Sisters will be disposed to go to any place in the world where obedience calls them, to work according to the spirit of their Institute."

[14]Msgr. de la Hailandière to Mother Mary, Le Havre, August 31, 1839. ASPR.

[15]Bailly, p. 21.

[16]Clementine de la Corbinière, <u>An Apostolic Woman</u>, English translation, St. Mary-of-the-Woods, 1934, p. 41, Letter to Elvire Payan.

[17]<u>Ibid</u>., p. 42.

[18]Bailly, p. 15.

[19]<u>An Apostolate Woman</u>, p. 54, letter to her sister Cecile, November 22, 1839.

[20]<u>Ibid</u>., p. 53.

[21]Marie Heurtel, first cousin of Sister Theodore, daughter of Julie Lefèvre and Pierre Heurtel, born March 20, 1797, died at Laval, in the convent of Nazareth, in 1877. Only one year older than her cousin, she remained devoted to her; several of her letters have been preserved. ASMW.

[22]<u>An Apostolic Woman</u>, p. 54.

[23]<u>Ibid</u>., p. 58, letter to her Aunt Cecile de la Salle, November 22, 1839.

[24]<u>Ibid</u>., p. 55, letter to her sister Eugénie.

[25]<u>Ibid</u>., p. 56, letter to her cousin Cecile, November 22, 1839.

[26]<u>Ibid</u>., p. 62, letter to her sister Elvire, December 7, 1839.

[27]<u>Ibid</u>., p. 64, letter to her mother, December 9, 1839.

[28]Msgr. de la Hailandière to Sister Theodore, Vincennes, December 17, 1839. ASMW.

Chapter 6 – Notes

[1]Bailly, p. 55.

[2]Msgr. de Lesquen to Sister Theodore, Rennes, December 31, 1839. ASMW, <u>Lesquen 10.</u>

[3]Msgr. Bouvier to Msgr. de la Hailandière, Le Mans, February 27, 1840. ASPR.

[4]<u>Constitutions et Regles des Soeurs de la Providence,</u> Part I, Ch. 14, art. 102-104.

[5]Msgr. de la Hailandière to Msgr. Bouvier, Vincennes, April 21, 1840. ASPR.

[6] Msgr. de la Hailandière to Mother Mary Lecor, Vincennes, April 29, 1840. ASPR.

[7] Msgr. de la Hailandière to Sister Theodore, Vincennes, March 29, 1840. ASMW.

[8]<u>Ibid.</u>

[9]Mother Theodore to Sister Maria, St. Mary-of-the-Woods, November 11, 1853. ASMW.

[10]M. Ivo Névo-Degouy to Sister Theodore, Angers, April 15, 1840. ASMW.

[11]Appendix E: Discourse Delivered on the Occasion of the Presentation of a Medal of Honor to Mother Theodore of Soulaines. English translation by Sister Mary Eudoxie Marshall. ASMW.

[12]Msgr. Bouvier to Sister Theodore, Le Mans, June 1, 1840. ASMW.

[13]<u>Registre des deliberations du Conseil particulier de la Congregation des Soeurs de la Providence,</u> Vol. I, pp. 55-56. A slight difference must be noted between this record, which names Sister Basilide, and the copy of the first draft of minutes brought to America by Mother Theodore, which names Sister St. Dominique. This final report of the meeting lists the Sisters who actually went to America.

[14]Mother Mary to Msgr. de la Hailandière, Ruillé, June 12, 1840. ASMW.

[15]Mother Mary to Sister Theodore, Ruillé, June 16, 1840. ASMW.

Chapter 7 – Notes

[1]Letter of Mother Mary to Sister Theodore, June 16, 1840. ASMW.

[2]Register of the deliberations of the particular Council of the Congregation of the Sisters of Providence, Vol. I, pp. 55-56. ASPR.

[3]Letter of Irma Le Fer to Madame Le Fer, Ruillé, July, 1840. An Apostolic Woman, pp. 100-101.

[4]Letters of Sister St. Charles to Canon Lottin, Ruillé, July 5 and 18, 1840. ASPR.

[5]Letter of Msgr. Bouvier, July 4, 1840. ASMW.

[6]Mairie d'Etables, Acte de deces, 1839, No. 34; Acte de Mariage, 1826, No. 23.

[7]Notes de notre voyage en Amérique. ASMW. The original journal, in Mother Theodore's handwriting, and entitled fully by her Brouillon de la rélation de notre voyage en Amérique 1840, is preserved in the archives at St. Mary-of-the-Woods. Citations are made with reference to the English version, Journals and Letters of Mother Theodore Guérin, St. Mary-of-the-Woods, 1937. p. 2.

[8]Ibid. p. 3.

[9]Letter to Canon Lottin, Le Havre, July 19, 1840. ASMW.

[10]Letter to Mother Mary Lecor, Le Havre, July 25, 1840. ASMW.

[11]Journal, p. 5.

Chapter 8 – Notes

[1]Unless otherwise indicated, Sister Theodore's comments on the voyage are quoted from her First Journal of Travel, published in Journals and Letters of Mother Theodore Guérin, edited by Sister Mary Theodosia Mug, St. Mary-of-the-Woods, 1937, 1978, pp. 1-70. Many details of the voyage are purposely omitted from this chapter to encourage the reader to consult this vibrant first-hand account.

[2]Letter to Mother Mary, on board ship, September 4, 1840. ASMW.

[3]Letter to Sister Eudoxie, to accompany third installment of the Journal, November 3, 1840. ASMW.

[4]Letter of September 4, cit.

[5]Ibid.

[6]Ibid.

[7]Continuation of letter on board ship, September 5, 1840. ASMW.

[8]Dr. Doane had studied medicine in Paris, where he became acquainted with the work of the religious in the hospitals. He was of a good New York family; his brother, a convert to Catholicism, became vicar-general of the

diocese of Newark, New Jersey; a relative was Protestant bishop of Albany. (Thomas Meehan, "A Century Ago," in <u>America,</u> vol. 57, No. 5, May 8, 1937, p. 114).

⁹Letter of September, <u>cit.</u>

¹⁰The Reverend Felix Varela (1788-1853), was born in Havana, where he became active politically. Exiled from Cuba in 1832 he went to New York, where he became pastor of the Church of the Transfiguration and vicar-general. A solid theologian, he wrote extensively in Spanish and in English.

¹¹Sylvie Parmentier was born in Louvain in 1793. She married a relative, André Parmentier, a noted horticulturist. The family came to America in 1824, and established the "Brooklyn Garden of Horticulture." Mme Parmentier was always a friend and benefactress to missionaries, especially the Sisters of Providence.

¹²Samuel Byerley was born in Staffordshire, England, July 31, 1796. He was a relative of the great English pottery manufacturer, Josiah Wedgwood. He served as dispatch carrier in the Napoleonic wars; then settled in Trieste, where he became partner in a large commercial house. When he came to the United States in 1832 his executive ability attracted the attention of one of the largest mercantile and shipping firms in the country, Howell and Aspinwall. He retired from business in 1843 and settled in South Bend, Indiana. When reverses overtook the family, Mother Theodore offered to educate his daughters, Louise and Josephine, at St. Mary-of-the-Woods. He died March 10, 1870.

¹³Letter of Sister Theodore to Sister St. Charles, Philadelphia, September 17, 1840. ASMW.

¹⁴<u>Ibid.</u>

¹⁵Marc Antony Frenaye (1783-1873), lawyer, friend of Msgr. de la Hailandière, confidential agent of the bishops of Philadelphia.

¹⁶Msgr. John Dubois (1764-1842). Ordained in Paris in 1787, he came to the United States in 1791. He rendered notable service to the diocese of Baltimore, founding the first church at Frederick, Maryland, helping in the establishment of St. Mary's College and Seminary and of Mother Seton's first convent of Sisters of Charity in 1809. In 1839, because of ill health, he resigned the active administration of the diocese to his coadjutor, Msgr. John Hughes.

¹⁷Msgr. John Hughes (1797-1864) was born in Ireland; immigrated with his father to Pennsylvania in 1816. While awaiting a vacancy in St. Mary's Seminary he worked for a year as gardener. Ordained in 1826

for diocese of Philadelphia. In 1838 he was consecrated coadjutor of the diocese of New York, succeeded to the See in 1842, and became the first archbishop in 1850. He successfully resisted anti-Catholic attacks, helped create parochial school system, took a leading part in the founding of the North American College in Rome.

[18]Msgr. Francis Patrick Kenrick (1796-1863) After leaving a brilliant record as student of theology in Rome, he taught at St. Joseph's Seminary, Bardstown, and acted as secretary to Bishop Flaget, whose theologian he was at the First Provincial Council of Baltimore, of which he was chosen Secretary. In 1832 he was consecrated coadjutor of Philadelphia, where the aged Bishop Conwell was having difficulties with the trustees. In 1842 he succeeded Bishop Conwell as Ordinary. In 1851 he was appointed Archbishop of Baltimore. He was considered the leading American moral theologian of his times.

[19]Letter to Sister St. Charles, Philadelphia, September 17, cit.

[20]Rev. William Stephen Chartier, Canadian missionary. After five years in the diocese of Vincennes he returned to Canada.

[21]Msgr. John Purcell (1800-1883), first archbishop of Philadelphia (1850).

[22]Alexis de Tocqueville, Democracy in America, English tr. by Reeves, New York, 1900, Vol. I, p. 322.

[23]Mother Mary Cecilia Bailly, Life of Mother Theodore Guérin, mss. St. Mary-of-the-Woods, 1873, p. 22.

[24]Ibid.

[25]Sisters of Charity of Nazareth, Kentucky, founded in 1812 at request of Bishop Flaget by Rev. (later Bishop) John Baptist David. In 1824 they opened the first Catholic school in Indiana, at Vincennes. Later a group formed a nucleus of Sisters of Charity of Leavenworth, Kansas.

[26]His name is not given, but it may well have been Rev. Anthony Deydier, pastor in Evansville at that time.

[27]The Sisters of Charity of Nazareth had left Vincennes in 1834. At Bishop Bruté's earnest request they returned in 1835. His attempt to form a diocesan congregation with these Sisters and two from Emmittsburg failed; Sisters from Emmittsburg were assigned to the diocese, but the Community could not found another Motherhouse.

[28]Letter to Mother Mary, New York, September 7, 1840. ASMW.

[29]Bailly, p. 25.

Chapter 9 – Notes

[1]Brown, ch. II, pp. 25-42. This chapter contains very helpful background details.

[2]Godecker, p. 297. Cf. also Alexis de Tocqueville, Oeuvres completes, Vol. I, De la démocratie en Amérique, Paris, 1951, pp. 343-345, and note, p. 211, which describes a "loghouse" and the life lived therein: "This dwelling is a little world in itself; it is the Ark of civilization lost in the middle of an ocean of foliage. A hundred paces farther on, the eternal forest stretches its shade all around, and solitude begins again."

[3]Bailly, p. 26.

[4]Journal and Letters, p. 61. This custode is still preserved in the Heritage Room at St. Mary-of-the-Woods.

[5]Bailly, p. 26.

[6]Conference on the eve of Corpus Christi, June 20, 1848. ASMW.

[7]Brown, p. 55.

[8]Journal and Letters, p. 62.

[9]Ibid.

[10]Ibid., p. 63.

[11]Father Buteux to Mrs. Williams, September 23, 1840. ASMW.

[12]Journal and Letters, p. 64.

[13]Ibid., p. 63.

[14]Josephine Pardeillan to Rev. Augustin Martin, November 24, 1839. ASMW.

[15]Josephine Pardeillan to Rev. Augustin Martin, November 30, 1839. ASMW.

[16]Célestine de la Hailandière to Mother M. Xavier Clark, May 21, 1840. ASCM.

[17]Hailandière to Mother M. Xavier Clark, August 17, 1840. ASCM.

[18]Mother Theodore to Mother Mary, November 14, 1840. ASMW.

[19]Hailandière to Mother Mary, October 29, 1840. ASMW.

[20]Bailly, p. 16.

[21] Hailandière to Msgr. Jean-Baptiste Bouvier, October 29, 1840. ADM, copy, ASMW.

[22]Journals and Letters, p. 63.

[23]Proceedings of Particular Council. ASMW.

[24]Hailandière to Mother Theodore, November 22, 1840. ASMW.

[25]Notes on the Establishment of St. Mary-of-the-Woods, ASMW.

[26]Mother Theodore to Mother Mary, November 14, 1840.

²⁷Journal abrégé. ASMW.
²⁸ Notes on the Establishment of St. Mary-of-the-Woods, ASMW.
²⁹ Journal abrégé.
³⁰Ibid.

Chapter 10– Notes

¹Community Diary.
²Sister Basilide to Mother Mary, January 20, 1841. ASMW.
³Sister St. Vincent to Mother Mary, January 18, 1841. ASMW.
⁴Msgr. de la Hailandière to Father Martin, January 26, 1841. ASMW.
⁵Msgr. de la Hailandière to Father Martin, February 13, 1841. ASMW.
⁶Msgr. de la Hailandière to Mother Mary, February 3, 1841. ASPR.
⁷Msgr. de la Hailandière to Msgr. Bouvier, February 3, 1841. ASPR.
⁸Community Diary.
⁹Mother Mary to the Sisters, December 7, 1840. ASMW.
¹⁰Msgr. de la Hailandière to Mother Theodore, February 14, 1841. ASMW.
¹¹ Msgr. de la Hailandière to Mother Theodore, February 21, 1841. ASMW.
¹² Msgr. de la Hailandière to Mother Theodore, February (n.d.) 1841.
¹³Community Diary.
¹⁴Mother Mary Cecilia Bailly, Life of Mother Theodore, p. 27.

Chapter 11 – Notes

¹Third Journal of Travel, Journals and Letters, pp. 176-177.
²Ibid.
³Mother Theodore to Father Martin, May 1, 1841. ASMW.
⁴Jean-Mari Marcile of St. Servan accompanied Monsignor de la Hailandière to Vincennes as his architect. He worked on the buildings at St. Mary's, the Village church, the cathedral at Vincennes, the University of Notre Dame, the parish church in Evansville. He died of cholera in 1851.

[5]Community diary.

[6]Mother Mary to Mother Thelodore, January 22, 1841. ASMW.

[7]Mother Theodore to Mother Mary, April 2, 1841. ASMW.

[8]Hailandière to Martin, April 17, 1841, ASMW.

[9]Mother Theodore to Mother Mary, April 2, 1841. ASMW.

[10] Mother Theodore to Bishop Bouvier, November 2, 1841. ASMW.

[11]Mother Theodore to Canon Lottin, May 25, 1841. ASMW.

[12] Charles Lemarié, <u>Monseigneur Bruté de Rémur, premier évêque de Vincennes, Indiana,</u> Paris 1973, p. 181.

[13]Celestin Rene Guynemer de la Hailandière was born at Combourg in Brittany May 2, 1798 and baptized the same day by a priest in hiding in his father's house. While he was still a child his family moved to Rennes, former capital of Brittany; he finished his classical studies at the College of Rennes. He studied law, and was just beginning a promising career when, at the age of 22, he renounced his post to enter the seminary. Ordained in 1825, he was appointed a short time after vicar at St. Germaine des Près, Rennes. Ten years later when Bishop Bruté on a visit to France, asked Bishop de Lesquen to recommend a zealous priest whom he could take as vicar general and later, perhaps, coadjutor, Msgr. de Lesquen recommended Father de la Hailandière. When he arrived in Vincennes in 1836 he was immediately appointed vicar general and pastor of the cathedral. Although Father de la Hailandière had never mastered English. Bishop Bruté listed him as one of the candidates for coadjutor after Father Nicholas Petit, SJ, who was his first choice. The fact that Father Petit was a Jesuit stood in the way of his nomination. See Ernest Audran, <u>Rt. Rev. Celestine de la Hailandière,</u> a discourse pronounced June 7, 1882, on the occasion of the solemn funeral service, Archives, Archdiocese of Indianapolis; Lemarié, <u>Les missionaries Bretons,</u> p. 13; Trisco, p. 86.

[14]Bailly, pp. 377-338.

[15]Mother Theodore to Mother Mary, November 14, 1840. ASMW.

[16]Mother Theodore to Father Martin, May 1, 1841; to Mother Mary, April 2, 1841. ASMW.

[17]Mother Theodore to S. St. Charles, September 17, 1840. ASMW.

[18]Hailandière to Mother Theodore, November 22, 1840; to Mother Mary, February 3, 1841. ASMW.

[19]Memorandum. May 1841. ASMW.

[20]Letter to Canon Lottin, <u>cit.</u>

[21]Community diary.

[22]<u>Ibid.</u>

Chapter 12– Notes

[1]Terre Haute *Wabash Courier,* June 19, 1841.
[2]Sister Mary Borromeo Brown S.P., History of the Sisters of Providence of St. Mary-of-the-Woods, 1949, p. 164.
[3]Ibid.
[4]Ibid., p. 107.
[5]Sister Joseph Eleanor Ryan, S.P., Positio-Part One – Beatification and Canonization of the Servent of God, Mother Theodore Guerin, 1798-1856, 1987, p. XXXV.
[6]Brown, p. 173.
[7]A Mere Marie Février, 1842. From the original letter of Mother Theodore to Mother Mary, in Ruillé, as translated in the Positio, Vol. 1, p. 267, ASMW.
[8]Sister Mary Cecilia Bailly, S.P., Life of Mother Theodore, p. 30.
[9]Brown, p. 218.
[10]Letters and Journals of Mother Theodore Guérin, p. 90.
[11]Letter of Bishop de la Hailandière to Mother Theodore Guérin, December 11, 1840, ASMW.
[12]Mother Theodore to Mother Mary, February 26, 1842, ASMW.
[13]Brown, p. 170.
[14]Mother Theodore to Mother Mary, December 3, 1841, ASMW.
[15]Mother Mary to Mother Theodore, December 10, 1841, ASMW.
[16]Brown, p. 173.
[17]Mother Theodore to Mother Mary, February 26, 1842, ASMW.
[18]Ibid., p. 265.
[19]Ibid., p. 266.

Chapter 13 – Notes

[1]Mother Theodore to Mother Mary, October 3, 1842, ASMW.
[2]First journal of travel, Journals and Letters, p. 64, ASMW.
[3]Mother Theodore to Bishop Bouvier, February 23, 1843, ASMW.
[4]Mother Theodore to Reverend A. Martin, July 3, 1846, ASMW.
[5]Mother Theodore to Mother Mary, April 2, 1841, ASMW.
[6]Mother Theodore to Mother Mary, October 3, 1842, ASMW.
[7]Mother Theodore to Bishop Bouvier, July 10, 1850, ASMW.

[8]Sister St. Francis Xavier to Mother Mary, December 3, 1841, ASMW.

[9]Mother Theodore to Bishop Bouvier, February 23, 1843, ASMW.

[10]Mother Theodore to her Sisters, March 8, 1846, ASMW.

[11]Bailley, p. 30.

[12]Mother Theodore to Bishop Bouvier, February 23, 1843, ASMW.

[13]Brown, p. 180.

[14]Bishop de la Hailandiere to Mother Theodore, December 19, 1841, ASMW.

[15]Mother Theodore to Father Kundek, October 15, 1841, ASMW.

[16]Mother Theodore to Mother Mary, February 26, 1842, ASMW.

[17]Brown, p. 198.

[18]Ibid., p. 199.

[19]Father Ducoudray to Mother Theodore, August 10, 1843, ASMW.

[20]Brown, p. 195.

[21]Ibid., p. 198.

[22]Ibid.

[23]Mother Theodore to Mme. Fer de la Motte, November 2, 1852.

Chapter 14 – Notes

[1]Positio – Vol. I, p. XXXVI.

[2]Mother Mary to Bishop Bouvier, June 21, 1843, ASPR.

[3]Brown, p. 55.

[4]Mother Theodore to Mother Mary April 8, 1843, ASMW.

[5]Brown, p. 245.

[6]Bishop de la Hailandière to Mother Theodore, April 30, 1843, ASMW.

[7]Brown, p. 250.

[8]Journals and Letters, p. 27.

[9]Positio – Vol. I, pp. 468, 469, 470.

[10]Journals and Letters, p. 167.

[11]Ibid., p. 138.

[12]Verification of Mother Theodore's credentials by Bishop Bouvier, June 9, 1843, ASMW.

[13]Leon Aubineau: Les Serviteurs de Dieu au XIX Siècle, p. 344.

[14]Brown, p. 254.

[15]Document written by Mother Theodore dated September 12, 1843. ASMW.

[16]Brown, p. 272.

[17]Journals and Letters, p. 200.

[18]Brown, pp. 272-273.

[19]Journals and Letters, p. 116.

[20]Ibid. p. 118

[21]Ibid.

[22]Ibid.

[23]Mother Mary to Mother Theodore, October 16, 1843, ASMW.

Chapter 15– Notes

[1]Annals of the Congregation of the Sisters of Providence, (Infra,D,2).

[2] Positio – Vol. I, p. 403.

[3]Annals of the Congregation of the Sisters of Providence, ASMW, SFX31.

[4]Constitutions et Regles des Soeurs de la Providence, Le Mans, 1835, pp. 6-7.

[5]Letters and Journals of Mother Theodore Guerin, p. 147.

[6]Ibid., p. 147.

[7]Ibid., p. 167.

[8]Letter of Mother Theodore to Mother Mary, January 24, 1843.

[9]Letters and Journals of Mother Theodore Guerin, p. 161.

[10]Ibid., p. 163.

[11]Ibid., p. 165.

[12]Ibid., p. 167.

[13]Ibid., p. 167.

[14]Letter of Sister Basilide to Mother Theodore, 21 Fevrier, 1844, ASMW.

[15]Annals, Book 13, p. 16, ASMW.

[16]Brown, p. 324.

[17]Journals and Letters, p. 168.

[18]Brown, p. 331.

[19]Letter of Mother Theodore Guerin to Bishop Bouvier, June 25, 1844. ASMW.

[20]Ibid. p. 332.

[21]Ibid.
[22]Ibid.
[23]Mother Mary to Mother Theodore, October 16, 1843, ASMW.

Chapter 16– Notes

[1]M. Nicholas Martin du Nord, Keeper of the Seals under Louis-Phillipe, who had shown marked kindness and courtesy to the servent of God during her quest in France, even to arranging for her an audience with Queen Amelia. V. ch. Y,C.

[2]Journals and Letters, p. 118.

[3]Ibid., p. 118.

[4]Positio – Vol. II, pp 622-623, ASMW.

[5]Journals and Letters, p. 183.

[6]Ibid., p. 97.

[7]Reflections for the Journey, pp. 1-7, Sister Paula Damiano and Sister Ruth Johnson, 1998.

[8]Journals and Letters, p. 418.

[9]Brown, p. 325.

[10]The Indianapolis Star, February 13, 1916, by Booth Tarkington.

[11]Brown, p. 532.

[12] Journals and Letters, pp. 191-192.

[13] Brown, p. 180.

[14]Mother Theodore Guérin – St. of God, Penny Mitchell, p. 107.

[15]Letter of Mother Theodore Guérin to Bishop Bouvier, June 25, 1844.

[16]Mother Theodore Guérin – St. of God, Penny Mitchell, p. 108.

[17]Ibid., p. 108.

[18]Letter of Mother Theodore Guérin to Bishop Bouvier, July 21, 1846, ASMW.

[19]Brown, p. 538.

[20]Letter of Mother Theodore to Bishop Bouvier, November 30, 1844, ASMW.

[21]Ibid.

[22]Ibid.

[23]Ibid.

[24]Letter of Mother Theodore to Mother Mar Lecor, June 25, 1847, ASMW.

²⁵Brown, p. 466.

²⁶Letter of Mother Theodore to Bishop Bouvier

²⁷Words of Bishop de la Hailandière to Mother Theodore, May 20, 1847.

²⁸Letter of Mother Theodore to Bishop Bouvier, July 8, 1847.

²⁹Holy Scripture.

³⁰Alering, History of Vincennes Diocese, p. 450.

³¹Letter from Bishop de la Hailandière to Father Corbe, May 30, 1847. ASMW.

³²Letter from Pope Pius IX to Diocese of Vincennes, Bishop de la Hailandière.

³³Letter of Mother Theodore to Bishop Bouvier, July 8, 1847. ASMW.

Chapter 17 – Notes

¹Constitutions et Reǵles, Le Mans, Art. 241., p. 55, ASMW.

²LeMarié, Les Missionnaires, cit., p. 322.

³Beste, p. 100, quoted by LeMarié, pp. 322-323.

⁴LeMarié, p. 323.

⁵Sister Mary Theodosia Mug, Mother Theodore Guerin, 1904, Benziger Brothers, p. 409-412.

⁶Journals and Letters of Mother Theodore Guerin, p. 279.

⁷The Gospel of Matthew 25:45..

⁸A Mère Marie, 10 Juillet, 1851, ASMW.

⁹Letter of Mother Theodore to Mère Marie, Dimanche de Pâques, 1852, ASMW.

¹⁰Letter of Mother Theodore to Mother St. Charles, 25 September, 1853, ASMW.

¹¹Brown, pp. 666.

¹²Community Diary, ASMW.

¹³Positio – Part II, P. 720.

¹⁴Journals and Letters of Mother Theodore Guerin, p. 412.

¹⁵Corbinière, Une Femme Apôtre, CT., p. 492.

¹⁶Letter of Mother Theodore Guerin to Sister Basilide, April 3, 1854, ASMW.

¹⁷Mug, p. 472.

¹⁸Positio – Vol. II, pp. 722-724.

[19]Letter of Mother Theodore Guerin to the Superiors at Ruillé, France, February 8, 1856, ASMW.

[20]Ibid., p. 773.

[21]Bailley, The Life of Mother Theodore, p. 40.

[22] Letter of Mother Theodore Guerin to the Superiors at Ruillé, France, February 8, 1856, ASMW.

About the Authors

The authors of this book, Sister Diane Ris, SP and Sister Joseph Eleanor Ryan, SP were steeped in the history of Mother Theodore Guerin from their entrance into the Sisters of Providence. Both authors had access to the originals and translations of Mother Theodore Guerin's diaries, instructions, journals, letters and other excellent materials related to Mother Theodore that were found in the congregation archives at Saint Mary-of-the-Woods and at the archives of Ruille, France.

When Sister Joseph Eleanor became ill and was unable to continue her writing, Sister Diane Ris was asked to complete Mother Theodore's life story. She was honored by the request and her "yes" was immediate.

PERSONAL BACKGROUND
Born - Port Chester, New York, July 16, 1932
Raised-New Rochelle, New York and Washington, D.C.

PROFESSIONAL BACKGROUND

Bachelor degree - Saint Mary-of-the-Woods College, Indiana

Master's degree - Indiana University, Bloomington, Indiana

Doctoral degree - Ball State University, Muncie, Indiana

TEACHING EXPERIENCE

Elementary Education - 21 years in Indiana, Illinois, and Maryland

Higher Education - 20 years at Morehead State University, Kentucky

ADMINISTRATIVE EXPERIENCE

Professor Emeritus - Morehead State University, Kentucky

Provincial Superior - Midwest and Southern States

General Superior - United States and Asia

Sister Joseph Eleanor Ryan, SP

You have most likely seen this name with mine on the cover of this biography. Sister Joseph Eleanor spent many years of her life researching the life of Mother Theodore. Her fluency in French enabled her to translate original documents found in the archives of Ruille, France. She was asked to compile the Positio Super Virtutibus for the Beatification and Canonization of Mother Theodore Guerin.

This was a 2 volume set that was thoroughly researched and sent to Rome for the Cardinals deliberations. Because of the completeness of Sister Joseph Eleanor's work, the Cardinals gave a unanimous vote of approval for Mother Theodore's Beatification.

Sister Joseph Eleanor was my high school teacher. She was all a good teacher should be. I am proud to have been asked to continue this book where she left off.

She died on May 7,1991. May she rest in peace.

— Sister Diane Ris, SP